Security, Conflict and Cooperation in the Contemporary World

The Palgrave Macmillan series, Security, Conflict and Cooperation in the Contemporary World aims to make a significant contribution to academic and policy debates on cooperation, conflict and security since 1900. It evolved from the series Global Conflict and Security edited by Professor Saki Ruth Dockrill. The current series welcomes proposals that offer innovative historical perspectives, based on archival evidence and promoting an empirical understanding of economic and political cooperation, conflict and security, peace-making, diplomacy, humanitarian intervention, nation-building, intelligence, terrorism, the influence of ideology and religion on international relations, as well as the work of international organisations and non-governmental organisations.

More information about this series at
http://www.palgrave.com/gp/series/14489

Nicholas Ferns

Australia in the Age of International Development, 1945–1975

Colonial and Foreign Aid Policy in Papua New Guinea and Southeast Asia

palgrave
macmillan

Nicholas Ferns
School of Philosophical, Historical
and International Studies
Monash University
Clayton, VIC, Australia

Security, Conflict and Cooperation in the Contemporary World
ISBN 978-3-030-50227-0 ISBN 978-3-030-50228-7 (eBook)
https://doi.org/10.1007/978-3-030-50228-7

Cover illustration: Photo by Rudolf Dietrich/ullstein bild via Getty Images

This Palgrave Macmillan imprint is published by the registered company Springer Nature Switzerland AG
The registered company address is: Gewerbestrasse 11, 6330 Cham, Switzerland

Acknowledgements

This project began as a doctoral thesis at Monash University in 2012. Over the past eight years I have benefitted from the advice and assistance of a huge range of people and institutions. I owe a particular debt of gratitude to my former supervisors, now mentors and colleagues, Agnieszka Sobocinska and Tom Heenan. Their support both during and following my doctoral studies has enabled me to finally complete this project. I have also benefitted from the kind support of staff members at Monash University, who have kindly offered their advice and assistance throughout my research.

I would also like to thank the staff members of the archives and institutions in which this research was undertaken. I am grateful to the staff of the National Archives of Australia, the National Library of Australia, the United States National Archives, the Mitchell Library and the United Nations Archives.

As this project neared completion, I received invaluable assistance from a number of helpful scholars. Kate Rivington, Emma Kluge, Jon Piccini, Evan Smith, Kirstie Close, Anisa Puri, Bernard Keo, Anna Kent and Sam Nicholls, all provided advice on chapters or full drafts. I am immensely grateful for their help.

Finally, I would like to thank my close friends for helping me get through everything. To Peter, Eamon, Martin, Chris, James and Daniel, your support has been invaluable. To my family, Julie, Dennis and Allyce, you have been there for me throughout the entire process.

But above all, I have to thank my beautiful wife Gaby. I could not have done this without you.

Contents

About the Author

Nicholas Ferns is a research and teaching associate at Monash University. He completed his Ph.D. in history at Monash University in 2017. His research examines the ways that, between 1945 and 1975, Australian colonial policy towards PNG and foreign aid policy towards Southeast Asia was driven by policymakers' engagement with post-war notions of international development. His research has been published in *The Australian Journal of Politics and History*, *The Australasian Journal of American Studies* and *Diplomacy and Statecraft*. In addition to his research on development and foreign aid, he has also published work on Australia's engagement with the American notion of "Manifest Destiny" between 1850 and 1900 and on the role of personal friendships in the diplomacy of Woodrow Wilson. He is currently working on a new project that explores the relationship between Australia and the World Bank in the several decades following the Second World War.

Abbreviations

ACFOA	Australian Council for Overseas Aid
ADAA	Australian Development Assistance Agency
ADAB	Australian Development Assistance Bureau
AIIA	Australian Institute of International Affairs
ALP	Australian Labor Party
ANGAU	Australian New Guinea Administrative Unit
ANU	Australian National University
ASOPA	Australian School of Pacific Administration
AusAID	Australian Agency for International Development
CPD	*Commonwealth Parliamentary Debates*
DFAT	Department of Foreign Affairs and Trade
DORCA	Directorate of Research and Civil Affairs
ECAFE	Economic Commission for Asia and the Far East
ECLA	Economic Commission for Latin America
ERP	European Recovery Program
ETA	Economic and Technical Assistance Branch
GATT	General Agreement on Tariffs and Trade
GNP	Gross National Product
IBRD	International Bank for Reconstruction and Development
ITO	International Trade Organisation
LSE	London School of Economics
MIT	Massachusetts Institute of Technology
NAA	National Archives of Australia
NARA	National Archives and Records Administration
NGO	Non-Governmental Organisation
NIEO	New International Economic Order

NLA	National Library of Australia
OECD	Organisation for Economic Co-operation and Development
PNG	Papua New Guinea
PWR	Post-War Reconstruction
UN	United Nations
UNA	United Nations Archives
UNCTAD	United Nations Conference on Trade and Development
UNDP	United Nations Development Program
UNRRA	United Nations Relief and Rehabilitation Agency
US	United States
USAID	United States Agency for International Development
USSR	Union of Soviet Socialist Republics
UWA	University of Western Australia
VGS	Volunteer Graduate Scheme

CHAPTER 1

Introduction

In late 1949, Department of External Affairs officials prepared a brief for the Australian delegation attending the upcoming Conference of Commonwealth Foreign Ministers to be held in Colombo in January 1950. They were commenting on the increasingly prominent post-war 'problem' of underdevelopment in Southeast Asian countries. In the brief, the departmental officials indicated that the Australian attitude towards technical assistance was favourable, given that "since the establishment of the United Nations, Australia has insisted upon the importance of providing the utmost assistance for the development of the under-developed countries."[1] More importantly, the department placed a clear emphasis on developmental objectives, arguing:

> The most important criterion for the selection of projects should be the effect of assistance on increasing productivity of the various factors of production (the essential characteristic of economic development).[2]

[1] Department of External Affairs, "Technical Assistance for Economic Development—Australian Policy," December 8, 1949, National Archives of Australia (hereafter cited as NAA): A1838, 532/5/2/2.

[2] Department of External Affairs, "Technical Assistance for Economic Development—Australian Policy."

N. Ferns, *Australia in the Age of International Development, 1945–1975*, Security, Conflict and Cooperation in the Contemporary World,
https://doi.org/10.1007/978-3-030-50228-7_1

Fast-forward almost three decades. By the 1970s, Australian aid policy had undergone numerous alterations that reflected the evolving nature of developmental ideas. Writing in 1973, Prime Ministerial advisor Peter Wilenski commented on Australian aid policy in the context of the proposed establishment of a stand-alone aid agency. He wrote that:

> Aid should be given very largely for developmental, humanitarian and social reasons within the broad framework of the various aspects of Australia's national interest rather than to seek political influence or favour. The use of aid to further political objectives may be counter-productive in the long run as the experience of some major aid donors has shown.[3]

In 1973, as in 1949, Australian aid policy was proposed as a solution to the developmental 'problem' in Papua New Guinea (PNG) and Southeast Asia.

Development was not invented in 1945, nor did it disappear after 1975. Nevertheless, the three decades following the Second World War mark a high point in thought and policy regarding the promotion of international development. During this period, the concept of 'development' was often seen at the time as interchangeable with terms such as 'modernisation', 'growth' and 'progress.' Eugene Staley was one of the clearest and earliest advocates for what, after 1945, would become 'development.'[4] In 1944, Staley asked himself the question, "What is Economic Development?" His answer typified the broad meaning of the idea:

> It is a combination of methods by which the capacity of a people to produce (and hence to consume) may be increased. It means introduction of better techniques; installing more and better capital equipment; raising the general level of education and the particular skills of labour and management; and expanding internal and external commerce in a manner to take better advantage of opportunities for specialisation.[5]

[3] "Report of the Task Force on a Unified Aid Administration," May 1973, NAA: M3383, 73.

[4] David Ekbladh, *The Great American Mission: Modernization and the Construction of an American World Order, 1914 to the Present* (Princeton: Princeton University Press, 2010), 68–74.

[5] Eugene Staley, *World Economic Development: Effects on Advanced Industrial Countries* (Montreal: International Labour Office, 1944), 5.

Over two decades later, Gunnar Myrdal, one of the World Bank's 'pioneers in development', presented a definition that also revealed the interchangeability of terminology.[6] In his 1968 *Asian Drama*, Myrdal demonstrated the compatibility of 'modernisation' and 'development': "The desire for development and planning for development flows directly from the quest for rationality and represents in the economic and social field the all-embracing and comprehensive expression of the modernization ideals."[7] The ambiguity as to the precise meaning of 'development' made it particularly useful to experts and policymakers in the decades following the Second World War.

In economic terms, Frederick Cooper argues that this semantic ambiguity rests in the simultaneous notions of "increasing production and increasing welfare."[8] As Staley showed in 1944, development was an economic process that was spurred by increased production. Nevertheless, the Myrdal quote reveals a broader meaning, with 'modernization ideals' involving shifts in a society's ways of thinking. Taking these observations as its starting point, this book understands development to be a comprehensive process of social, economic and political progress that was largely perceived as positive until at least the mid-1970s. More specifically, economic development was seen as a process that would improve people's standard of living as a result of increased production. This improvement in living standards was expected to then lead to positive social and political change.

Modernisation was one form of development that revolved around the belief that social, economic and political change had a specific destination, which was generally exemplified by 'modern', Western civilisation. The definitive statement of modernisation theory was Walt Rostow's 1960 *The Stages of Economic Growth*.[9] Rostow's central premise was that all societies go through a series of stages, from 'the traditional society' through to 'the age of high mass-consumption.' The pivotal stage was

[6] Gerald M. Meier and Dudley Seers, eds., *Pioneers in Development* (New York: Oxford University Press, 1984).

[7] Gunnar Myrdal, *Asian Drama: An Inquiry into the Poverty of Nations*, vol. 1 (New York: Pantheon, 1968), 58.

[8] Frederick Cooper, *Decolonization and African Society: The Labor Question in French and British Africa* (Cambridge: Cambridge University Press, 1996), 206.

[9] Walt W. Rostow, *The Stages of Economic Growth: A Non-Communist Manifesto* (London: Cambridge University Press, 1960).

the third, the 'take-off', where societies would make the transition from the 'traditional' to the 'modern.' While Rostow's analysis mostly revolved around the economic processes required to progress through the stages, he also engaged with the social and cultural features of modernisation. In the conclusion to *The Stages of Economic Growth*, Rostow argued that a loosely defined 'democratic creed', marked by acceptance of diversity and support for "private areas of retreat and expression," would be "what most human beings would choose, if the choice were theirs."[10] For Rostow, the United States was the epitome of modernity, and all other societies were to emulate their historical development. The intellectual and political influence of these ideas was enhanced by Rostow's involvement in the Kennedy and Johnson Administrations. The combination of the intellectual and emotional appeal of American-style modernity with the political ability to promote that process overseas caused modernisation to reach the peak of its influence in the early 1960s.[11] This was as much the case in Australia as in the United States.

More broadly, developmentalism was the ideological belief held by many experts and policymakers that the process of development was an inherently positive thing and was something to be actively encouraged. For much of the post-Second World War period, modernisation was the orthodox conception of this belief. While most commonly associated with Walt Rostow and reaching its peak in the early 1960s, this orthodoxy did not emerge out of nowhere. In the mid-1940s, Eugene Staley and Paul Rosenstein-Rodan emphasised the role of government policy in driving economic growth, which would thereby facilitate the development process.[12] For these theorists, increased production needed to be actively encouraged in order to safeguard the welfare of poorer peoples. It was in this capacity that development took on what Gilbert Rist refers to as a "transitive meaning." No longer was development a process that just

[10] Rostow, *Stages of Economic Growth*, 165.

[11] Ekbladh, *The Great American Mission*; Michael E. Latham, *Modernization as Ideology: American Social Science and "Nation Building" in the Kennedy Era* (Chapel Hill, NC: University of North Carolina Press, 2000); Nils Gilman, *Mandarins of the Future: Modernization Theory in Cold War America* (Baltimore: Johns Hopkins University Press, 2003).

[12] Staley, *World Economic Development*; P.N. Rosenstein-Rodan, "The International Development of Economically Backward Areas," *International Affairs* 20, no. 2 (1944).

happened; "now it was possible to 'develop' a region."[13] This growth-centric model assumed its level of orthodoxy throughout the 1950s and 1960s, enhanced first by the work of West Indian born-British economist, W. Arthur Lewis, and then by American modernisation theorists such as Rostow.[14] In Australia, this approach was epitomised in the immediate post-war period by John Crawford and Douglas Copland, and then later by Heinz Arndt.[15]

Alternatively, another set of ideas aimed to revise the Western-oriented, growth-centric assumptions of Rostow and his international counterparts. From the 1950s onward, economists—mostly in the Global South—challenged the orthodox position, arguing that developmental policy brought benefits not to the poor, but rather to those already in a position of economic and political power. Argentinian economist Raul Prebisch developed the earliest iteration of what would eventually become known as dependency theory in 1950, and by the mid-1960s, the notion had taken hold.[16] The earliest demonstration of the political power of dependency theory was the 1964 United Nations Conference on Trade and Development (UNCTAD), which posed significant challenges to Australia's previous conception of its own developmental position. By the late 1960s, dependency theory attracted an Australian following, most evident in the work of Rex Mortimer.[17] Entering the 1970s, dependency theory was joined by numerous other theoretical concepts and positions that challenged the growth orthodoxy. Self-reliance and basic needs

[13] Gilbert Rist, *The History of Development: From Western Origins to Global Faith*, 3rd ed. (London: Zed, 2008), 73.

[14] W. Arthur Lewis, *The Theory of Economic Growth* (London: Allen & Unwin, 1955).

[15] John Crawford and A.A. Ross, *Wartime Agriculture in Australia and New Zealand 1939–50* (Stanford, CA: Stanford University Press, 1954); D.B. Copland, *The Changing Structure of the Western Economy* (Montreal: McGill University Press, 1963), 18; H.W. Arndt, *A Small Rich Industrial Country: Studies in Australian Development, Aid and Trade* (Melbourne: Cheshire, 1968).

[16] United Nations Economic Commission for Latin America, *The Economic Development of Latin America and Its Principal Problems* (Lake Success: United Nations Department of Economic Affairs, 1950); H.W. Arndt, *Economic Development: The History of an Idea* (Chicago: University of Chicago Press, 1987), 120; Andre Gunder Frank, *Capitalism and Underdevelopment in Latin America: Historical Studies of Chile and Brazil*, rev. ed. (Harmondsworth: Penguin, 1971).

[17] Rex Mortimer, ed., *Showcase State: The Illusion of Indonesia's "Accelerated Modernisation"* (Sydney: Angus & Robertson, 1973).

approaches exemplified the shift away from growth as the fundamental goal of developmental theory and policy and found a ready audience in Australia in the 1970s. Crucially, even these critical stances aimed to promote development, albeit in the context of attempted structural change.[18]

The Age of International Development

The period spanning from the mid-1940s through to the mid-1970s can be characterised as the 'age of development.' Gilbert Rist presents the establishment of the American Point Four program of 1949, which was the United States' first major attempt to provide bilateral aid, as having "*inaugurated the 'development age*."[19] This program built on the work of scholars such as Staley and Rosenstein-Rodan, whose post-war vision of international development was taken up by President Harry Truman.[20] The end of the Second World War was marked by a global impulse to not just prevent another war of its kind but to also create a better, more prosperous world. The international symbols of this were the United Nations, formed in 1945 in San Francisco, as well as the Bretton Woods institutions formed in 1944, with the International Bank for Reconstruction and Development (World Bank) providing the clearest example of increased interest in developmental concerns. Aside from the institutional changes that occurred in the aftermath of war, politicians and experts throughout the world also sought to 'improve' peoples' lives. This was seen in the establishment of a welfare state in the United Kingdom. This was partly a result of states feeling the need to repay the wartime sacrifices of their populations but was also motivated by evolving ideas of welfare and development.[21]

This was not just a domestic process. A growing number of experts and politicians observed the poor living conditions of those people most

[18] Daniel Immerwahr, *Thinking Small: The United States and the Lure of Community Development* (Cambridge, MA: Harvard University Press, 2015), 172.

[19] Rist, *History of Development*, 71 (Emphasis in original); Frederick Cooper, "Writing the History of Development," *Journal of Modern European History* 8, no. 1 (2010): 8; Corinna R. Unger, *International Development: A Postwar History* (London: Bloomsbury, 2018).

[20] Ekbladh, *The Great American Mission*, 77–78.

[21] Chris Renwick, *Bread for All: The Origins of the Welfare State* (London: Penguin, 2017).

affected by the war, as well as in areas that remained under colonial rule. A growing number of scholars have traced this process, demonstrating that over time Western civil society came to accept a degree of responsibility to prevent the suffering of others. As Didier Fassin contends, humanitarianism "concerns the victims of poverty, homelessness, unemployment, and exile, as well as of disasters, famines, epidemics, and wars – in short, every situation characterised by precariousness."[22] Motivated by this sense of responsibility and a growing faith in government's role in ameliorating social ills, after the Second World War economists and other scholars conceived of ways to ensure that the precariousness associated with poverty could be overcome.

The age of international development emerged out of the integration of these humanitarian and economic impulses. Throughout the 1950s and 1960s, international development entered its golden era. Driven by the modernisation orthodoxy, experts and leaders throughout the Global North promoted development projects throughout the Global South. This was partly a product of the Cold War, which often saw American-led development compete with its Soviet counterparts.[23] This only tells part of the story, however, as development also had an energy of its own. As David Ekbladh explains, "modernisation ideas worked their way into Cold War policies, they were not created by them."[24] Foreign aid budgets were at their historical peak for many countries during this period, as the confluence of political, humanitarian, and developmental impulses drove the Global North to offer assistance to the Global South. This was also a time of sustained economic growth throughout the North, which eased the financial 'sacrifice' of providing foreign aid. The power of these ideas can be seen in the words of Eugene Staley in 1961, at the height of the development era:

[22] Didier Fassin, *Humanitarian Reason: A Moral History of the Present* (Berkeley: University of California Press, 2012), x. Other examples of this scholarship include Michael N. Barnett, *Empire of Humanity: A History of Humanitarianism* (Ithaca, NY: Cornell University Press, 2011); Ian R. Tyrrell, *Reforming the World: The Creation of America's Moral Empire* (Princeton, NJ: Princeton University Press, 2010).

[23] Latham, *Modernization as Ideology*; David C. Engerman, "West Meets East: The Center for International Studies and Indian Economic Development," in *Staging Growth: Modernization, Development, and the Global Cold War*, ed. David C. Engerman, et al. (Amherst: University of Massachusetts Press, 2003), 202; Gilman, *Mandarins of the Future*, 3.

[24] Ekbladh, *The Great American Mission*, 4.

> Large segments of the human race that for the last several centuries have been relatively weak in comparison with the West because of their technological and economic 'backwardness' are now resolved to modernize their economies as rapidly as they can. Compelling reasons of enlightened self-interest, reinforced by humanitarianism, lead the West to hasten this process by making international aid of various kinds available.[25]

For experts like Staley, development was a goal sought by all, and foreign aid was the means by which it would be achieved.

While 1945 and the end of the Second World War marks a clear dividing point in international history, the end of the age of international development was a product of much more complex forces. By the mid-1970s, the formal international process of decolonisation was effectively complete, as new states embarked on the process of consolidating their newfound independence. While the lingering effects of colonial rule continue to be felt through to the twenty-first century, it is important not to understate the significance of this process. It resulted in a brief shift in international relations, as the bloc of newly independent, developing countries took a much greater degree of control over their place in the international development system.[26] In the words of Gilbert Rist, "The 1970s will go down in history as the decade when the South's power seemed to be growing. It was a time of hope and enthusiasm about the role that had finally been recognized for it within the international order."[27]

The result was a push for a New International Economic Order (NIEO), which aimed at structural change in the global economy. As Nils Gilman explains:

> Its fundamental objective was to *transform the governance of the global economy to redirect more of the benefits of transnational integration toward 'the developing nations'* – thus completing the geopolitical process of decolonization and creating a democratic global order of truly sovereign states.[28]

[25] Eugene Staley, *The Future of Underdeveloped Countries: Political Implications of Economic Development*, rev. ed. (New York: Praeger, 1961), 7.

[26] Nils Gilman, "The New International Economic Order: A Reintroduction," *Humanity: An International Journal of Human Rights, Humanitarianism, and Development* 6, no. 1 (2015).

[27] Rist, *History of Development*, 140.

[28] Gilman, "The New International Economic Order," 1, (Emphasis in original).

Shaped by the work of dependency theorists alongside the ambitious ideas of post-colonial leaders throughout the Global South, the NIEO reached its peak in the 1970s before its quite rapid collapse. This collapse was due to a range of factors, including Global North resistance, divisions within the Global South and the global downturn in the capitalist world economy.[29]

The changes to international capitalism, driven by economic and energy crises in the West and the neoliberal challenge to post-war Keynesianism, spelled the end of the post-war age of international development by the mid-1970s.[30] They had a detrimental effect on Global North attitudes towards foreign aid, producing a significant decline in developmental assistance by the late 1970s. This process is depicted vividly by Vijay Prashad:

> The Third World's NIEO faltered, as did Atlantic liberalism. The space abandoned by them was occupied by a philosophy that descended from the stale air of Mont Pelerin, Switzerland, where Friedrich Hayek, Milton Friedman, Ludwig von Mises, and their comrades had incubated the theory of neoliberalism in the 1940s. From the ashes of Atlantic liberalism and the Third World project rose global neoliberalism.[31]

The age of international development was a product of the rise of 'Atlantic liberalism' and Keynesian economics. It was shaped by the tenets of modernisation until the process of decolonisation and the rise of the NIEO challenged the primacy of the Global North. By the mid-1970s, however, this system had broken down, to be replaced by a new neoliberal orthodoxy. Development did not disappear, but it was to enter a new age.

[29] Rist, *History of Development*, 153; Vijay Prashad, *The Poorer Nations: A Possible History of the Global South* (London: Verso, 2012), 17.

[30] Stuart Hall, "The Neoliberal Revolution," *Soundings*, no. 48 (2011): 9–11.

[31] Prashad, *The Poorer Nations*, 17.

Australia in the Age of International Development

Australia was an active participant in international development between 1945 and 1975. As this book will show, many of the ideas and policies implemented by Australian experts and policymakers drew on international influences. As the post-war years progressed, however, an Australian developmentalism emerged. As with Staley and Rosenstein-Rodan, Australian economists were shaped by the experiences of war and their visions of development reflected this. The demands of what became known in Australia as Post-War Reconstruction (PWR) also facilitated the rise of Australian developmentalism through the emergence of economists in the centre of policymaking in Canberra. Nicholas Brown has explained the modernist impulses behind PWR's objective of 'governing prosperity' after 1945.[32] In his biography of H.C. 'Nugget' Coombs, the Departmental Head of the Post-War Reconstruction Department from 1943 to 1948, Tim Rowse suggests that "World War II was the making of economists," due to the perception that economic thinking was needed to solve the pressing post-war problems.[33] Stuart Macintyre, in his comprehensive study of PWR, makes a similar point, claiming that:

> No-one questioned the decision to entrust reconstruction planning to economists. It was simply taken as axiomatic that they possessed the expertise that was needed to break down the components of the task, calculate the dimensions, devise the most appropriate mechanisms and forecast the outcomes.[34]

The rise of economists and the developmental challenges of PWR provided the perfect context for Australia to enter the age of international development.

[32] Nicholas Brown, *Governing Prosperity: Social Change and Social Analysis in Australia in the 1950s* (Cambridge: Cambridge University Press, 1995).

[33] Tim Rowse, *Nugget Coombs: A Reforming Life* (Cambridge: Cambridge University Press, 2002), 145.

[34] Stuart Macintyre, *Australia's Boldest Experiment: War and Reconstruction in the 1940s* (Sydney: NewSouth Publishing, 2015), 73.

One tension that quickly emerged in Australian developmentalism in the PWR period (1945–1949) was between Australian and international development. Much of the published work on development in Australia published in the 1940s focused on telling the Australian story.[35] These scholars generally attributed Australian development to agricultural improvement and maintained the argument that, as G.L. Wood argued in 1947, "Australia's development is still in its infancy."[36] Still, these observers, along with policymakers in Canberra, maintained an international outlook. Development is inherently comparative, and Australia's economy was regularly contrasted with the 'developed' economies of North America and Western Europe, as well as with the 'underdeveloped' regions of Asia, Africa and the Pacific. This tension between domestic and international development was most pronounced in Australian perceptions and policies towards its colonial possession of PNG. Ian Downs, the official historian of Australian post-war rule in PNG, argued that the development of PNG was inhibited by "the post-war reconstruction program in the hands of authorities more concerned with problems on the Australian mainland."[37] In contrast, historians of PWR suggest that the development of PNG received substantially more attention after 1945.[38] Both positions have merit, as this book will show. Australian engagement with international development significantly increased after 1945, but it was often tempered by a sense of anxiety about Australia's own developmental status.

Much as development entered its golden era in the 1950s and 1960s, Australian developmentalism also consolidated itself during this period. The modernisation orthodoxy was persuasive in Australia, with economists such as Douglas Copland embracing some of the key principles found in the work of Rostow. Copland, one of the pre-eminent Australian economists of the mid-twentieth century, regularly reflected

[35] A.G.L. Shaw, *The Economic Development of Australia*, rev. ed. (London: Longmans, Green, 1946); G.L. Wood, ed., *Australia: Its Resources and Development* (New York: Macmillan, 1947).

[36] Wood, *Australia*, vii.

[37] Ian Downs, *The Australian Trusteeship Papua New Guinea, 1945–75* (Canberra: Australian Government Publishing Service, 1980), 54.

[38] Macintyre, *Australia's Boldest Experiment*, 310; Kate Darian-Smith, "World War 2 and Post-War Reconstruction," in *The Cambridge History of Australia*, ed. Alison Bashford and Stuart Macintyre (Port Melbourne: Cambridge University Press, 2013), 110.

on both Australian and international development.[39] For instance, in his 1963 *The Changing Structure of the Western Economy*, Copland wrote:

> The West has pioneered the development of modern techniques, as well as initiated the egalitarian features of the modern welfare state. It is therefore in a position to guide and assist the underdeveloped countries along the same path and in the process to enrich its own experience, in both economic and human terms.[40]

This was language reminiscent of Rostow's depiction of the modernisation process, published only three years earlier.

The modernisation orthodoxy also filtered through to Australian analysis of PNG. As early as 1951, the language of modernisation could be seen in Cyril Belshaw's analysis of Australian goals in the colony. He wrote, "the people of the South-Eastern Division [of Papua] are waiting for a lead, and it is only their lack of education in the techniques and customs of modern life that is preventing them taking that lead themselves."[41] Belshaw had just completed an Australian National University (ANU)-sponsored report on PNG, alongside Oskar Spate and prominent development expert Trevor Swan. The terminology used by Belshaw was still quite general, but his emphasis on the need for Australian leadership and the goal of a 'modern life' were key features of modernisation thinking. This kind of analysis became more refined entering into the 1960s, as could be seen in David Bettison's analysis of PNG. Bettison, who had established his developmental credentials in Southern Africa, had moved to the ANU New Guinea Research Unit in the early 1960s. In his analysis of PNG, Bettison employed the language of modernisation to explore the psychological impacts of the process, writing "The major towns and their hinterlands contain a class of indigenous person who

[39] Marjorie Harper, *Douglas Copland: Scholar, Economist, Diplomat* (Carlton, Victoria: Miegunyah Press, 2013). Alex Millmow has written a fascinating piece on Copland's 'battle' with younger post-war Australian economists. While Copland may have dissented from orthodox views regarding Australian development, if anything this brought him closer to the international orthodoxy. Alex Millmow, "Douglas Copland's Battle with the Younger Brethren of Economists," *Australian Economic History Review* 53, no. 2 (2013).

[40] Copland, *The Changing Structure of the Western Economy*, 64–65.

[41] Cyril S. Belshaw, "Native Administration in South-Eastern Papua," *Australian Outlook* 5, no. 2 (1951): 115.

is looking to the future with ambitious eyes, a rapidly growing competence and a willingness to experiment with new and modern forms of organisation."[42] Just as Walt Rostow foresaw the need for a fundamental reconfiguration of 'traditional' societies—in Australia the word 'primitive' was more common—Bettison approved of a similar process in PNG. This kind of thinking dominated Australian attitudes towards international and colonial development well into the 1960s.

Just as Australian developmentalism revolved around questions of domestic development in the early stages of the post-war period, a similar process occurred throughout the 1950s and 1960s. Once again Douglas Copland was at the centre of the story. His most memorable contribution to Australian thinking at this time was that Australia was a 'milk bar' economy that involved significant increases in consumerism alongside inefficiencies in other areas of the economy.[43] This perpetuated the Australian anxiety regarding its own development, which impacted upon the depth of Australia's engagement towards the promotion of development overseas. Nevertheless, Australian developmentalism assumed its own twist during this period, which largely revolved around this very question. For prominent economists such as John Crawford, Australia's development, which largely revolved around improvements in agricultural efficiency, offered a useful model to those 'developing' countries that were the subject of intense academic analysis during this period. As Groenewegen and McFarlane point out, Crawford took a slightly different line to the more conventional modernisation theory: "While not opposing industrialisation, he advocated taking agriculture and pastoral sectors as the main base in these cases."[44] For Crawford, the United States and Western Europe were not the best models on which to base the modernisation process. Instead, it was Australia, with its modern infrastructure and society alongside an economy based around primary exports, that offered the most useful guide. This was largely a disagreement over detail,

[42] David George Bettison, "The People of Papua-New Guinea," in *The Independence of Papua-New Guinea: What Are the Pre-Requisites?—Four Lectures Presented under the Auspices of the Public Lectures Committee of the Australian National University*, ed. David George Bettison, E.K. Fisk, F.J. West and J.G. Crawford (Sydney: Angus and Robertson, 1962), 10.

[43] Brown, *Governing Prosperity*, 88–89; Peter D. Groenewegen and Bruce J. McFarlane, *A History of Australian Economic Thought* (London: Routledge, 2011), 140–141.

[44] Groenewegen and McFarlane, *A History of Australian Economic Thought*, 222.

however, as it was still clear that some kind of model should be offered to those countries seeking to modernise.

The modernisation orthodoxy continued to exert some influence as the 1960s progressed. Heinz Arndt emerged as a pre-eminent developmental expert in Australia. An assistant of Paul Rosenstein-Rodan (whom he referred to in his memoir as 'Rosi') in London during the Second World War, Arndt moved to Canberra to work at the Canberra University College in the war's immediate aftermath.[45] After assuming a research chair at the Australian National University (ANU) in 1963, he specialised in the study of Indonesia, but regularly also commented on Australia's development. During the 1960s, his work largely corresponded with the orthodox emphasis on modernisation and growth, which reflected the influence of Rosenstein-Rodan.[46] His most important contribution in the 1960s was *A Small Rich Industrial Country*, which was a compilation of his developmental thinking throughout the decade and which commented on both Australia's development as well as that of its neighbours.[47] It is driven by a rather conventional understanding of the development process and can be seen as the culmination of the 1960s' orthodoxy in Australian developmentalism.

Alongside all of this emerged an alternative set of views that challenged the dominant modernisation orthodoxy. As with many aspects of Australian developmentalism, the emergence of this alternative mirrored international processes, as demonstrated by the rise of dependency theory and ideas of self-reliance that were a product of the decolonisation process. This shift was exacerbated by the link between modernisation and the increasingly unpopular Vietnam War, which was personified by Walt Rostow's involvement in the Kennedy and Johnson Administrations. Australian observers also took note of these shifts and developed an alternative vision of development. This was perhaps most clearly shown in the work of Monash University academic Rex Mortimer. A long-time communist and somewhat late entrant into the field of development (he completed his PhD at Monash in 1971 at the age of 45), Mortimer quickly became a prominent voice for a

[45] H.W. Arndt, *A Course through Life* (Canberra: National Centre for Development Studies, Australian National University, 1985). He then moved to the ANU in the early 1960s.

[46] Groenewegen and McFarlane, *A History of Australian Economic Thought*, 181.

[47] Arndt, *A Small Rich Industrial Country*; Groenewegen and McFarlane, *A History of Australian Economic Thought*, 183.

vision of development that opposed Heinz Arndt.[48] This was partly a product of institutional rivalries between Mortimer's Monash University and Arndt's ANU, but also clearly reflected the competing strands of Australian developmentalism that had emerged by the end of the 1960s.[49]

The debate revolved around each scholar's analysis of Indonesia's development following Suharto's rise to power in 1965. For Mortimer, Arndt was "to a greater degree than most Indonesianists in Australia, and most Indonesian intellectuals outside the governmental in-group... highly optimistic about the progress of Indonesia's Western-conceived development effort."[50] In contrast, Mortimer suggested:

> The division of the world into countries that are growing relatively richer and countries that are growing relatively poorer is not simply the product of some historical accident ... but constitutes a network of interactions which is systematically enforced by the wealthy club.[51]

This dependency-inspired critique illustrated the divisions within the two dominant Australian understandings of economic development that emerged in the late 1960s and early 1970s. Indeed, Mortimer also applied these ideas to Australia's colonial administration in PNG, arguing alongside Azeem Amarshi and Kenneth Good that Australian development policy was "so insidious in its fostering of dependence" amongst the Indigenous population.[52] The brief rise and fall of this school of thought—Mortimer's untimely death in 1979 weakened this movement—coincided with significant changes in Australian and international developmentalism.

[48] T.H. Irving, "Mortimer, Rex Alfred (1926–1979)," *Australian Dictionary of Biography*, National Centre of Biography, Australian National University, http://adb.anu.edu.au/biography/mortimer-rex-alfred-11181/text9925, published first in hardcopy 2000.

[49] Arndt, *A Course through Life*, 65; Jemma Purdey, *From Vienna to Yogyakarta: The Life of Herb Feith* (Sydney: University of New South Wales Press, 2011), 363–364.

[50] Mortimer, *Showcase State*, 121.

[51] Mortimer, *Showcase State*, 129.

[52] Azeem Amarshi, Kenneth Good and Rex Mortimer, *Development and Dependency: The Political Economy of Papua New Guinea* (Melbourne: Oxford University Press, 1979), x.

The conclusion of the age of development in Australia was a product of both the global end of development's 'golden age' as well as some occurrences that were particular to Australia. The brief rise and fall of the Labor Whitlam Government from 1972 to 1975 offers a clear impetus to identifying 1975 as a dividing point in Australia's perception of itself and its relationship with the Global South. Whitlam's firm anti-colonial beliefs pervaded his government and shaped Australian policy and ideas during the period.[53] The proliferation of new developmental ideas and actors in Australia at this time speaks to the reformist energy that came with the Whitlam Government. However, the most obvious moment to demonstrate the conclusion of the golden age of development in Australia is PNG's independence, achieved in September 1975.[54] While analysing the development of PNG continues to be at the heart of Australian developmentalism, the end of the colonial administration marked a clear end of an era.

Australian Aid in the Age of International Development—The Colombo Plan *and* Papua New Guinea

Given that Australian developmentalism was preoccupied with the 'underdeveloped' regions to Australia's north, it is little surprise that Canberra's foreign aid policy was mostly in this direction as well. The vast majority of Australian aid spending—almost ninety per cent between 1945 and 1975—went either to the newly independent countries of South and Southeast Asia or to PNG.[55] This aid satisfied both the developmental claims of people discussed in the previous section, as well as concerns over national interest and regional politics. Australian diplomats and policymakers pursued a genuine policy of development that was

[53] Michael Sexton, *The Great Crash: The Short Life and Sudden Death of the Whitlam Government*, rev. ed. (Melbourne: Scribe, 2005); Jenny Hocking, *Gough Whitlam: His Time—The Biography Volume II* (Carlton: Miegunyah Press, 2012), 189–190.

[54] Hank Nelson, *Taim Bilong Masta: The Australian Involvement with Papua New Guinea* (Crows Nest: ABC Enterprises, 1990), 217–219; Donald Denoon, *A Trial Separation: Australia and the Decolonisation of Papua New Guinea* (Canberra: ANU E Press, 2012).

[55] Alan E. Wilkinson, "The Politics of Australian Aid Policy, 1950–1972" (PhD Thesis, ANU, 1976), 371–376.

more than a fig leaf covering political goals, and which was inspired by modernisation theory in concert with global trends. The developmental imperatives for aid policy following the Second World War were a product of a complex intersection of economic and humanitarian impulses.

There has often been a tension in examining Australian policy between 1945 and 1975 towards Southeast Asia alongside that of its colonial administration of PNG. Scholars of Australian foreign policy tend to emphasise the Colombo Plan and downplay PNG. Alternatively, scholars of Australian colonialism often sidestep the developmental parallels with Australia's other major aid program from the period. For instance, in his early analysis of the evolution of Australian aid, Frank Jarrett treated the Colombo Plan as a "significant departure point" in Australia's aid program.[56] Other scholars, such as David Lowe, Daniel Oakman and Nicholas Brown, have produced detailed studies of the Colombo Plan as the primary medium through which Australian technical assistance was provided after the Second World War.[57] This pioneering work has expanded our understanding of the utility of aid in both traditional and cultural diplomacy. However, Australian attempts to promote development beyond its shores were not limited to the Colombo Plan, and the resources given to the administration in PNG generally dwarfed those devoted to the Plan.

By the early 1960s, policymakers in Canberra counted grants made to both Southeast Asia and PNG in external aid calculations. Examining colonial and foreign aid policy alongside one another allows a new understanding of Australian aid. This is not a new approach in the international scholarship on aid and development. The connections between development, aid, and colonialism in the British, French and Dutch Empires have

[56] F.G. Jarrett, *The Evolution of Australia's Aid Program* (Canberra: Australian Development Studies Network, 1994), 1.

[57] Daniel Oakman, *Facing Asia: A History of the Colombo Plan* (Canberra: Pandanus Books, 2004); David Lowe, "The Colombo Plan," in *Australia and the End of Empires: The Impact of Decolonisation in Australia's Near North, 1945–65*, ed. David Lowe (Geelong: Deakin University Press, 1996); David Lowe, "Canberra's Colombo Plan: Public Images of Australia's Relations with Post-Colonial South and Southeast Asia in the 1950s," *South Asia: Journal of South Asian Studies* 25, no. 2 (2002); David Lowe, "Journalists and the Stirring of Australian Public Diplomacy: The Colombo Plan Towards the 1960s," *Journal of Contemporary History* 48, no. 1 (2013); Nicholas Brown, "Student, Expert, Peacekeeper: Three Versions of International Engagement," *Australian Journal of Politics and History* 57, no. 1 (2011): 39–45.

been shown by historians Frederick Cooper, Joseph Hodge, Marc Frey and Suzanne Moon amongst others.[58] This provides an entry point into understanding Australian foreign aid and colonial policies as being part of a single process. Taking this approach, Eddie Ward's 'New Deal' in PNG, established in 1945, marks the new beginning point for post-war Australian aid, rather than the Colombo Plan of 1950.

Development provides the link between the two spheres of aid. As Scott MacWilliam points out: "Throughout the entire period from 1945 until PNG's independence, no term appeared more often than development as the objective of state policies."[59] With regard to the Colombo Plan, David Lowe emphasises political considerations while also acknowledging the place of development, writing that Australian policymakers quickly recognised that "the best way to exert political influence … was by fostering economic development in the region."[60] This is not to deny that self-interested political motivations were not involved in the formulation of Australian aid policy in the age of international development. One of the central claims of this book is that the political imperatives behind Australian aid policy in PNG and Southeast Asia have been slightly overstated, and that development was just as powerful a force in guiding experts and policymakers in Canberra and Port Moresby.

This is largely a response to scholarship that either downplays or ignores the place of development altogether. For over thirty years, historians of Australia's foreign policy have regarded the Colombo Plan as a tool to improve Australia's strategic relations with a decolonising Asia

[58] Marc Frey, "Control, Legitimacy, and the Securing of Interests: European Development Policy in South-East Asia from the Late Colonial Period to the Early 1960s," *Contemporary European History* 12, no. 4 (2003); Joseph Morgan Hodge, *Triumph of the Expert: Agrarian Doctrines of Development and the Legacies of British Colonialism* (Athens: Ohio University Press, 2007); Véronique Dimier, *The Invention of a European Development Aid Bureaucracy: Recycling Empire* (Basingstoke: Palgrave Macmillan, 2014); Daniel Gorman, "Britain, India, and the United Nations: Colonialism and the Development of International Governance, 1945–1960," *Journal of Global History* 9, no. 3 (2014); Suzanne Moon, *Technology and Ethical Idealism: A History of Development in the Netherlands East Indies* (Leiden: CNWS Publications, 2007).

[59] Scott MacWilliam, *Securing Village Life: Development in Late Colonial Papua New Guinea* (Canberra: ANU E Press, 2013), 3.

[60] David Lowe, "Percy Spender and the Colombo Plan 1950," *Australian Journal of Politics and History* 40, no. 2 (1994): 163.

during the Cold War.[61] Daniel Oakman centres on the political motivations behind the Colombo Plan, describing it as "a facade, a device intended to lure independent Asia into an alliance with the Western bloc."[62] Significantly, this analysis has influenced scholars of contemporary Australian aid policy, who emphasise the strategic purposes of aid in the immediate post-war period.[63] Andrew Rosser goes so far as to say that the "main driver of Australian aid policy has always been the government's foreign policy and security objectives."[64] Some scholars, such as Faye Sutherland, deny the place of development. Sutherland argued that during the 1960s, "in the areas of relief, development and sending personnel overseas ... the government's aid agenda was not driven by developmental concerns."[65] I firmly disagree with this position. Australian aid was more than a diplomatic tool to achieve closer relations with Asia; it was a product of the age of international development.

With regard to PNG, scholars have observed the rhetoric of development, but historians including Ian Downs, William Hudson and James Griffin have regarded development less as a historical process and more as an economic good. As a result, they have criticised the Australian

[61] P. Gifford, "The Cold War Across Asia," in *Facing North: A Century of Australian Engagement with Asia*, ed. David Goldsworthy and P.G. Edwards (Carlton South: Melbourne University Press, 2001), 174; P.G. Edwards and Gregory Pemberton, *Crises and Commitments: The Politics and Diplomacy of Australia's Involvement in Southeast Asian Conflicts, 1948–1965* (North Sydney: Allen & Unwin, 1992), 343; Gregory Pemberton, *All the Way: Australia's Road to Vietnam* (Sydney: Allen & Unwin, 1987), 38; Christopher Waters, "A Failure of Imagination: R.G. Casey and Australian Plans for Counter-Subversion in Asia, 1954–1956," *Australian Journal of Politics and History* 45, no. 3 (1999): 352.

[62] Oakman, *Facing Asia*, 67.

[63] Shahar Hameiri, "Risk Management, Neo-Liberalism and the Securitisation of the Australian Aid Program," *Australian Journal of International Affairs* 62, no. 3 (2008): 357–359.

[64] Andrew Rosser, "Neo-Liberalism and the Politics of Australian Aid Policy-Making," *Australian Journal of International Affairs* 62, no. 3 (2008): 372. A similar point is raised in Jack Corbett, *Australia's Foreign Aid Dilemma: Humanitarian Aspirations Confront Democratic Legitimacy* (Abingdon: Routledge, 2017), 20–21.

[65] Faye Sutherland, "The Dynamics of Aid and Development: Australian and Asian Responses to Poverty in the Region 1950s–1990s" (PhD Thesis, University of NSW, 1997), 165.

government's prioritising of social stability above development, particularly during the Hasluck period from 1951 to 1963.[66] Recent studies of Australian colonial policy take a more critical approach. Donald Denoon makes the important observation that development and the end of Australian colonial rule were deeply intertwined.[67] Scott MacWilliam presents a detailed examination of Australian developmental policy in PNG, with some analysis of the origins of the development idea.[68] However, there has yet to be a comprehensive analysis of developmental policy in PNG that takes the full gamut of Australian aid policy into account. While some scholars of Australian colonial policy have recognised the shift in emphasis on development in the 1940s, they have not investigated how this shift was a product of broader international processes.[69] What previous analyses lack, and what this book makes clear, is that Australia's colonial development policy did not take place in a political and intellectual vacuum. Australian colonial experts and policymakers were deeply interested in the evolution of international developmental ideas and policy, and this was reflected in the policies they introduced. This was true of both colonial and foreign policy; it is therefore necessary to examine the two together. Therefore, to examine the Colombo Plan or Australian policy in PNG in isolation is to look at only half the story. By revealing the interaction between Australian foreign aid and colonial policy, we gain a new, more comprehensive understanding of post-war Australian aid policy and its place in the age of international development.

[66] Downs, *The Australian Trusteeship Papua New Guinea*, 116; W.J. Hudson and Jill Daven, "Papua and New Guinea since 1945," in *Australia and Papua New Guinea*, ed. W.J. Hudson (Sydney: Sydney University Press, 1971), 158; James Griffin, Hank Nelson and Stewart Firth, *Papua New Guinea: A Political History* (Richmond: Heinemann Educational Australia, 1979).

[67] Donald Denoon, Philippa Mein Smith and Marivic Wyndham, *A History of Australia, New Zealand, and the Pacific* (Malden, MA: Blackwell Publishers, 2000), 400; Denoon, *A Trial Separation*, 32.

[68] MacWilliam, *Securing Village Life*, 5–7. Huntley Wright takes a similar approach to MacWilliam. Huntley Wright, "Protecting the National Interest: The Labor Government and the Reform of Australia's Colonial Policy, 1942–45," *Labour History* 82, no. May 2002 (2002).

[69] I.C. Campbell, "The ASOPA Controversy: A Pivot of Australian Policy for Papua and New Guinea, 1945–49," *The Journal of Pacific History* 35, no. 1 (2000): 98–99; Brian Jinks, "Alfred Conlon, the Directorate of Research and New Guinea," *Journal of Australian Studies* 7, no. 12 (1983): 28.

CHAPTER 2

"Stone Age to the Twentieth Century": Trusteeship and the New Deal for Papua New Guinea, 1945–1949

On September 21, 1943, Eddie Ward, the Labor member of parliament for East Sydney, took over the federal portfolios of External Territories and Transport. This was perceived as a demotion from his previous role as Minister for Labour and National Service, with Ward complaining that the "Japs have got the external territories and the army's got the transport."[1] Despite this complaint, immediately after taking his new position Ward outlined his vision for Australia's largest external territory, Papua New Guinea (PNG). Described in the press as a "New Deal" for PNG, Ward called for a new Australian policy for the colony's Indigenous population. In an attempt to overcome the "shabby" pre-war treatment of Papua New Guineans, Ward emphasised the need to improve medical and educational facilities in PNG.[2] This marked a decisive shift from earlier policies, which generally left the hitherto separate territories of Papua and New

[1] Ross McMullin, "Ward, Edward John (Eddie) (1899–1963)," Australian Dictionary of Biography, National Centre of Biography, Australian National University, http://adb.anu.edu.au/biography/ward-edward-john-eddie-11959/text21435, published first in hardcopy 2002.

[2] "Post-War New Deal for New Guinea Natives," *Canberra Times*, September 23, 1943. The "New Deal" terminology was used in a variety of ways in the Australian press during the war, as seen in the "new deals" for Education, the elderly, and returning soldiers.

N. Ferns, *Australia in the Age of International Development, 1945–1975*, Security, Conflict and Cooperation in the Contemporary World, https://doi.org/10.1007/978-3-030-50228-7_2

Guinea to fend for themselves.[3] The imperatives of the Second World War, which involved heavy fighting in New Guinea, prevented Ward from implementing any of these changes until 1945. Nevertheless, the terms of Australia's post-war colonial administration of PNG had been set.

In July 1945, with the war winding down in the Southwest Pacific, Ward now had the opportunity to give more details regarding his New Deal. Speaking to the House of Representatives, he presented his proposed bill for the provisional civil administration of PNG. This bill reinstated civilian control over PNG, after several years of military administration. In his second reading speech on July 4, Ward repeated his criticism of the pre-war neglect of PNG's Indigenous population.[4] For the Minister, civilian administration was to be accompanied by an increased interest in the development of the colony. This meant a removal of the indentured labour system and increased spending on Indigenous health and education, alongside a shift towards an economy that took both European and Indigenous enterprise into account. As part of his defence of the new policy, Ward expressed hope that the Australian administration of PNG would "set an example to the world by the conditions we establish there."[5] This "new deal" for PNG was driven by Ward's belief that it was the Commonwealth's responsibility to provide for the welfare of the colony's Indigenous population. In order to "improve" the lives of those in PNG, Ward felt it would be necessary to take a more active role in developing the colony. As such, the New Deal marks the first step in Australia's involvement in the post-war age of international development, which lasted into the mid-1970s.

Over the next four years, the Labor government, guided by international principles of trusteeship, instituted the New Deal in its attempt to promote development in PNG.[6] This was marked by a rejection of the

[3] J.D. Legge, "The Murray Period: Papua 1906–40," in *Australia and Papua New Guinea*, ed. W.J. Hudson (Sydney: Sydney University Press, 1971), 52.

[4] *Commonwealth Parliamentary Debates* (Hereafter cited as *CPD*), House of Representatives, no. 27, 1945, July 4, 1945, 4052.

[5] *CPD*, House of Representatives, no. 29, 1945, July 19, 1945, 4306.

[6] Downs, *The Australian Trusteeship Papua New Guinea, 1945–75*, 3; MacWilliam, *Securing Village Life*, 38–39; Margriet Roe, "Papua-New Guinea and War 1941–5," in *Australia and Papua New Guinea*, ed. W.J. Hudson (Sydney: Sydney University Press, 1971), 146–149; Elwyn Spratt, *Eddie Ward: Firebrand of East Sydney* (Adelaide: Rigby, 1965), 143–145; Arthur Hoyle, *Eddie Ward: The Truest Labor Man* (Canberra: A. Hoyle, 1994), 127–161.

pre-war notion that PNG would have to fend for itself, with little or no Commonwealth assistance. It also challenged the expatriate business interests' notion that they could rely on a system of indentured labour.[7] The New Deal sought to improve living conditions of Indigenous Papua New Guineans through the removal of indentured labour and the promotion of agricultural development. In order to achieve these goals, the Commonwealth Government significantly increased its financial assistance to PNG. From a pre-war (1938/9) level of £42,500 per annum, the Australian grant to Papua New Guinea had risen to £3.2 million by 1948/1949.[8] This significant increase in funding set the tone for the next three decades of Australian colonial rule, and economic assistance to PNG became the dominant component of Australian aid.

This chapter explores how the New Deal for PNG emerged as the first post-war attempt by Australia to provide 'aid' to 'underdeveloped' parts of the world. While political and strategic imperatives were present in post-war Australian colonial policy, a humanitarian and developmental desire to improve the standard of living of the Indigenous population was a major consideration. The emphasis on development in the New Deal was a result of shifting Australian and international attitudes towards colonialism, which were manifested most clearly in the UN concept of trusteeship. Central to this vision was the belief in a more active government role in providing developmental assistance. This was pronounced in PNG, where experts and policymakers alike were struck by the extreme 'primitiveness' of the Indigenous population. Whereas prior to the war Australian colonial rule was dictated by a paternalistic "protection" of the Indigenous population alongside expatriate economic exploitation, the New Deal sought to actively improve the living standards of the Papua New Guineans.

[7] Griffin, Nelson, and Firth, *Papua New Guinea*, 11.

[8] Paul Hasluck, *Australian Policy in Papua and New Guinea* (University of Sydney, 1956), 3–4.

Development at the End of the Second World War

The New Deal was part of a new development paradigm that emerged in the 1940s, which attracted debate within the Commonwealth bureaucracy. International forces, both academic and political, worked to influence the Australian attitude towards its colonial possessions. Outside Canberra, the expatriate community in PNG provided considerable resistance to the new developmental approach in the belief that the increased awareness of Indigenous welfare posed a threat to their interests. They sought a return to the pre-war system of local control that was heavily influenced by expatriate needs.[9] The New Deal challenged these interests by suggesting more explicit attention be given to the development of the Indigenous population. Nevertheless, Ward and his department saw a place for expatriate enterprise. As such, the New Deal came to reflect both the complexities within Australia's understanding of development, as well as the difficulties in implementing the ideas through policy. Ultimately, while the New Deal marks the first Australian attempt to provide developmental assistance after the Second World War, its implementation was limited by political imperatives. This would emerge as a motif in Australian aid between 1945 and 1975.

Scholarly understanding of development underwent a shift in the mid- to late 1940s. Central to this shift was the recognition that global peace and prosperity depended on increased economic development in poorer parts of the world. When combined with increasing governmental interest in development, the stage was set for the rise of the age of international development. The two key scholars who helped to propel this new understanding were Paul Rosenstein-Rodan and Eugene Staley. Born in Krakow, Poland in 1902, Rosenstein-Rodan worked in Vienna before moving to Britain in 1930, working at University College, London, and then, the London School of Economics (LSE) until moving to the World Bank in 1947.[10] Staley was born in Nebraska in 1906 and received his Ph.D. in economics from the University of Chicago in 1928. Following a brief tenure as assistant professor at Chicago, he moved to Tufts University where he worked with the American Council on Foreign Relations and the International Labour Organisation (ILO).[11] It was through the

[9] *CPD*, House of Representatives, no. 29, 1945, July 18, 1945, 4204.

[10] Meier and Seers, *Pioneers in Development*, 205.

[11] Ekbladh, *The Great American Mission*, 65.

ILO that Staley began to take an increased interest in the question of economic development.

Writing in 1944, Rosenstein-Rodan presented a strong case for increased international attention to 'backward' economies.[12] Staley expanded upon Rosenstein-Rodan's call in the same year, in his book, *World Economic Development*.[13] The strength of his views can be gleaned from its opening pages, where Staley writes: "It cannot be too often repeated that improvement in living standards depends fundamentally on improvement in the capacity of a people to produce. No programme of charity can abolish want."[14] For Staley, economic assistance had to go beyond the simple protection of peoples' welfare; rather, development would take place when people were given the means to increase their own production. This idea was central to developmental thinking in the decades following the Second World War. Over time, Staley's ideas were steadily incorporated into international policies towards the 'underdeveloped' parts of the world.[15]

In Australia, a number of prominent economists were involved in research into the development process, establishing connections between Australian foreign policies and global trends. Many focused on their own country's historical development, producing a burgeoning domestic field of developmental theory. Edward Shann, Brian Fitzpatrick and Alan Shaw produced extensive histories of Australian development in the 1930s and 1940s, building towards a consensus that increased efficiency in primary industry had been the engine for Australian growth and improved living standards.[16] One of the foremost interwar economists in Australia, Shann

[12] Rosenstein-Rodan, "International Development of Economically Backward Areas."

[13] Staley, *World Economic Development*.

[14] Staley, *World Economic Development*, 2.

[15] For discussion of the incorporation of Staley's ideas into American policy, see David A. Baldwin, *Economic Development and American Foreign Policy, 1943–62* (Chicago: University of Chicago Press, 1966), 53; Ekbladh, *The Great American Mission*, 65–69. A connection can also be drawn between this process and the work of industrial missions throughout the Pacific, discussed in Kirstie Close-Barry, *A Mission Divided: Race, Culture and Colonialism in Fiji's Methodist Mission* (Acton: ANU Press, 2015), 81.

[16] E.O.G. Shann, *An Economic History of Australia* (Cambridge: University Press, 1930); Brian Fitzpatrick, *The British Empire in Australia: An Economic History 1834–1939* (Melbourne: Melbourne University Press in association with Oxford University Press, 1941), 502; Shaw, *The Economic Development of Australia*, 89, 173.

was also Arthur Tange's father-in-law. Tange would become the long-term Secretary of the Department of External Affairs, and a central figure in the rise of development as a component of Australian foreign policy. According to Lionel Frost, both Shann and Fitzpatrick emphasised that Australian "improvements" in agriculture had been achieved in the interests of Empire as opposed to strictly nationalist goals.[17] Importantly, in the pre-war period these experts presented development as a process divorced from state intervention.

Two members of this burgeoning field of economists, H.C. 'Nugget' Coombs and John Crawford, were called upon to serve the Commonwealth, as wartime needs strengthened links between government and academia. Crawford had established himself as a prominent Australian economist prior to the Second World War, as seen in his collaboration with British-born Colin Clark, one of Australia's earliest developmental theorists. This collaboration culminated in a pioneering study of national income statistics, an area of research that assumed great prominence in developmental studies.[18] Recruited into the Department of Post-War Reconstruction (PWR), which oversaw Australian planning for the transition back to a peacetime economy, Crawford quickly adapted to the bureaucratic environment.[19] During this period, he steadily refined his understanding of the importance of agriculture in the process of economic development, identifying PNG and India as areas where increased agricultural production would lead to significant economic development.[20] Reflecting upon the work of PWR a quarter of a century later, Coombs identified Crawford as giving "Australian political and economic thinking its characteristic patterns during the forties and early fifties."[21]

Australian experts and policymakers were particularly drawn to the ideas of Eugene Staley. A 1946 briefing document prepared by PWR cites

[17] Lionel Frost, "The Economy," in *The Cambridge History of Australia*, ed. Alison Bashford and Stuart Macintyre (Port Melbourne, VIC: Cambridge University Press, 2013), 320.

[18] Colin Clark and John Crawford, *The National Income of Australia* (Sydney: Angus & Robertson, 1938).

[19] Macintyre, *Australia's Boldest Experiment*, 142.

[20] Groenewegen and McFarlane, *A History of Australian Economic Thought*, 222.

[21] H.C. Coombs, Farewell speech for J.G. Crawford, Australian National University, March 9, 1973, State Library of New South Wales, Mitchell Library, Coombs Papers, MLMSS 4268, Box 1.

Staley's work in discussing the link between manufacturing and industrial development.[22] Interestingly, this paper cited Staley in the context of describing the United States as the epitome of the developmental process, a notion that assumed greater importance over the next two decades. In his analysis of modernisation theory as the orthodox American understanding of development, Nils Gilman writes that this way of thinking represented "the most explicit and systematic blueprint ever created by Americans for reshaping foreign societies."[23] Staley's academic authority was also highlighted at a meeting organised by the Australian Institute of International Affairs (AIIA) during the war. In discussions of post-war international reconstruction, Staley's work, with its emphasis on international organisations, was presented as an example of the approach that produced the best results following the end of hostilities.[24] These meetings were attended by PWR personnel and provided them with information that guided policy in the latter part of the Second World War.

While PWR was primarily concerned with domestic policy, a related group of experts worked on Australia's policy towards PNG. This was Alfred Conlon's Directorate of Research and Civil Affairs (DORCA), which brought together an eclectic mix of scholars and bureaucrats to study the post-war needs of PNG and to make policy recommendations.[25] Its membership included anthropologists such as Camilla Wedgwood, Lucy Mair and W.E.H. Stanner; the poet James McAuley; and economist

[22] Untitled PWR paper, Brief for Australian delegation to International Trade Organisation Conference, 1946, National Library of Australia (Hereafter cited as NLA), Crawford Papers, MS 4514, Box 1.

[23] Gilman, *Mandarins of the Future*, 5.

[24] K.H. Bailey, "Political Setting of Economic Reconstruction," June 4, 1942, National Archives of Australia (Hereafter cited as NAA): A989, 1943/735/651. The discussion centred around Staley's examination of "The Economic Organisation of the Peace," which built on ideas made in Eugene Staley, *World Economy in Transition* (New York: Council on Foreign Relations, 1939).

[25] Peter Ryan, "Conlon, Alfred Austin Joseph (Alf) (1908–1961)," Australian Dictionary of Biography, National Centre of Biography, Australian National University, http://adb.anu.edu.au/biography/conlon-alfred-austin-joseph-alf-9804/text17331, published in hardcopy 1993. Graeme Sligo, *The Backroom Boys: Alfred Conlon and Army's Directorate of Research and Civil Affairs, 1942–46* (Newport: Big Sky Publishing, 2013); Cassandra Pybus, "Conlon's Remarkable Circus," in *Scholars at War: Australasian Social Scientists, 1939–1945*, ed. Geoffrey Gray, Doug Munro, and Christine Winter (Canberra: ANU E Press, 2012).

and future Secretary of the Department of External Affairs, James Plimsoll. Conlon is a fascinating figure and has attracted polarised accounts from his contemporaries and historians. As the philosopher John Passmore recalled, "Of course one trouble with talking about Alf Conlon is that one never knows quite where fact starts and ends and where legend starts and ends."[26] He was renowned for his intense working habits; he kept a cot in his office and regularly stayed at work overnight. He was also criticised by the future Minister for Territories Paul Hasluck as leading a "barrel of ratbags" in DORCA.[27] Personal quirks notwithstanding, his desire to utilise academic expertise in the pursuit of Australian objectives in PNG was central to the work of DORCA in 1944 and 1945.

The post-war Administrator of PNG, Keith Murray, testified to DORCA's historical importance. At the second Waigani Seminar, held in Port Moresby in 1968, Murray recalled that Conlon and his Directorate had played a "decisive" role in calling for a "revolutionary new system" in PNG following the war.[28] For Murray, the newfound governmental interest in 'native advancement' was a radical departure from the pre-war situation and was the central component of the post-war "Rooseveltian New Deal" in PNG.[29] After the war, some members of DORCA continued to exert an influence on Australian colonial policy through the short-lived Australian Pacific Territories Council, which was loosely modelled on the British Colonial Research Committee.[30] The New Deal, with its promises of development for the Indigenous population of PNG, was a product of academically trained bureaucrats applying their academic and economic training to the 'problem' of Australia's post-war colonial administration.

[26] John Thompson, ed. *Alfred Conlon: A Memorial by Some of His Friends* (Sydney: Benevolent Society of New South Wales, 1963), 11.

[27] G.C. Bolton, *Paul Hasluck: A Life* (Crawley: UWA Publishing, 2014), 119.

[28] J.K. Murray, "In Retrospect 1945–1952: Papua-New Guinea and Territory of Papua and New Guinea," in *The History of Melanesia*, ed. Ken Inglis (Port Moresby: University of Papua New Guinea, 1969), 178.

[29] Murray, "In Retrospect 1945–1952," 181.

[30] J.R. Halligan, "Proposed External Territories Research Council," January 31, 1945, NAA: A518, R815/1/1 PART 1.

Trusteeship and Colonial Development

Australian colonial officials were not solely dependent on Staley's conception of development. The principle of trusteeship, which had underpinned British colonial practices since the middle of the nineteenth century, was also influential. For historian William Bain, trusteeship is "an idea that sanctions the rule of one man over another, in lands that are not his own, so long as the power of dominion is directed towards the improvement of the disadvantaged."[31] The French word *tutelle*, meaning "guardianship" or "tutelage" (the French name for the UN Trusteeship Council is *Conseil de tutelle des Nations unies*), is informative in understanding the motivations behind trusteeship. The idea was most clearly exemplified in the first half of the twentieth century by the Lugardian notion of the 'dual mandate.' According to Lord Frederick Lugard, who obtained his colonial experience in West Africa, British colonial rule was expected to ensure that Indigenous welfare and economic development (which at that time meant the exploitation of natural resources) co-existed, and that ultimately "development should be undertaken in such a way as to benefit the people of the country equally with others."[32] This approach informed some pre-war Australian colonial practices, particularly in Papua under Sir Hubert Murray, whose paternalistic policies led to a colonial administration that was less interested in overt economic exploitation than in neighbouring New Guinea.[33] Importantly, trusteeship shared many similarities to post-war developmental thought, particularly as both were interested in "lifting the ignorant and the infirm into the ranks of civilized life."[34]

After the Second World War, the concepts of trusteeship and development coalesced, with significant implications for Australian colonial policy in PNG.[35] The post-war notion of trusteeship was formalised through

[31] William Bain, "The Idea of Trusteeship in International Society," *The Round Table* 92, no. 368 (2003): 70. See also Camilla Boisen, "The Changing Moral Justification of Empire: From the Right to Colonise to the Obligation to Civilise," *History of European Ideas* 39, no. 3 (2013): 336.

[32] F.D. Lugard, *The Principle of Trusteeship for Backward Races* (Marlborough, England: Adam Matthew Digital, 2007), 162.

[33] Hubert Murray, *Papua of To-day: Or an Australian Colony in the Making* (London: P. S. King & Son, 1925), viii.

[34] Bain, "The Idea of Trusteeship in International Society," 72.

[35] Gorman, "Britain, India, and the United Nations," 486.

the UN Charter and the establishment of the UN Trusteeship Council, which oversaw former League of Nations mandates such as New Guinea. Australia's obligations were set out in the trusteeship agreement for New Guinea, signed in December 1946. According to this agreement, Australia was responsible for the promotion of "economic, political, social and educational advancement" in the trust territory.[36] This was in accordance with Article 73 of the UN Charter, which advised that the advancement of the Indigenous population had to occur "with due respect for the culture of the peoples concerned."[37] According to historian Neta C. Crawford, this phrasing, drafted by African-American political scientist, colonial expert and wartime diplomat Ralph Bunche, encapsulated the "core idea of trusteeship—the benevolent governance of the incapable by the capable outsider."[38] Under this system, Australia was obliged to promote the advancement of the Indigenous people in a manner that respected their cultural traditions. This provided a framework for Ward and officials in the Department of External Territories, led by departmental secretary J.R. Halligan, to implement the New Deal. Nevertheless, while the international concept of trusteeship offered some guidance to policymakers, the notion of "economic, political, social and educational advancement" offered a large degree of discretion for Australians to apply their own conception of how this process might take place.

Ward, Halligan and other members of External Territories were conscious of the international pressure applied through the UN Trusteeship Council. In response to Australia's 1946–1947 report on New Guinea, the Council expressed "concern at the inadequacy of educational facilities in the Territory and at the consequently high rate of illiteracy, which is hindering the political advancement of the Indigenous

[36] "Trusteeship Agreement for the Territory of New Guinea," in *Australia and Papua New Guinea*, ed. W.J. Hudson (Sydney: Sydney University Press, 1971), 189. The formal establishment of administrative union in 1949 between Papua and New Guinea confirmed a unity of policy that had existed from the end of the Second World War.

[37] Article 73, United Nations Charter, http://www.un.org/en/sections/un-charter/chapter-xi/.

[38] Neta C. Crawford, "Decolonization Through Trusteeship: The Legacy of Ralph Bunche," in *Trustee for the Human Community: Ralph J. Bunche, the United Nations, and the Decolonization of Africa*, ed. Robert A. Hill and Edmond J. Keller (Athens: Ohio University Press, 2010), 109.

inhabitants."[39] The oversight provided by the Trusteeship Council forced Australian policymakers to ensure new levels of support for development in PNG.

Ward and his advisors engaged with other international practices regarding colonial development. At an inter-departmental meeting in 1949, External Affairs Secretary, John Burton, circulated a paper on British colonial policy in Fiji, which invoked some of the principles of trusteeship, as it denied that attempts were being made to turn Fiji into a "tolerable likeness of Australia or New Zealand." According to the document, British policy was directed at making limited improvements in agriculture, infrastructure and social services, as a consequence of its inflexible budget of £3 million.[40] This was a useful report for Commonwealth planners, as financial constraints and a shortage of supplies was a major obstacle to long-term development planning for PNG. The British colonial example provided inspiration for policymakers who sought to understand how an administering power could direct the use of limited funds. From its earliest origins, Australian aid policy was hamstrung by limited resources.

'Primitive' Papua New Guinea

One of the assumptions that shaped Australian colonial policy in PNG was the colonists' perception of the Indigenous population as being particularly 'primitive.' Comments regarding the extreme 'primitiveness' of the Papua New Guineans were ubiquitous in the decades following the Second World War, and were made by both experts and officials in their descriptions of PNG.[41] This terminology carried a developmental undertone, as it served to highlight the stark difference between 'civilised'

[39] U.N. Trusteeship Council, *Report of the Drafting Committee on the Report on the Administration of the Trust Territory of New Guinea for the Year 1 July 1946 to 30 June 1947*, UN Doc T/202 (Lake Success, NY: UN, 1948), 213.

[40] Fijian Administration, "Revised Development Plan," attached to J. Burton to H.J. Goodes, December 8, 1949, NAA: A1838, 301/9.

[41] Hudson and Daven touch on the continued influence of the idea that the Indigenous population of PNG were living in 'stone age' conditions, Hudson and Daven, "Papua and New Guinea Since 1945," 155.

(read 'developed') Australia and its colonial possession.[42] At the official level, invocations of the 'primitive' were common throughout the New Deal. Not long after Ward's appointment to the portfolio of External Territories, a departmental paper commented on the job he faced: "It is necessary to guide them from the Stone Age to the Twentieth Century, and all that this implies without impairing, or at least seriously damaging, the original structure."[43] In 1947, the administration in Port Moresby described the Indigenous population as "for the most part primitive, illiterate in the vernacular as well as in English, inexperienced and quite untried in modern techniques."[44] Australian experts also employed this kind of language, with British-born DORCA member Lucy Mair observing the 'natives' in their "primitive state", and James McAuley suggesting that the population was still "neolithic in culture."[45] The pervasiveness of the Australian perception of the 'primitiveness' of PNG underpinned the establishment and progress of the New Deal and of post-war Australian colonial policy more broadly.

Not only did the 'primitiveness' of the Indigenous population guide Australian attitudes towards colonial policy, but it also demonstrated the scope of the Australian developmental task. Australian officials repeatedly referred to the 'primitive' PNG population to explain the difficulties they faced in the attempt to promote development. T.P. Fry, a legal scholar who worked for DORCA, provided a clear example of this logic when explaining the nature of PNG society:

> The fact is that in these Territories there are a million natives still living primitive lives in village communities, a small European community which provides the rulers, managers and experts and has entirely different cultural and economic functions and requirements, and other small communities

[42] Brown, *Governing Prosperity*, 8; Edward W. Said, *Orientalism* (London: Penguin, 1995), 232.

[43] Department of External Territories, "The Territories of Papua and New Guinea Under Australian Control," January 17, 1944, NLA, Ward Papers, MS 2396, Box 43A.

[44] Territory of Papua-New Guinea, "Memorandum on the Policy of the Administration," September 8, 1947, NLA, Ward Papers, MS 2396, Box 43A.

[45] Lucy Mair, *Australia in New Guinea* (London and Melbourne: Christophers, 1948), 6; A.H. McDonald, ed. *Trusteeship in the Pacific* (Sydney: Angus & Robertson, 1949), 36.

> such as the Chinese and half-castes whose functions and requirements are different again.[46]

The syllabi for the training of colonial officials at the Australian School of Pacific Administration (ASOPA) also emphasised the contrasts between 'European' and 'Melanesian' systems of living, influencing a further generation of colonial officials.[47] Australian officials perceived their task as being particularly difficult because of the extreme primitiveness of the population.

Ward's New Deal for Papua New Guinea

The New Deal for PNG was a product of both trusteeship and post-war ideas of development. It exemplified the international reconfiguration of colonialism that in the British context has been referred to by historians D.A. Low and John Lonsdale as the 'second colonial occupation.'[48] The welfare of the Indigenous population was to be protected through labour reform, in particular the abolition of indentured labour. As important was Canberra's acknowledgement that the Commonwealth had a responsibility to fund PNG's development, echoing Staley and Rosenstein-Rodan. Commonwealth spending was vastly increased to promote development through the improvement of agriculture, health and education. The post-war era of governmental financial assistance for development had begun.

Following the resumption of civil administration at the end of 1945, over £7 million was spent by the Commonwealth Government in PNG during Ward's tenure as Minister for External Territories.[49] In recognition of the international climate of support for colonial development, Ward recommended that Commonwealth funds should be provided "not

[46] T.P. Fry, "Relief and Rehabilitation in Australia's Territories in New Guinea," January 1945, NLA, Ward Papers, MS 2396, Box 43A.

[47] "Syllabus of Short Course—The Australian School of Pacific Administration, Mosman NSW," June 1946, NAA: A518, A114/1/1 PART 1; Rist, *The History of Development*, 69–79; Gilman, *Mandarins of the Future*, 5–8; Said, *Orientalism*, 326–327.

[48] D.A. Low and J.M. Lonsdale, "Introduction: Towards the New Order 1945–1963," in *History of East Africa*, ed. D.A. Low and Alison Smith (Oxford: Clarendon Press, 1976), 12–16.

[49] Department of Territories, "Papua and New Guinea," n.d. [December 1964], NAA: A1838, 2020/1/24/23.

only to assist the Administration to meet its expenditure but also to finance native welfare schemes."[50] A number of factors affected the Department of Territories' capacity to implement their goals of protecting Indigenous welfare and promoting development in PNG between 1945 and 1949. These ranged from disagreements within the Commonwealth bureaucracy over the best way to promote development to tension between Canberra and Port Moresby. Nevertheless, once the Commonwealth Government accepted the Trusteeship agreement for New Guinea, development became a dominant feature of Australian policy for PNG.

Contests Over Development: Within the Bureaucracy

While External Territories had direct control over policy in PNG, there were numerous other groups in Canberra that took an interest in colonial development. On the one hand, this demonstrated the increased level of Australian interest in the economic, developmental and security concerns regarding PNG. On the other, the diversity of developmental attitudes complicated officials' attempts to devise the best method to implement the New Deal. Ward's goals were obstructed by different political objectives within the Canberra bureaucracy. Development as a broad component of Australian policy attracted almost universal acceptance. How to implement it was another matter altogether.

On three occasions during the New Deal, in 1944, 1947 and 1949, an Inter-Departmental Committee was assembled to devise a plan for the development of PNG. The committees frequently became bogged down with bureaucratic minutiae, as the specifics of various programs undermined the New Deal's broad goal of promoting Indigenous development. The number of false starts can be explained by frequent changes in administration both in Canberra and in Port Moresby, as well as the growing number of Commonwealth departments that claimed an interest in PNG. Each committee almost had to start again as new developmental strategies and shifting departmental interests were put forward.

[50] E.J. Ward draft agendum, "Territories of Papua and New Guinea. Ministerial Sub-Committee: Economic Development of the Territories," June 29, 1945, NLA, Ward Papers, MS 2396, Box 43A.

The 1949 version was a product of Prime Ministerial intervention, as Ben Chifley instructed Ward to reconstitute the Committee and establish a development plan, expressing his belief that it was "desirable that the consideration of plans for the development of the Territory of Papua-New Guinea should be pursued actively."[51] Clearly, the Prime Minister was frustrated at the lack of progress. These meetings involved numerous individuals and government departments whose conception of development played an important role in Australia for many years to come. In attendance at the meeting of September 26, 1949, were Halligan, External Affairs Secretary John Burton and John Crawford in his capacity as Director of the Bureau of Agricultural Economics.[52] At this meeting, Crawford explained that three objectives were necessary for any plan to promote the development of PNG: developing the territory's resources in the interests of the Indigenous population of PNG and raising their standard of living; using the resources to meet Australian requirements; and finding an international market for PNG's resources.[53] This was a vision for PNG that sought to incorporate the Indigenous economy into the international economy, with the expectation of improved standards of living that came with it.

This vision of PNG development was undermined by inter-departmental differences that established a pattern of debate that would persist throughout the age of international development. In the 1949 meetings of the committee, H.J. Goodes, the Assistant Secretary of the Treasury Department, argued for a clearer sense of the relationship between welfare and development, emphasising the "considerable sums" that the Commonwealth Government had already spent on PNG.[54] In response, Burton challenged Treasury's distinction between welfare and development, arguing that "economic development must in the long

[51] J.B. Chifley to E.J. Ward, August 1, 1949, NAA: A518, A927/1.

[52] Department of External Territories, "Territory of Papua and New Guinea—Reconstitution of Ministerial and Inter-Departmental Committee to Plan the Development of Papua and New Guinea," September 1949, NAA: A1838, 301/9. Other departments represented included Treasury, Works and Housing, and the PNG Administration, with an observer from the Commonwealth Bank.

[53] Department of External Territories, "Reconstitution of Ministerial and Inter-Departmental Committee."

[54] Department of External Territories, "Reconstitution of Ministerial and Inter-Departmental Committee."

run benefit the welfare of the native people provided that such policy was developed thoroughly."[55] This foreshadowed future debates between Treasury and External Affairs over the objectives and scale of Australian aid. The differences between the departments point to the notion that "welfare" was understood as a domestic (which for Treasury excluded PNG) concern, while "development" was something to be promoted overseas.

Little progress was made by the Committee, despite its recognition of the need for a developmental plan for PNG. T.A. Pyman, an External Affairs expert on trusteeship matters, was deeply critical of the Committee. Writing in 1949, Pyman targeted the "disjointed" work of the 1944 and 1947 Committees, which had the effect of producing "desultory investigations of isolated topics." What was needed was "a more limited programme with far greater emphasis upon the inter-relationship between economic, social and political development in the Territories."[56] The lack of will to implement developmental policy was at least in part a product of the absence of an agreed set of steps to follow. Ironically, while Pyman suggested a need for more focused policies, he did not elaborate on how to achieve a plan that satisfied his own recommendations. The debate over the best way to implement development was reflective of the diversity of developmental attitudes in Canberra. Unfortunately for the New Deal, the differences of opinion were such that a decisive program for developmental assistance could not be drawn up.

Indentured Labour and the Expatriate Community

At the heart of Ward's vision of agricultural improvement was increased Indigenous production. This was linked to both the trusteeship notion of improving Indigenous welfare, as well as the recognition that a self-governing PNG (still a distant vision in 1945) would require a local economic base. Ward and his Department agreed that the indentured labour system had to be abolished but accepted that it would take until 1950 to be completely removed. In the meantime, they failed to produce a clear vision of the system to replace indentured labour. By 1949, there

[55] Department of External Territories, "Reconstitution of Ministerial and Inter-Departmental Committee."

[56] T.A. Pyman for J. Burton, September 26, 1949, NAA: A1838, 301/9.

was little achievement in this regard. With indentured labour about to come to a complete end, it was replaced with vague references to labour policy that sought to balance Indigenous welfare with the establishment of an efficient labour force. Rather than leap forward with an active labour policy, departmental officials, led by Halligan, repeatedly sent the reform back for further inter-departmental discussion.[57] This reflected the importance of getting the policy right, as labour was an essential component of economic development.[58] In effect, however, the continued debates simply added more voices to the policymaking process, increasing the delay in implementing the New Deal.

As with many features of the New Deal, the desire to abolish indentured labour was in keeping with international shifts taking place following the Second World War. Writing in the British context, Hodge explains that post-war colonialism employed "science and technology in opening up the tropics not only for the benefit of European trade and industry but also for the moral and material advancement of colonial peoples."[59] In keeping with the emphasis on Indigenous economic activity, European enterprise was to be regulated to prevent a return to the pre-war system of exploitation. This was strongly opposed by the expatriate community in PNG, parts of which were firmly opposed to the New Deal. Self-interested business owners expressed concern over the consequences of colonial development policies that supposedly privileged Indigenous interests. The *Pacific Islands Monthly* served as the mouthpiece for anti-Ward sentiment, regularly criticising how PNG had become the "socialist plaything" of the Minister.[60]

The government was not well-disposed to the expatriates' argument. W. Cottrell-Dormer, the Administration Director of Agriculture, Stock and Fisheries, opposed any increase to the European-run plantation system. While recognising the economic potential and increased export

[57] Downs describes Halligan as being reluctant to impose radical reform after the war. Downs, *The Australian Trusteeship Papua New Guinea, 1945–75*, 15.

[58] Rosenstein-Rodan, "International Development of Economically Backward Areas," 161; Kurt Mandelbaum, *The Industrialisation of Backward Areas* (Oxford: B. Blackwell, 1945), 1; T.P. Fry, "Papua and Mandated New Guinea Today," *Pacific Affairs* 19, no. 2 (1946): 159.

[59] Hodge, *Triumph of the Expert*, 7.

[60] "Progress of Rehabilitation in Papua-New Guinea," *Pacific Islands Monthly* 16, no. 6 (1946): 3.

earnings that could come from new plantations, Cottrell-Dormer opposed expatriate proposals to expand the cocoa industry:

> If European settlement is excessive the peoples of the Territory will become a race of wage-earners dependant [sic] upon European industry for their livelihood and losing the greater part of their native self-reliance; under such conditions these peoples would gradually find themselves in the same plight as the people of the West Indies and similarly be landless and poverty-stricken in times of depressed prices for the commodities grown by their European masters.[61]

By avoiding the mistakes of other colonial powers, Australian officials such as Cottrell-Dormer sought to maximise the role Indigenous Papua New Guineans could play in their own development.

The expatriate community opposed the new government's attitude and protested against reforms to labour, fearing that it would impact on mining and plantation interests. The New Deal's abolition of indentured labour and new attitudes towards Indigenous agriculture produced a hostile reaction amongst some expatriates. Expatriate organisations including the New Guinea Planters' Association argued that because "the native lacks any sense of responsibility", some kind of employment contract was "absolutely essential in the present stage of native development."[62] Again, the *Pacific Islands Monthly* revealed the views of colonial business interests. Written in the context of a proposed visit by Ward to PNG (which never eventuated), an article imagined a scenario where he was 'Shanghai-ed' up the Sepik River, discovering the 'real' New Guinea in the process. For the anonymous author:

> Of such things are planters' dreams made. It is scarcely possible that anything so unfortunate and realistic could happen to the man who made New Guinea safe for Fuzzy Wuzzy, freed the slaves from the evil machinations of predatory planters, and tied a tin-can to the tail of the exploiters.[63]

[61] W. Cottrell-Dormer to J.R. Halligan, n.d. [c. May 1946], NAA: A518, A58/3/3.

[62] Minutes of Native Labour Conference, December 2, 1944, NLA, Ward Papers, MS 2396, Box 43A.

[63] *Pacific Islands Monthly*, November 1947, NAA: A518, T800/1/7.

This expatriate opposition was a problem for government authorities, as Australian planters still had an important role to play in PNG development. The humanitarian impulses behind the New Deal were a particular target of expatriate interests, as they clearly posed a threat to their vision of a European-centric economy.

PNG Administrator Keith Murray acted as a kind of middleman between expatriate interests and New Deal officials in the Territories Department. His approach was informed by both the developmental and political imperatives that guided Australian aid. Writing to Ward in 1947, Murray emphasised the significance of production in tropical products for the Australian market. Identifying that this production would be optimised with "a healthy and contented native people", the Administrator argued that his views were "not a starry-eyed idealism, nor sentimental; they are merely realistic and humanitarian."[64] For Murray, the primary consideration was the Indigenous population, as the encouragement of their "educational, social, economic and political development" would ensure a humanitarian colonial policy.[65] As the New Deal progressed, however, Murray found himself increasingly frustrated by Canberra's apparent inability to implement developmental policy. In 1947, a frustrated Murray wrote to the Inter-Departmental Committee, stating that while "Australia can and does produce concrete, soundly based, realistic thinking in relation to New Guinea, there has seemed to be difficulty in providing the administrative basis of action."[66] The Administrator was particularly concerned at the lack of personnel to implement these plans. For Murray, the "fundamental problem" was "one of recruitment and supply."[67] From the viewpoint of Port Moresby, it was one thing to meet and discuss developmental ideas with regard to PNG, but another thing completely to fund and implement them.

Partly to overcome this issue, Murray established his own committees for developmental policy, but he acknowledged that they lacked one important thing—economists. This was "a most serious handicap" and ensured that the PNG Administration continued to be dependent upon

[64] J.K. Murray to E.J. Ward, September 10, 1947, NLA, Ward Papers, MS 2396, Box 43A.

[65] Murray, "In Retrospect 1945–1952," 178.

[66] J.K. Murray to Chairman, Inter-Departmental Committee on the Planning and Development of New Guinea, April 27, 1947, NLA, Ward Papers, MS 2396, Box 43A.

[67] J.K. Murray to Chairman, Inter-Departmental Committee, April 27, 1947.

advice and guidance from Canberra.[68] This had the effect of further exasperating the Administrator, who let out his frustrations on Christmas Day 1948, in a handwritten letter to Ward. Murray was firm in his attitude:

> The Inter-departmental Committee on New Guinea has not produced a plan for the economic development of the Territory. The finalisation of policy regarding the economic development of the native people and of the Territory is basic, and the Committee should be made capable of producing it; they simply must be aware of its importance.[69]

Similar to the expatriate disapproval, Murray's criticism of Ward pointed to differing attitudes between Canberra and Port Moresby. This was to become a common refrain plaguing development policy in the future. Criticism of Canberra's supposed lack of understanding of local conditions became a regular feature of Australian aid between 1945 and 1975, in regard to both PNG and Southeast Asia.

Agriculture as the Basis for Development

While External Territories and other departments interested in PNG struggled to come up with a clear developmental policy for the colony, there was a general agreement regarding the promotion of agricultural development. It was largely accepted that agricultural improvement was central to the development of PNG. This was in keeping with colonial development practices throughout the world.[70] However, there was disagreement about how to use the limited (albeit significantly increased from before the war) resources of the Administration in Port Moresby to fund specific agricultural programs. The policy discussions on agricultural development in the New Deal highlight some of the persistent issues involved in post-war Australian aid. Australian expertise in agriculture was repeatedly drawn upon throughout the age of international development, but this expertise was not resourced to ensure the best results.

[68] J.K. Murray to J.R. Halligan, August 22, 1947, NLA, Ward Papers, MS 2396, Box 43A.

[69] J.K. Murray to E.J. Ward, December 25, 1948, NLA, Ward Papers, MS 2396, Box 43B.

[70] Hodge, *Triumph of the Expert*, 250.

As with later attempts to promote development in Southeast Asia, developmental policy was vulnerable to debates over best practice and the most appropriate allocation of resources.

Agricultural improvement was a core component of Ward's vision for colonial development. In December 1946, Ward argued that agriculture must form "the main basis for the ultimate prosperity" of the Indigenous population, outlining the state of Indigenous agriculture in the following terms:

> Relatively speaking, the native peoples are at present in a primitive stage of agricultural development; but it is believed they can gradually be instructed and led into the cultivation of such crops as coffee, tea, cocoa, cinchona, fibres etc. eventually reaching a stage where a mutual trade will be established between the Commonwealth and her dependencies.[71]

This was analysis that could have been taken straight from the pages of Staley or Rosenstein-Rodan, which also emphasised the role of 'advanced' countries in providing technical assistance to improve agricultural production.[72]

Administrator Keith Murray was also a strong advocate for increased Commonwealth assistance to agricultural improvement in PNG. In a gesture to his own career as a former professor of agriculture at the University of Queensland, Murray was interested in the role of Australian agricultural experts in providing a colonial version of technical assistance.[73] At a conference on the work of ASOPA, the Administrator presented his views:

> The attempt to get the New Guinea economy developed in the way it ought to be developed, the integration of that economy into the Australian economy, if we are going to do that, we won't do it until the agriculturalist

[71] E.J. Ward, "External Territories of the Commonwealth," December 6, 1946, NLA, Ward Papers, MS 2396, Box 43A.

[72] Rosenstein-Rodan, "International Development of Economically Backward Areas," 160; Staley, *World Economic Development*, 75.

[73] Brian Jinks, "Murray, Sir Jack Keith (1899–1979)", Australian Dictionary of Biography, National Centre of Biography, Australian National University, http://adb.anu.edu.au/biography/murray-sir-jack-keith-11209/text19983, published first in hardcopy 2000.

> has gone through a School of Colonial Administration as well as knowing the technical side of agriculture.[74]

Murray's vision of the connection between agricultural development and technical assistance was typical of the post-war developmental age. As he noted in the context of calling for a more decisive policy from Canberra:

> The future prosperity of the Territory will be dependent upon a steady rise in the economic productivity of the native people. This can be achieved by the stimulation of an improved subsistence agriculture linked with native production of revenue crops – European technical assistance and control being in accordance with what particular circumstances require.[75]

Like Ward, Murray placed agricultural improvement at the heart of PNG's overall development plan.

Ward's emphasis on agriculture had been inspired by Australia's own development, which was often linked to the increased efficiency in agricultural production.[76] 'Nugget' Coombs commented on the fact that, similar to Australia, "the future development of the Territory seems to depend on the development of agricultural products produced for export."[77] In late 1949, External Territories official, E.J. Wood, re-examined the centrality of agriculture within a broader developmental program for PNG. He identified three basic components of a "balanced plan for development": improved economic standards, "better methods of carrying out agricultural production", and how those methods could be taught.[78] The fact that this paper was produced in late 1949 demonstrates two things. First, it shows the continued relevance of improved agricultural practices in the Commonwealth vision of PNG's development. Second, it suggests that little progress had been made between Ward's statement of 1946 and the end of his tenure in late 1949. In a process

[74] Minutes, "Conference Concerning the Future Activities of the Australian School of Pacific Administration," Sydney, April 19, 1947, NAA: A518, A114/1/1 PART 2.

[75] Territory of Papua and New Guinea, "Memorandum on the Policy of the Administration," September 8, 1947, NLA, Ward Papers, MS 2396, Box 43A.

[76] Shaw, *The Economic Development of Australia*, 173.

[77] H.C. Coombs to J.B. Chifley, July 7, 1949, NAA: A518, A927/1.

[78] E.J. Wood, "Agricultural Policy," November 15, 1949, NAA: A518, B927/1 PART 1.

that would become familiar over the next three decades, the implementation of Australian developmental policy was obstructed by bureaucratic debate and administrative difficulties.

A number of agricultural programs had been initiated during the New Deal, including a series of District Agricultural Stations that provided "research, extension, and native project development activities."[79] This was technical assistance work that aimed to improve agricultural production in PNG. Also, "the foundations of future progress" were being laid, with seeds distributed by district officers to establish Indigenous food production.[80] This was aimed at overcoming what Administration officials identified as 'native' practices that were "wasteful of effort" and "wasteful of resources."[81] But while increased funds were going to the Administration in Port Moresby, personnel difficulties and bureaucratic inertia prevented more resources from being devoted to specific agriculture programs. This illustrates the gradual nature of Australian colonial development policy in the early post-war years.

The New Deal: Australia's First 'Aid' Program

A product of the intersection of ideas of international development and trusteeship, the New Deal illustrates the connection between Australian policy and global intellectual trends. In 1940, the British Government passed the Colonial Development and Welfare Act, which set aside an annual figure of £5 million for the development of its colonies. Arising out of the need to rally colonial support for the war and British concerns over American anti-imperialism, this policy served as an early example of the connection between colonialism and the age of international development.[82] Joseph Hodge and Frederick Cooper have shown that development became a central feature of British colonial policy after the Second World War, departing from earlier policies that regarded it as a

[79] Commonwealth of Australia, "Report to the General Assembly of the United Nations on the Administration of the Territory of New Guinea, July 1, 1947 to June 30, 1948," 21, NLA, Ward Papers, MS 2396, Box 43A.

[80] "Report to the General Assembly of the United Nations on the Administration of the Territory of New Guinea, July 1, 1947 to June 30, 1948," 51.

[81] Wood, "Agricultural Policy."

[82] Frey, "Control, Legitimacy, and the Securing of Interests," 397–398.

process outside the remit of government.[83] Similar changes took place in Australia. Ward demonstrated his awareness of the British Colonial Development and Welfare Act when identifying the need for increased spending for colonial development. Writing in mid-1945, he stated:

> In this connection attention is directed to the provision made by the British Government for the welfare and development of British Colonies – a sum of £12,000,000 has been provided by the British Treasury for such expenditure over a period of years.[84]

Departmental secretary J.R. Halligan also commented on the new British colonial development policy, observing: "The primary aim of Colonial policy is to protect and advance the interests of the inhabitants of the colonies."[85] Health and education were a central part of British attempts at colonial development in Africa, and they were also at the heart of the New Deal.

Ward's New Deal for PNG was the first post-war example of Australian policy that sought to promote development in an 'underdeveloped' area through the use of Commonwealth resources. Conceived through the international principle of trusteeship, it was a departure from pre-war colonial policy in its emphasis on Indigenous economic activity. By the end of Ward's tenure as Minister at the end of 1949, there were mixed feelings about the achievements of the New Deal. Murray exemplified the competing feelings of frustration and satisfaction in his letter of condolence to Ward following the defeat of the Chifley Labor Government in the Federal election of December 1949. Encapsulating his continued desire for active Federal government involvement, Murray wrote: "The groundwork for economic development is being surely done, but much

[83] Hodge, *Triumph of the Expert*, 209; Cooper, "Writing the History of Development," 10.

[84] E.J. Ward draft agendum, "Territories of Papua and New Guinea. Ministerial Sub-Committee: Economic Development of the Territories," June 29, 1945, NLA, Ward Papers, MS 2396, Box 43A.

[85] J.R. Halligan, "Colonial Development and Welfare Act 1940," January 31, 1945, NAA: A518, R815/1/1 PART 1.

remains to be expected because of the dependence of economic development on major discussions which the Inter-Departmental Committee on N.G. was to work on."[86]

Numerous obstacles undermined the implementation of development policy. These included continued negotiations over the exact meaning of development and resistance to increased Commonwealth intervention in the PNG economy. The debate over labour policy exemplified two of the dominant conceptions of development in PNG between 1945 and 1949. Expatriate Australians with business interests in PNG desired a return to the pre-war situation, where exploitative labour practices produced a process of development with very limited beneficiaries. In contrast, Ward and his Department, guided by the principles of trusteeship, were more interested in creating policy that benefitted the Indigenous population. While this did not preclude expatriate interests, it required a significant shift in attitudes and policy both in Canberra and Port Moresby. In the absence of this shift, the implementation of development programs was delayed. While the broad framework of developmental policy had more or less been identified by 1949, debate over the most effective method of implementation continued.

Another important factor was the competition for resources that emerged out of policies directed at Australia's own development. The debates in the Inter-Departmental Committee over the purpose of assistance to PNG between External Affairs and Treasury demonstrated that there were limits to the amount of resources that Australia could provide. Knowing this, Ward was loath to ask Cabinet for significant amounts of money for PNG, as he was aware of the pressing concerns for domestic programs.[87] This pattern continued for the next three decades, as Australian aid spending was limited by the requirements of domestic development. The perception of Australia's developmental position by government officials impacted upon aid policy. As a rich country with colonial responsibilities, Australia was considered to be an 'advanced'

[86] J.K. Murray to E.J. Ward, December 21, 1949, NLA, Ward Papers, MS 2396, Box 43B.

[87] Department of External Territories, Notes on Meeting to discuss the legislative provisions to be made for an administrative union of the Territory of Papua with the Trust Territory of New Guinea, May 18, 1948, NLA, Ward Papers, MS 2396, Box 43B.

(soon to be rephrased as 'developed') economy.[88] This was obvious when comparing Australia with 'primitive' PNG. The post-war requirements of trusteeship and development left Australia with a responsibility to provide economic assistance to its dependent territories, with the transfer of developmental resources that entailed. Similar questions would be raised by Australia's involvement in the Colombo Plan, which is discussed in the next chapter. Ward's New Deal for PNG, as Australia's first attempt to participate in the international system of developmental assistance, established many of the trends that would define Australian policy over the next three decades.

In spite of Ward's enthusiasm for the New Deal and the increased Commonwealth expenditure on PNG, the lofty goals outlined by the Minister in 1945 were not achieved. By the middle of 1948, around one-third of the Indigenous workforce in New Guinea continued to work under indenture.[89] Health reform was limited by a "lack of staff and adequate supply of materials", while a housing shortage (which was also an issue in Australia) undermined attempts to improve living standards.[90] Slow progress was expected, owing to the 'primitiveness' of the Indigenous population. Nevertheless, the fact that around three quarters of Australia's grant to PNG was being spent on "welfare, development and reconstruction" (compared to zero before the war) indicates that a new phase in Australian policy had begun.[91]

[88] United Nations. Department of Economic Affairs, ed. *Economic Development in Selected Countries: Plans, Programmes and Agencies* (Lake Success, 1947), 33.

[89] "Report to the General Assembly of the United Nations on the Administration of the Territory of New Guinea, July 1, 1947 to June 30, 1948," 51.

[90] "Report to the General Assembly of the United Nations on the Administration of the Territory of New Guinea, July 1, 1947 to June 30, 1948," 36, 40.

[91] "Report to the General Assembly of the United Nations on the Administration of the Territory of New Guinea, July 1, 1947 to June 30, 1948," 15.

CHAPTER 3

"By Every Means in Our Power": The Establishment of the Colombo Plan, 1949–1957

On January 11, 1950, Australian External Affairs Minister, Percy Spender, presented a proposal to the Commonwealth Meeting of Foreign Ministers in Colombo. Addressing the political crisis facing South and Southeast Asia in the aftermath of the 1949 communist revolution in China, Spender asserted that "the problem in Asia lies in the poverty of the region."[1] The solution was to provide developmental assistance, thereby improving the standard of living in the poor countries of the region. In addition to improving the lives of millions, this would undermine the appeal of communism, which according to the collective wisdom of the time, thrived in places that suffered from widespread poverty.[2] The plan that emerged from the conference, and that was formalised by two further Consultative Committee meetings throughout 1950, became the Colombo Plan. For over two decades, the Colombo Plan was Australia's primary means of assisting South and Southeast Asian countries in furthering their plans for economic development. Cold War calculations were clearly significant in the formation of the Colombo Plan. They formed a core argument for why increasing spending in foreign

[1] Commonwealth Meeting on Foreign Affairs, "Economic Policy in South and South-East Asia: Memorandum by the Australian Delegation," January 11, 1950, NAA: A10617, 1950/1.

[2] Ekbladh, *The Great American Mission*, 97–99.

N. Ferns, *Australia in the Age of International Development, 1945–1975*, Security, Conflict and Cooperation in the Contemporary World,
https://doi.org/10.1007/978-3-030-50228-7_3

nations was in Australia's national interest. However, as this chapter shows, the anti-Communist argument formed only one part of a broader developmentalist rationale for the Plan.

Like the New Deal for PNG, the Colombo Plan was the product of Australian policymakers' engagement with international ideas of development. The intellectual and political origins of the Plan reveal the incorporation of international ideas of development into post-war Australian foreign policy towards Asia. This process reflected Australia's involvement in the American-led post-war global order. In the years immediately preceding the establishment of the Colombo Plan, American officials employed the emerging field of developmental theory as a component of foreign policy through the establishment of the Point Four program. Central to Point Four was the belief that technical assistance and technological improvement would facilitate the process of development.[3] Similar assumptions operated in the Colombo Plan.

However, these assumptions were not shared by all. Inter-departmental differences, primarily between External Affairs and Treasury, evolved into ideological distinctions in the decades following the Second World War, and represented competing Australian understandings of international development. Ultimately, and again like the New Deal in PNG, the enthusiasm felt by Australian officials for development in the early days of the Colombo Plan was challenged by the difficulties of putting the idea into practice. This challenge reflected the tension at the heart of Australian aid policy, as developmental and political imperatives were constantly in competition.

Scholarship on the Australian experience of the Colombo Plan largely revolves around its importance to Australian foreign policy towards Asia in the 1950s and 1960s.[4] David Lowe demonstrates that the Colombo

[3] Ekbladh, *The Great American Mission*, 77–78.

[4] Oakman, *Facing Asia*; Lowe, "The Colombo Plan"; Brown, "Student, Expert, Peacekeeper"; Lowe, "Journalists and the Stirring of Australian Public Diplomacy"; "Australia's Colombo Plans, Old and New: International Students as Foreign Relations," *International Journal of Cultural Policy* 21, no. 4 (2015). Examples of analysis of the Colombo Plan outside of the Australian context include: Shigeru Akita, Gerold Krozewski, and Shōichi Watanabe, eds., *The Transformation of the International Order of Asia: Decolonization, the Cold War, and the Colombo Plan* (Milton Park, Abingdon, Oxon: Routledge, 2014); Keith Spicer, "Clubmanship Upstaged: Canada's Twenty Years in the Colombo Plan," *International Journal* 25, no. 1 (1969); Nicholas Tarling, "The United Kingdom and the Origins of the Colombo Plan," *The Journal of Commonwealth and Comparative Politics* 24, no. 1 (1986).

Plan was a means by which Australian policymakers sought to negotiate the complexities surrounding the Cold War and decolonisation in Asia.[5] Daniel Oakman has emphasised its centrality to Australian attempts to engage with Asia, as shown by the acceptance of significant numbers of Asian students to Australian universities in the decades following its establishment in 1950.[6] There is more to the Colombo Plan than this, however, as developmental imperatives also guided the establishment of the Plan. Recently, American historians, including Ekbladh, Latham and Cullather, have established that development discourse and ideology made its way into the formation of American foreign aid policy.[7] This chapter employs a similar approach to demonstrate the place of development in the minds of policymakers in establishing the Colombo Plan. The Plan, alongside the growing developmental interest in PNG discussed in the previous chapter, served as the two prongs of Australian aid through to the mid-1970s.

Developmental Theory and the Shift from Relief to Development

After the Second World War, moral and political claims for global economic equality became internationally prominent. As historian Michael Barnett puts it: "Humanitarianism went global after World War II."[8] In order to repair the destruction wrought by years of war, international agencies, both public and private, worked to provide relief to those suffering in war-torn areas. These same agencies soon moved into the field of development, as the objective of providing "help" turned into one of achieving "self-help."[9] Development therefore emerged as an extension of humanitarianism. Moreover, improvements in the standard of living of poorer peoples were seen as preventing future crises. In this

[5] David Lowe, *Australian Between Empires: The Life of Percy Spender* (London: Pickering & Chatto, 2010), 130–131; "The Colombo Plan," 105.

[6] Oakman, *Facing Asia*, 1–3.

[7] Ekbladh, *The Great American Mission*; Latham, *Modernization as Ideology*; Nick Cullather, *The Hungry World: America's Cold War Battle Against Poverty in Asia* (Cambridge, MA: Harvard University Press, 2010).

[8] Barnett, *Empire of Humanity*, 118.

[9] Barnett, *Empire of Humanity*, 105.

context, developmental economists assumed an important position as they provided the intellectual framework for this new kind of aid.

The Atlantic Charter provided the inspiration for post-war developmental theorists. The fifth article of the Charter pledged to "secur[e] for all, improved labour standards, economic advancement and social security."[10] Eugene Staley opened his 1944 *World Economic Development* by quoting the fifth article, though he also argued that simply protecting these economic rights was not enough.[11] Elizabeth Borgwardt makes the persuasive case that the Atlantic Charter formed the basis for an American attempt to produce a "New Deal for the World."[12] By internationalising the principles of the New Deal, the Charter brought questions of economic welfare and development to a global stage.

Staley and his colleagues argued that living standards could only be improved through increased governmental intervention in the promotion of development. In *World Economic Development*, he drew together the call for development with the post-war vision of a more prosperous global society:

> A great international programme of development, fitting the capital needs of some areas to the abundant savings of other areas, might provide just the extra stimulus needed to put the post-war era into the upward phase of a new "long wave" in economic activity.[13]

With its roots in the international appeal of the Atlantic Charter, Staley's work drew explicit links between international political action and the necessity of promoting economic development throughout the world. W. Arthur Lewis, one of the "founding fathers" of developmental economics,

[10] "The Atlantic Charter," August 14, 1941, http://avalon.law.yale.edu/wwii/atlantic.asp.

[11] Staley, *World Economic Development*, 1–2.

[12] Elizabeth Borgwardt, *A New Deal for the World: America's Vision for Human Rights* (Cambridge, MA: Belknap Press of Harvard University Press, 2005), 34. Mark Mazower spends some time explaining the ways that the Charter facilitated both anti- and pro-imperial understandings of the post-war world. Mark Mazower, *No Enchanted Palace: The End of Empire and the Ideological Origins of the United Nations* (Princeton: Princeton University Press, 2009), 55.

[13] Staley, *World Economic Development*, 45.

built on Staley's work.[14] Saint Lucian by birth, and Professor of Political Economy at the University of Manchester, Lewis argued that:

> The crux of the problem is usually a backward system of agriculture – lack of scientific knowledge, poor equipment, inefficient marketing, insecure tenure, an uneconomically small scale of operation, and, frequently also, rural overpopulation. There are recognised remedies – an agricultural extension service, cooperative and other provision of credit, cooperative and other reorganisation of marketing, legislation to protect the security of tenants.[15]

International assistance would be required to implement these so-called remedies. In a 1951 study commissioned by the UN, Lewis and his colleagues suggested that the development process also required a change in mindset, "for what is required is a radical change in the outlook of the peoples of the under-developed countries."[16] According to the authors, technological improvement in the United States and Europe had been a product of a "long scientific tradition", something clearly lacking in the 'underdeveloped' world. Tacit in this analysis was the view that reforms in 'underdeveloped' countries would lead them to resemble the modern, industrial, 'developed' West.

As developmental thought became more internationally prominent, policymakers throughout the 'developed' world took note of Staley and Lewis' calls for official assistance to poorer nations. Lewis presented these ideas in their clearest form in 1949, when he argued that "planning is at the same time much more necessary and much more difficult to

[14] H.W. Arndt, "Economic Development: A Semantic History," *Economic Development and Cultural Change* 29, no. 3 (1981): 465; Cullather, *The Hungry World*, 148; Ekbladh, *The Great American Mission*, 165; Meier and Seers, *Pioneers in Development*, 147. Staley also commented on the importance of Lewis' work in his 1961 study of "underdeveloped" economies, Staley, *The Future of Underdeveloped Countries*, 421.

[15] William Arthur Lewis, *Principles of Economic Planning* (Washington, DC: Public Affairs Pr., 1951), 122–123.

[16] United Nations Department of Economic Affairs, *Measures for the Economic Development of Under-Developed Countries: Report by a Group of Experts Appointed by the Secretary-General of the United Nations* (New York: United Nations Publications, 1951), 30. The other economists involved in the study were Alberto Baltra Cortez, D.R. Gadgil, George Hakim and Theodore W. Schulz.

execute in backward than in advanced countries."[17] For Lewis, planning was required in these countries because of the lack of existing development, which meant that a much more active government was necessary than in 'advanced' countries, where national income enjoyed a steady increase "from decade to decade."[18] Lewis' understanding of the role of international capital and the need for substantial provision of developmental assistance was incorporated into his 1951 UN report, *Measures for the Economic Development of Under-developed Countries*. Working with a number of other economists, Lewis concluded that "the transfer of capital that is required to raise rapidly the living standards of under-developed countries is far beyond what is currently envisaged."[19] Foreign aid needed to become a significant part of international policy.

Discussion of international developmental problems made its way into Australian academic circles in the post-war period. In 1948, E.E. Ward, the Australian delegate to the UN Economic Commission for Asia and the Far East (ECAFE) and later Lecturer in Political Science at the University of Melbourne, wrote that:

> As the world becomes smaller in communications, and education spreads, more people in Asia are becoming conscious of their relatively poor conditions of life and believe that the benefits of scientific and technical progress and advanced economic organisation can, and should, be realised just as much in the East as in the West.[20]

This was an Australian analysis in the same vein as that of Staley and Lewis, and provides an example of the transnational spread of developmental thought in the second half of the 1940s. A similar call was put forward by Hans Leyser of the University of Melbourne's Law Faculty, who suggested that Southeast Asian countries required "great numbers of technical experts to advise them in the establishment of industrial, health and educational facilities, and Australia could provide a number of these

[17] Lewis, *Principles of Economic Planning*, 121.

[18] Lewis, *Principles of Economic Planning*, 122.

[19] Department of Economic Affairs, *Measures for the Economic Development of Under-Developed Countries*, 75.

[20] E.E. Ward, "The Economic Commission for Asia and the Far East," *Australian Outlook* 2, no. 3 (1948): 142.

experts."[21] This scholarly work paved the way for an intensified Australian attempt to promote development in South and Southeast Asia.

Yet, anxiety about the level of Australia's own development shadowed discussions about its potential to become involved in international development. As seen in the previous chapter, Australian economists had long taken an interest in the process of development. Much of their work focused on Australia's own development. The underdeveloped North of the continent had posed a 'problem' to Australian experts and policymakers for decades.[22] Where Australia's historical development had been premised on agricultural improvement, Douglas Copland famously coined the term "Milk Bar economy" to express his fear that Australia was specialising in consumer industries at the expense of more basic products.[23] According to Nicholas Brown, Copland's analysis portrayed Australia's progress as fragile and prone to upsets by imbalanced attitudes towards consumption.[24] At the heart of this was uncertainty over Australia's status as a 'developed' country, and its capacity to sustain further development. Copland's long-time colleague at Melbourne University, G.L. Wood, expressed a more confident attitude regarding Australia's development, depicting the country as having "all the equipment and trappings of a modern industrial state."[25] Nevertheless, this anxiety resurfaced regularly in discussions of Australia's capacity to finance international development projects.

[21] J. Leyser, "Australia and the Post-War Settlement in South-East Asia," *Australian Outlook* 3, no. 3 (1949): 189.

[22] Russell McGregor, *Environment, Race, and Nationhood in Australia: Revisiting the Empty North* (New York: Palgrave Macmillan, 2016). Northern development continues to be an issue in Australian politics, as demonstrated by the publication of a government white paper in 2015. Commonwealth of Australia, *Our North, Our Future: White Paper on Developing Northern Australia* (Canberra: Commonwealth of Australia, 2015).

[23] D.B. Copland, "Balance of Production in the Australian Post-War Economy," *Economic Record* 25, no. 2 (1949): 4.

[24] Brown, *Governing Prosperity*, 88–89.

[25] Wood, *Australia*, 14.

Aid Becomes Foreign Policy

Early post-war programs tended to focus on reconstructing parts of the world affected by the Second World War, particularly in Europe. The UN Relief and Rehabilitation Agency (UNRRA) provided economic assistance to countries both in Europe and in Asia. Australia was the fourth highest contributor to UNRRA, a fact emphasised repeatedly by Australian policymakers.[26] Australia's involvement in UNRRA provided an early example of the competition between the developmental and political imperatives in Australian aid policy. In commenting on what would replace UNRRA following its conclusion in 1947, the *Sydney Morning Herald* editorialised that if UNRRA's work was to be discontinued, "human misery on a vast and tragic scale is certain to result."[27] In contrast, Assistant Secretary of the Treasury, Frederick Wheeler, when commenting on an External Affairs request for increased post-UNRRA funds, argued that the submission was motivated by the "political advantage" that would accrue to the Minister for External Affairs as a result of a generous Australian contribution.[28] From its earliest stages, Australian aid policy was a product of both humanitarian (soon to become more overtly developmental) and political motives.

In 1947, around the same time as UNRRA concluded, the UN established the Economic Committee for Asia and the Far East (ECAFE), which had the explicit goal of assisting in the reconstruction and development of Asian countries.[29] Commenting several years after the establishment of the Colombo Plan, R.G. Neale identified ECAFE as one of the Plan's intellectual antecedents. Importantly, Neale also identified the "lesser known" British programs of colonial development in his analysis,

[26] The bulk of Australia's UNRRA contribution went to China. "Statement on Australia's Contribution to Humanitarian Funds," NAA: A1068, R47/3/1.

[27] "After UNRRA," *Sydney Morning Herald*, May 14, 1947.

[28] F.H. Wheeler to J.B. Chifley, June 15, 1948, NAA: A571, 1947/1529 PART 2.

[29] H.V. Evatt, Ministerial Statement on Foreign Affairs, June 6, 1947, State Library of New South Wales, Mitchell Library, Dr. H.V. Evatt Papers, MS 1309, Folder 1. Ekbladh explains the distinction between "reconstruction" and "development" after the Second World War, in Ekbladh, *The Great American Mission*, 94.

providing an indication of the shared intellectual origins of the Colombo Plan and the New Deal for PNG.[30]

As the 1940s progressed, the United States established their own economic reconstruction programs, with the most notable being the European Recovery Program (ERP), more commonly known as the Marshall Plan, which was sometimes presented as a precursor to the Colombo Plan.[31] By providing European countries with American dollars, the ERP also indirectly funded programs of colonial development in Asia, including in British Malaya and French Indochina.[32]

The American Point Four program was the most important example of the incorporation of development into policy. The fourth point of President Truman's 1949 Inaugural Address called for a "bold new program" to provide technical assistance to the poorer parts of the world.[33] The key to Point Four was its plan to provide expert advice to the underdeveloped countries, a policy in keeping with the ideas of scholars such as Lewis.[34] In his inaugural address, Truman expressed his faith in American technological skill, claiming: "The material resources which we can afford to use for the assistance of other peoples are limited. But our imponderable resources in technical knowledge are constantly growing and are inexhaustible."[35] Over the following years, Point Four technical assistance

[30] R.G. Neale, "Australian Interests in and Attitudes Towards Economic Assistance to Asia," in *Australian Policies toward Asia: Australian Papers, Institute of Pacific Relations Conference, 1954*, ed. Gordon Greenwood (Melbourne: Australian Institute of International Affairs, 1954), 1–2.

[31] John Carr-Gregg, "The Colombo Plan: A Commonwealth Program for Southeast Asia," *International Conciliation*, no. 467 (1951): 18; L.P. Singh, *The Colombo Plan: Some Political Aspects* (Canberra: Dept. of International Relations, Research School of Pacific Studies, Australian National University, 1963), 7.

[32] Members of the United States State Department expressed concern over British economic issues and the effect it might have on the ability of the United Kingdom to provide aid funding in Southeast Asia, State Department, "Southeast Asia & Philippines," April/May 1951, Box 2854, Decimal File, 1950–54, Central File for State Department Records, RG 59, National Archives at College Park, MD (Hereafter cited as NACP).

[33] Truman Inauguration Speech, January 20, 1949 in Dennis Merrill, ed. *Documentary History of the Truman Presidency*, vol. 27 (Bethesda, MD.: University Publications of America, 1995), 4.

[34] Ekbladh, *The Great American Mission*, 77–78.

[35] Merrill, *Documentary History of the Truman Presidency*.

projects were launched in numerous countries including Iran, Indonesia and Pakistan. By 1950, development was becoming incorporated into the heart of American policies towards 'underdeveloped' regions.

Southeast Asia quickly became the primary area of interest for Australian policymakers with an interest in the economic development of 'backward' countries. In this context, the arrival of academically trained bureaucrats during the Second World War impacted upon Australian foreign policy in a similar way to the effect of DORCA on Australian colonial policy. These experts folded the latest international theoretical developments into Australian foreign policy. One key figure was Arthur Tange, who began his career in PWR before moving to the fledgling Department of External Affairs, where he eventually rose to become departmental head. Tange played a pivotal role in the formation of the Colombo Plan proposal.[36] Prior to entering PWR, Tange received postgraduate training in economics at the University of Western Australia under the prominent economic historian Edward Shann. Another important official was John Burton, who was Secretary of the Department of External Affairs at the time of the 1950 Colombo Conference. A recipient of a doctorate from the London School of Economics, Burton rose quickly to become departmental secretary under H.V. Evatt.[37] Despite his departure shortly after the establishment of the Colombo Plan, Burton remained committed to development. In his 1954 book, *The Alternative*, Burton argued for the "giving of economic and technical assistance on a much increased scale to governments prepared to institute fundamental reforms for the sake of world peace."[38] These observations demonstrate the commitment of influential Australian scholars-turned-bureaucrats to the moral cause of developmentalism.

Enthusiasm for overseas development was bolstered by events in Asia, which married political imperatives to the developmental rhetoric. The fall of China to communism in late 1949 complicated existing issues regarding peace with Japan and the economic, political and security

[36] Arthur Tange, *Defence Policy-Making: A Close-Up View, 1950–1980* (Canberra: ANU E Press, 2008), 2.

[37] Adam Hughes Henry, "John Burton: Forgotten Mandarin?" in *The Seven Dwarfs and the Age of the Mandarins: Australian Government Administration in the Post-War Reconstruction Era*, ed. Samuel Furphy (Acton, ACT: ANU Press, 2015), 223.

[38] John W. Burton, *The Alternative: A Dynamic Approach to Our Relations with Asia* (Sydney: Morgans Publications, 1954), 115.

consequences of decolonisation in the region.[39] Australian diplomatic representatives in the region were called to Canberra to meet and discuss how to respond. The views put forward were presented in a document written by External Affairs official L.R. 'Jim' McIntyre, in consultation with Tange and Burton. McIntyre drew a direct relationship between the low standard of living in the 'underdeveloped' countries of Southeast Asia and the threat of communism. According to McIntyre:

> For Australia the problem is at present political and economic; it calls for sustained and co-ordinated action to encourage and strengthen established governments throughout the area, to cultivate and maintain the goodwill of the peoples, and to help them raise their standards of living and thereby increase their resistance to Communism.[40]

According to this view, increased developmental assistance to Southeast Asian countries would produce increased political stability, which would undermine the appeal of communism throughout the region. In following this logic, McIntyre drew on a connection that had already been established in the United States, and which has been examined by Nick Cullather.[41] According to McIntyre, Australian policy ought "to be determined largely, even though not entirely, by the extent to which we can help to foster the economic development of the region."[42] The Colombo Plan, proposed a month after McIntyre drafted his memorandum, joined colonial policy in PNG as the second facet of the Australian contribution to the age of international development.

At the time that McIntyre wrote his analysis of Australian policy towards Southeast Asia, the Commonwealth Government provided small-scale programs of technical assistance to Indonesia and Malaya. A small

[39] Gifford, "The Cold War across Asia"; David Lowe, ed., *Australia and the End of Empires: The Impact of Decolonisation in Australia's Near North, 1945–65* (Geelong, VIC: Deakin University Press, 1996).

[40] L.R. McIntyre, "Australian Policy in South East Asia," December 12, 1949, NAA: A1068, DL47/5/6.

[41] Cullather, *The Hungry World*, 7.

[42] McIntyre, "Australian Policy in South East Asia."

number of Commonwealth scholarships were offered, whereby Indonesian scholars could attend courses at Australian universities.[43] This funding was taken from Australia's contribution to post-UNRRA relief, revealing the way that humanitarian assistance was becoming increasingly developmental.[44] McIntyre's arguments, circulated to Burton and Tange, were therefore not produced in a policy vacuum. Tange's responsiveness to these ideas undoubtedly drew upon his wartime experiences of flying to the United Kingdom via cities like Karachi, where he was exposed to the "extremes of wealth and poverty" in what became known as 'underdeveloped' countries.[45] It also drew on his familiarity with theoretical and policy advances overseas, particularly the United States' Point Four program.

The Colombo Plan

External Affairs officials were still in the process of refining their plans when the Menzies Liberal Coalition government came to power on December 19, 1949. The new Minister for External Affairs, Percy Spender brought a different perspective to the Department on many issues.[46] Spender had served as Treasurer during Menzies' first government in the early stages of the Second World War and quickly emerged as one of the leading figures in the government after the 1949 election. His earlier experiences both as a politician and a private citizen influenced his approach to the 'problem' of development in Asia. David Lowe, in his biography of Spender, tells the story of the Minister's encounters with poverty in Asia in the 1930s. According to Lowe, Spender's experiences "drove home the lack of general Australian awareness about such endemic poverty."[47] These experiences, combined with his university education in economics (a similar combination to that of Arthur Tange),

[43] McIntyre, "Australian Policy in South East Asia."

[44] *Sydney Morning Herald*, May 29, 1948, NAA: A571, 1947/1529 PART 2.

[45] A.H. Tange to Mrs Elsie Tange, September 16, 1945, Tange Papers, NLA, MS 9847, Box 2.

[46] Percy Spender, *Exercises in Diplomacy: The Anzus Treaty and the Colombo Plan* (Sydney: Sydney University Press, 1969), 32; Lowe, *Australian Between Empires*.

[47] Lowe, *Australian Between Empires*, 35.

provided fruitful ground for Spender to engage with the growing field of development.

Spender shared the previous government's view regarding development assistance. Less than a month after becoming External Affairs Minister, Spender represented Australia in Colombo. Although Spender claimed that the Colombo Plan was formulated en route to the conference, in fact it built upon the plan previously formulated by the Department of External Affairs.[48] McIntyre recounted Spender pacing the halls of his guesthouse in Jakarta, excitedly outlining his plan before heading to Colombo.[49] While there is little reason to doubt that discussions between the new minister and his departmental officials added flesh to the bones of the Australian proposal, these individuals were building on ideas that had evolved throughout the previous year.

Australian recommendations, in conjunction with papers presented by the Ceylonese and New Zealand delegations, became the foundation of the Colombo Plan.[50] Two consultative committee meetings were held in Sydney in May 1950 and London in September and October. The Sydney meeting was marked by disagreement between Australia and the United Kingdom over whether the program should emphasise long or short-term planning. The Australian delegation was in favour of urgent action, largely because they sought immediate American involvement in the Plan.[51] Other parties, particularly the British, were more cautious, and tensions emerged. At the second ministerial meeting, Spender was quoted as explaining: "While Australia did not deny the necessity for long term study and planning, he [Spender] felt that the United Kingdom point of view was disturbing in that it implied a lack of any real attempt to carry out the decisions of the Colombo Conference."[52] David Lowe suggests

[48] Spender, *Exercises in Diplomacy*, 214.

[49] L.R. McIntyre, Presentation to Conference on South-East Asia, Goulburn College of Advanced Education, July 7, 1976, McIntyre Papers, NLA, MS 7662, Folder 3.

[50] Commonwealth Meeting on Foreign Affairs, Final Communique, January 14, 1950, NAA: A4639, 37.

[51] Telegram from Australian Government to United Kingdom Government, April 19, 1950, David Lowe and Daniel Oakman, eds., *Australia and the Colombo Plan, 1949–1957* (Barton, ACT: Dept. of Foreign Affairs and Trade, 2004), 115; Cablegram from Spender to Harrison, May 10, 1950, ibid., 131.

[52] Minutes of the Second Plenary Session, Commonwealth Consultative Committee Meeting, Sydney, May 15, 1950, NAA: A10617, 1950/5. In the same address, Spender

that Spender's "over-stepping of the mark" threatened not only British interest in the Plan, but also that of the United States.[53] Nevertheless, in spite of Spender's behaviour (or perhaps because of it), a compromise agreement was reached in Sydney that established a Bureau to provide technical assistance to all countries in the region, as well as calling for another meeting in London in September to continue examining the development programs submitted by the Commonwealth countries in the region.[54]

Throughout 1950, Spender repeatedly explained the motivations behind the Colombo Plan, even as negotiations continued. On one side were the imperatives of maintaining political and economic stability in an area of strategic importance to Australia. However, the Minister also provided developmental arguments for the Plan. Following the Sydney conference, Spender outlined in parliament the rationale for Australian assistance. Rather than opening with the political benefits of aid, the Minister explained that "on humanitarian grounds we cannot ignore the basic needs of such a large and important section of the world's population."[55] In the External Affairs notes on the London conference of September, reference was made to the fact that the Australian delegation fought to ensure that "humanitarian" concerns were present in the face of British emphasis on balance of payments issues.[56] Even before the Plan's formal beginning, tension between political and developmental objectives was coming into conflict. Press reports on the 1950 conferences also commented on this tension. After the Colombo meeting, the Brisbane *Courier-Mail* suggested that in the Australian proposal "the humanitarian motive either comes first or last – according to the viewer."[57] This apt reading of Australian aid policy did not detract from the fact that the

threatened to postpone further meetings until other delegations demonstrated "signs of any action" of the agreements from the Colombo conference.

[53] Lowe, "Percy Spender and the Colombo Plan 1950," 170–171.

[54] Department of External Affairs Notes on London Meeting of Commonwealth Consultative Committee, October 1950, NAA: A9879, 2202/E PART 1.

[55] *CPD*, House of Representatives, no. 23, 1950, June 6, 1950, 3723.

[56] Department of External Affairs, "Departmental Notes on the London Meeting of the Commonwealth Consultative Committee, September 6 to October 4, 1950," NAA: A9879, 2202/E PART 1.

[57] "Spender Plan Emerges," *The Courier-Mail*, January 14, 1950.

improvement of the welfare of Asian peoples was a goal in itself of the Colombo Plan.

In March 1950, Spender secured £13 million as the Australian contribution to the Colombo Plan for its first year.[58] This can be seen as a substantial gesture of support for the Plan in its very early stages, as well as an indication of Spender's ability to achieve his policy goals in Cabinet. As it transpired, this figure was whittled down in Cabinet to £8.75 million and then only £4.225 million in Colombo Plan aid was actually provided in 1951–1952, the first full financial year of the Plan.[59] Difficulties at both the donor and recipient ends explain the shortfall. In recipient countries, developmental plans were often vague, and the equipment and resources needed to put them into action were also required in Australia. As such, it took Australian officials far longer to identify and organise aid projects than Spender and his department had anticipated. After negotiations between officials of the Departments of External Affairs and Treasury, Australia went on to pledge £31.25 million in developmental funding for the first six years of the Plan. Of the £8.75 million allocated in the financial year 1951/1952, £4.2 million went to India, £2 million to Pakistan, £300,000 to Ceylon and the remaining £2.25 million was held in reserve for potential new members, such as Indonesia.[60] The Australian commitment to India and Ceylon primarily comprised gifts of flour and wheat, but by January 1952 none of the £2 million for Pakistan had been allocated. The purpose of these gifts was to generate counterpart funds that would enable government investment in developmental projects.

The Colombo Plan provided for technical as well as economic assistance. Australian technical assistance comprised of scholarships for Asian students to study in Australia and the sending of Australian experts overseas to assist in local development projects. For Oakman, this part of the

[58] Minutes, Cabinet Committee on Aid to South-East Asia, March 22, 1950, NAA: A1209, 1957/5406.

[59] Department of External Affairs press release, June 15, 1951, NAA: A1209, 1957/5406. Annex to Department of External Affairs, "Papua/New Guinea: The Australian Effort," n.d. [Written at some point in the middle of 1964], Tange Papers, NLA, MS 9847, Box 6. To put this into perspective, the Australian grant to PNG was over £5.5 million in 1951–1952.

[60] Department of External Affairs, "Colombo Plan—Progress Report of the Australian Effort, April 17, 1951 to September 17, 1951," NAA: A1838, 2020/1/12 PART 1.

Plan was most important. As he suggests: "Just as the presence of international students challenged racial stereotypes, so the expert program changed Australian perceptions of Asian people and work practices."[61] At the end of the first term of the Colombo Plan in mid-1957, Australia had provided 2041 Training Awards for study in Australia, while 237 Australian experts had been sent to recipient nations to provide technical assistance. These figures were second only to the United States during the same period and demonstrate one area where Australian assistance was substantial in international terms.[62] Australian economic assistance involved food gifts, as well as funds and equipment for specific programs. Early examples of Colombo Plan programs included a hydroelectric scheme in India, a mass literacy program in Indonesia and an irrigation scheme in Pakistan.[63] These programs fitted neatly with the dominant developmental ideas of the time, which emphasised the importance of improved infrastructure and education as key requirements for growth.[64] By the end of the Plan's first six-year term, Australia had spent £18.5 million on economic assistance and almost £3.5 million on technical assistance.[65] While dwarfed by aid provided by countries like the United States, this was a clear sign that Australia was a part of the international system of developmental assistance in Asia.

In the early years of the Colombo Plan, Australian assistance was largely directed towards the newly independent states of India, Pakistan and Ceylon. This was partly a product of their status as independent nations, which meant they were responsible for drafting their own developmental programs. It was also due to the perception, held by countries such as Australia and Great Britain, of their extreme plight with regard to food production.[66] In contrast, Malaya and British Borneo, which were still under British colonial control, received far less economic assistance from Australia in the Plan's early years. This was mainly because the British

[61] Oakman, *Facing Asia*, 206.

[62] Department of External Affairs, "The Colombo Plan's First Six Years—Australia's Part to June 30, 1957," August 23, 1957, NAA: A1838, 740/4/5 PART 1.

[63] R.G. Casey, "The Colombo Plan: Report Presented to the Australian Parliament on 9 April, 1954," NAA: A1838, 740/4/5 PART 1.

[64] Cullather, *The Hungry World*, 108.

[65] Department of External Affairs, "The Colombo Plan's First Six Years."

[66] Department of External Affairs Notes on London Meeting of Commonwealth Consultative Committee, October 1950.

continued to direct the development of these colonies, using funds allocated by the Colonial Development and Welfare Act.[67] Australia did provide scholarships to these colonies, and 492 students from British Southeast Asian colonies came to Australia in the first six years of the plan. Nevertheless, the fact that Australian Colombo Plan aid was predominantly given to India, Pakistan and Ceylon in its very early years suggests a distinction between colonial development and foreign aid. This can be linked also to Australian assistance to PNG, which continued to grow as the Colombo Plan was created. In the early 1950s, there was little interaction between the two dominant spheres of Australian aid, despite Spender briefly also occupying the portfolio of External Territories.[68] While driven by the same intellectual framework, it would not be until the early 1960s that Australian policymakers started to conceive of assistance to PNG and the Colombo Plan as being closely connected.

The Colombo Plan's International Dimensions

Australia's role in the creation of the Colombo Plan demonstrates the importance of the circulation of transnational ideas and policies in the establishment of Australian policy. While Australian officials were undoubtedly motivated by the political and diplomatic benefits that would accrue as a result of providing aid to Asian countries, the Plan should be seen as a product of the international rise of developmental assistance in the late 1940s and early 1950s. External Affairs officials took particular note of Point Four. In his review of the Colombo Conference, the Counselor of the American Embassy in Colombo observed: "In this connection it has been learned that the Department's booklet, POINT 4 (revised December 1949), which had been loaned to the Ceylon legation, was passed on to the Australians."[69] In March 1950, John Burton issued a memorandum to the heads of all government departments reflecting on the nature of American foreign aid policy towards Southeast Asia. In his observations on American policy, Burton suggested that "an initiative by Commonwealth countries is expected to have a favourable reaction upon

[67] Frey, "Control, Legitimacy, and the Securing of Interests," 401.

[68] MacWilliam, *Securing Village Life*, 79–80; Lowe, *Australian Between Empires*, 140.

[69] John B. Ketcham to the Department of State, January 25, 1950, Box 3519, Decimal File, 1950–54, RG 59, NACP.

the United States and it is the intention to keep the United States fully informed of the broad lines of Australian intentions."[70] This was a clear indication that Colombo Plan aid would interact with the American aid program.

American officials also commented on the interaction between the two programs. The American Consul-General in Singapore, William R. Langdon, called for the Colombo Plan to be given "financial and moral aid" by the United States.[71] The report of the International Development Advisory Board (better known as the Rockefeller Report), published in March 1951, advocated a strong American response to the problem of economic development, in conjunction with the rest of the 'free world' (in other words, the Colombo Plan).[72] The United States' Ambassador in Canberra, Pete Jarman, considered the Colombo Plan as being "complementary to our own plans and policies including Point Four."[73] Similar sentiments were also found in an early Australian publicity piece for the Colombo Plan. In the introduction to *New Hope for Asia*, published in 1951, Spender wrote that:

> It is in countries with low living standards and little hope for improvement in the future that extremist political doctrines find fertile ground. This Plan is a major part of the answer of the Western World to any questions which may be raised in the minds of the peoples of these countries by Communist influences.[74]

Together, the Colombo Plan and Point Four sought to establish a 'free world' system of technical and economic assistance to the 'underdeveloped' countries of the world. This would serve humanitarian goals by lifting the standard of living across the 'underdeveloped' world. It also

[70] Memorandum from Burton to Heads of Departments, March 13, 1950, Lowe and Oakman, *Australia and the Colombo Plan, 1949–1957*, 74.

[71] William R. Langdon to the Department of State, October 30, 1950, Box 2854, Decimal File, 1950–54, RG 59, NACP.

[72] Report, International Development Advisory Board, March 1951, Merrill, *Documentary History of the Truman Presidency*, vol. 27, 525.

[73] Pete Jarman to Dean Acheson, March 24, 1950, *FR-US*, 1950, vol. 4, 66.

[74] Australian Dept. of External Affairs, *New Hope for Asia: The Colombo Plan for Co-operative Economic Development in South and South-East Asia*, Australian ed. (Sydney: F.H. Johnston, 1951), 6.

satisfied political goals, by ameliorating the attractions of communism and binding peoples to donor nations.

Australian officials were also mindful of the UN program of technical assistance. Importantly, while the Colombo Plan was established in the context of Commonwealth relations, the UN technical assistance program often clashed with the imperatives of the Cold War and decolonisation.[75] Within External Affairs, there was a feeling that while the UN program was worthwhile, more needed to be done. When discussing the potential for Australian aid to Indonesia in 1949, McIntyre argued: "It is desirable that Australia should consider ways and means of extending technical assistance to Indonesia over and above whatever general contribution we may make to the United Nations technical assistance programme."[76] The Prime Minister, Robert Menzies, also indicated that the Colombo Plan should supplement UN attempts to provide technical assistance.[77] Following the negotiations in Sydney and London, the Colombo Plan emerged as a product of these observations. The global dimensions of the Colombo Plan can be seen in External Affairs' commentary on the London meeting in September 1950:

> This scheme will not compete with existing organisations ... The expansion of the technical aid programme of the United Nations and Specialised Agencies and of United States activities in this field through the Point Four programme underlines the need for close liaison and co-operation among the various agencies now operating in the field of technical assistance if the available man-power is to be used to best advantage.[78]

From its very beginning, Australian policymakers perceived the Colombo Plan as being part of a broader international developmental project.

[75] David Webster, "Development Advisors in a Time of Cold War and Decolonization: The United Nations Technical Assistance Administration, 1950–59," *Journal of Global History* 6, no. 2 (2011).

[76] McIntyre, "Australian Policy in South East Asia."

[77] R.G. Menzies, quoted in Department of External Affairs press release, "The Ceylon Conference," January 16, 1950, NAA: A3318, L1950/3/2/28.

[78] Department of External Affairs Notes on London Meeting of Commonwealth Consultative Committee, October 1950.

Developmental Debates: External Affairs and Treasury

Australia's involvement in attempts to promote economic development in the 'underdeveloped' countries of Southeast Asia and PNG signified its membership of a small group of 'developed' nations. Yet in Australia, debate continued about the degree to which Australia should be considered 'developed.' This debate was foreshadowed in the establishment of the New Deal for PNG, but it became much more pronounced in 1950. The two key Commonwealth departments involved in this debate were External Affairs and Treasury.

External Affairs was the strongest advocate for the notion of Australia as a 'developed' nation, with a responsibility to provide assistance to the 'underdeveloped' world. External Affairs devised both the developmental and political rationales for the Colombo Plan. In September 1951, the department prepared a brief for new Minister Richard Casey to be used in a meeting with Indonesian Foreign Minister, Ahmad Subardjo. Casey had enjoyed a privileged upbringing, studying at Cambridge, and while he was in no way an economic expert, he managed to obtain a reasonable understanding of economic ideas. This intellectual background was combined with his wartime experience as Governor of Bengal, a position he obtained at the urging of Winston Churchill. According to his biographer, W.J. Hudson, "the Indian experience was good for Casey," as it opened his eyes to the poor standards of living in that country and caused him to pay increased attention to Australia's relationship with newly independent Asian countries.[79] Once he became Minister for External Affairs, Casey used these experiences to take a close interest in the Colombo Plan.[80]

In preparing Casey for his meeting with Subardjo, the departmental brief explained Australia's dual reasons for supporting the Colombo Plan:

[79] W.J. Hudson, *Casey* (Melbourne: Oxford University Press, 1986), 156–179. Allen Gyngell also comments on Casey's loose relationship with theoretical ideas, in *Fear of Abandonment: Australia in the World Since 1942* (Carlton: La Trobe University Press, 2017), 26.

[80] Adam Henry, *The Gatekeepers of Australian Foreign Policy 1950–1966* (North Melbourne: Australian Scholarly Publishing, 2015), 36.

> The Plan was conceived not only for humanitarian reasons, but as a counter to internal and external communist influences and activities, and to bring South and South-East Asian countries into a closer relationship with the 'Western' developed and democratic countries.[81]

Three years later, Casey presented a further report to Parliament that explained the rationale behind the Colombo Plan, along with its early achievements. In explaining "Australia's interest" in the Plan, Casey presented Australia as one of the world's "economically more developed countries."[82] Throughout his tenure, Casey evoked two key notions related to post-war Australian developmentalism—faith in Australian development and acceptance of the responsibilities that come with that status. These comments share striking similarities with E.E. Ward's 1951 analysis, which contrasted the characteristics of "modern democratic states" such as Britain and Australia, with the absence of these features in 'underdeveloped' recipient states.[83] For External Affairs officials and academic observers, the Colombo Plan both signified and reinforced Australia's status amongst the 'developed' economies.

In contrast, Treasury officials were inclined to place Australian aid spending in the context of broader domestic priorities. For them, every pound spent on development overseas undermined Australia's own development. Given Treasury's ongoing concern over Australian economic growth, departmental officials were more likely to present Australia as a 'developing' country in its own right. Greg Whitwell observes that during the 1950s Treasury officials were committed to the notion that "balanced growth necessitated recognising limits and not exceeding them."[84] This position assumed a level of orthodoxy in the Treasury and would be the cause of ongoing tension with External Affairs. Treasurer Arthur Fadden presented this view to Menzies in 1951, citing budgetary difficulties as a reason for limiting Australian spending on the Colombo Plan.[85] Several

[81] Economic and Technical Assistance Section, "Notes for the Minister, Proposed Meeting with Dr. Subardjo on the Colombo Plan," September 19, 1951, NAA: A1838, 3004/11 PART 1.

[82] R.G. Casey, "The Colombo Plan: Report Presented to the Australian Parliament," April 9, 1954, NAA: A1838, 740/4/5 PART 1.

[83] E.E. Ward, "The Colombo Plan," *Australian Outlook* 5, no. 4 (1951): 196.

[84] Greg Whitwell, *The Treasury Line* (Sydney: Allen & Unwin, 1986), 122–123.

[85] A.W. Fadden to R.G. Menzies, March 15, 1951, NAA: A1209, 1957/5406.

years later, at an inter-departmental meeting in 1955, Treasury raised objections to Colombo Plan spending, again citing budgetary concerns. In a moment that encapsulated the differences between the two departments, the External Affairs representative exclaimed: "Australia could hardly say to South East Asia and her partners in the Colombo Plan, such as the United States, that she could not afford to do what she was doing."[86]

The difference in attitudes between External Affairs and Treasury demonstrated the vulnerability of developmental policy to political debate. The clearest demonstration of this in the early 1950s emerged over the amount of funding to be devoted to the Colombo Plan. Spender's original goal was to secure £13 million for the first year of the Plan, with no clear indication of how much would be spent over the entire six-year term.[87] However, the spending limit was gradually worn down, largely through the efforts of the Treasurer, Arthur Fadden. The Treasurer, with some support from Menzies, managed to whittle down the Australian commitment for the first six-year phase of the Colombo Plan to a total of £25 million.[88] He attributed the need for a lower figure to budgetary concerns, presenting what would become familiar arguments that revolved around the need to balance spending for domestic and international development. Spender and officials inside the Department of External Affairs were disappointed with the reduction in funds for the Plan, although they did manage to get the figure raised to £31.25 million for the first six years of the plan. External Affairs official Thomas Critchley, who led the Australian delegation to the meeting of officials in Colombo in February 1951, expressed his regret "that the Australian Government, which had large and increasing demands at present on its financial resources, was not in a position to make available greater assistance than that announced."[89] External Affairs was regularly rebuffed in its attempts to secure increased funding for the Colombo Plan.

[86] Minutes of Inter-departmental Meeting on the Colombo Plan, May 19, 1955, NAA: A1838, 740/4/5 PART 1.

[87] R.G. Menzies to P.C. Spender, September 21, 1950, NAA: A1209, 1957/5406.

[88] F.H. Wheeler to A.S. Brown, October 4, 1950, NAA: A1209, 1957/5406; A.W. Fadden to R.G. Menzies, March 15, 1951, NAA: A1209, 1957/5406.

[89] Minutes of First Business Meeting of Colombo Plan Consultative Committee, Colombo, February 13, 1951, NAA: A9879, 2202/E PART 1. External Affairs officials raised a similar point in a memorandum on March 27, 1952, where it was commented

The Early Years of the Colombo Plan

Following the formal establishment of the Colombo Plan at the end of 1950, Australian policymakers devised ways of responding to the developmental plans of the inaugural recipient countries. Developmental and political imperatives continued to guide policymakers. Projects that satisfied both of these imperatives tended to be favoured, with mixed success. In the early years of the Colombo Plan, the Department of External Affairs' zeal for development resulted in the selection of projects that were difficult to implement. Exacerbating this was the fact that many of the developmental needs of recipient nations required resources that were in short supply in Australia.

As the Colombo Plan evolved, Australian officials worked with their Commonwealth counterparts to expand its membership. Australian policymakers were particularly determined to extend the Colombo Plan to the United States (as a donor) and Indonesia (as a recipient). National and regional interests were clearly influential in this regard. American involvement would significantly increase the amount of assistance that could be provided through the plan and Australian officials were very interested in maintaining close ties with Indonesia. Nevertheless, the early expansion of the Plan also reflects the internationalisation of developmental assistance after 1949 and demonstrates the Australian recognition that the Plan needed to go beyond the Commonwealth.

Securing American involvement in the Colombo Plan was a primary consideration for both Australia and the United Kingdom at the London meeting of the consultative committee in 1950. Spender best expressed this in a cablegram to Menzies during the conference. Commenting on his priorities at the conference, the External Affairs Minister wrote: "The first is the vital importance for Australia's long-term security of a United States commitment to sustain the economic (and indirectly the political) stability of this area."[90] Political concerns were prominent in Spender's mind. Still, there were also developmental reasons behind Australia's desire for American involvement. The technical assistance component of the Plan was also a signal to the United States, with their Point Four

that a demonstration of American interest in increased resources might convince Treasury to agree to increased Australian spending. NAA: A1838, 3004/11 PART 1.

[90] Cablegram from Spender to Menzies, September 27, 1950, Lowe and Oakman, *Australia and the Colombo Plan, 1949–1957*, 241.

program that the Commonwealth was willing to invest in the development of the region. The report of the London conference drew explicit influence from the American Point Four program, which had recently been formally established by the Act for International Development.[91] Ultimately, these tactics achieved their desired aim, as the United States joined the Colombo Plan at the beginning of 1951.

Following this, Australian officials' ongoing concern over American commitment to the Colombo Plan was rooted in developmental language. For instance, a Department of External Affairs memorandum from 1952 commented:

> The Colombo Plan must be regarded as a bid to interest the United States in providing an enlarged volume of economic aid to South and South-East Asia. Without it, the prospects of reaching the modest targets of the Colombo Plan are remote.[92]

The developmental requirements of Colombo Plan recipients were huge. India's development program for the period 1951–1957 alone required over £600 million in external capital, which was well beyond the capabilities of the British Commonwealth.[93] American involvement was therefore required to satisfy the developmental goals of the Plan. In the first full year of the Colombo Plan (1951–1952), the United States provided $282.5 million to 'Asia and the Pacific', which included Colombo Plan countries as well as countries such as Taiwan and South Korea.[94] The involvement of the United States served to both internationalise the Colombo Plan and expand its developmental resources.

[91] "The Colombo Plan for Co-operative Economic Development in South and South-East Asia," London, October 1950, NAA: A9879, 2202/E PART 1. State Department memorandum, "Point IV Legislation," July 12, 1950, Merrill, *Documentary History of the Truman Presidency*, vol. 27, 421.

[92] Department of External Affairs Memorandum, March 19, 1952, NLA: A1838, 3004/11 PART 1. A similar point is raised in A.H. Tange to T.K. Critchley, February 10, 1950, Lowe and Oakman, *Australia and the Colombo Plan, 1949–1957*, 61.

[93] "The Colombo Plan for Co-operative Economic Development in South and South-East Asia".

[94] Department of External Affairs, "Colombo Plan Economic Development and Technical Co-operation Programmes—Progress Report of the Australian Effort, April 17, 1951 to September 17, 1951."

Australian attempts to bring Indonesia into the Colombo Plan also demonstrated the international forces that underpinned Australian aid policy. Well before 1950, Australian experts and officials recognised the importance of providing developmental assistance to Indonesia. According to William MacMahon Ball, political scientist turned diplomat who toured Southeast Asia in 1948, Indonesia needed help, and "they would prefer it to come from Australia than from the United States."[95] According to Ball, this was because Australia's relatively low level of global power made it less likely to pose a political threat to countries emerging out of colonial rule. In his December 1949 memorandum, McIntyre identified Indonesia as the place where Australian assistance efforts should be focused:

> In the economic field, however, the effectiveness of what Australia may be able to do will be determined rather more by the extent to which we are prepared to divert resources from other uses. The fact that our capacity to do this is limited is, as was stated earlier, the principal argument in favour of concentrating on the territory where economic assistance promises to be most effective – at the present time Indonesia.[96]

Here, we see McIntyre engaging with developmental arguments in recommending that aid should be sent to Indonesia. McIntyre argued that Australian funds would have the greatest developmental impact there. The notion of aid 'effectiveness' would become an ongoing concern in External Affairs, as officials were constantly required to monitor whether or not Australian aid had a positive impact on the development of the recipient country. This was generally done in an informal way, through high commission and embassy reports, as well as tours by departmental officials. Despite strong Australian pressure from the earliest days of the Colombo Plan, Indonesia did not join until 1953. This was partially due to the perceived Commonwealth-centric nature of the Colombo Plan, alongside the gradual nature of the Plan's build-up. As a consequence,

[95] W. MacMahon Ball, "Interim Notes on Netherlands East Indies," attached to W. MacMahon Ball to J. Burton, June 7, 1948, Ball Papers, NLA, MS 7851, Box 29. Christopher Waters, "The Macmahon Ball Mission to East Asia 1948," *Australian Journal of Politics and History* 40, no. 3 (1994).

[96] McIntyre, "Australian Policy in South East Asia."

Australian aid spending was spread over a wide number of countries, creating a precedent that guided Australian aid to Asia for the next several decades.

The wide spread of Colombo Plan aid was a product of political imperatives, as the perceived political benefits that came from aid projects in a large number of countries trumped the developmental arguments for concentrating aid in fewer locations. Nevertheless, the developmental basis of the Colombo Plan remained. A 1952 External Affairs discussion noted that the Plan was "a humanitarian attack on poverty" and not just a response to "the menace of Communism."[97] Richard Casey, who had a strong interest in the public relations aspects of the Colombo Plan, was also keen to stress the Plan's developmental imperatives. In a 1954 report to Parliament on the Colombo Plan, Casey explained that:

> In extending aid to countries of the area, Australia has recognised that the economically more developed countries have a responsibility to see that the peoples of less developed areas of the world should receive the opportunity to improve their standards of living towards that level enjoyed by countries of the Western World.[98]

This notion of responsibility conjured up a vision of Australia's developmental obligations in PNG. While Casey was a keen proponent of the political objectives of the Colombo Plan, he also had a firm sense of the place of development within the Plan.

As the Plan progressed, Australian officials were faced with the challenge of implementing their vision of developmental assistance. This proved difficult. Almost exactly two years after the Colombo conference, of the budgeted £8.75 million, over half had yet to be provided to recipient countries.[99] This slowness persisted, as the machinery for providing large-scale aid to South and Southeast Asia required much more administrative work than the technical assistance component of the Plan. Indeed, Australian journalist Creighton Burns aptly identified this issue in a 1954

[97] External Affairs Notes on the "Political Objectives of the Colombo Plan," March 27, 1952, NAA: A1838, 3004/11 PART 1.

[98] Report on the Colombo Plan Presented to the Australian Parliament by the Minister for External Affairs the Rt. Hon. R.G. Casey, April 1954, NAA: A1209, 1957/5406.

[99] Economic and Technical Assistance Section, "The Colombo Plan—Present Status of the Australian Effort," January 8, 1952, NAA: A1838, 2020/1/12 PART 1.

piece for *Australia's Neighbours*, when he wrote: "By 1952 the exuberant idealism of the original conception had hardened into restrained optimism. This has now given way to set-jaw determination which seems to carry with it a hint of disillusionment."[100] Officials in Canberra held a similar view. Commenting on the lack of progress in providing assistance to Pakistan, an official in the Economic and Technical Assistance section of the Department of External Affairs wrote: "Taking the Colombo Plan as a whole, it is probably fair to say that the Australian effort is not, at this stage at least, as impressive as might have been hoped."[101] Similar observations were made at the end of the Plan's first term, with External Affairs Assistant Secretary, Keith Waller, explaining:

> Many of the projects to which we are now wholly or partly committed seem, for this distance, to have been badly chosen, despite our commendable desire to get the Plan into top gear. In my opinion, this poor selection was partly because of haste to commit funds, partly because the Minister yielded too easily to pressure at Consultative Committee meetings and partly because we did not think out thoroughly what was involved.[102]

This commentary points to the tension between political and developmental imperatives in Australian aid policy. Because the Plan had both political and developmental objectives, Australian officials ran the risk of choosing projects that might not be the best for the development of a recipient country. This was often the case and helps to explain why External Affairs felt disappointed with the progress of the Plan.

Throughout the 1950s, Australian involvement in the Colombo Plan continued to be guided by the principles established by Percy Spender and his department. The initial six-year term of the plan was extended to 1961 at the Singapore meeting of the Consultative Committee in 1955. The spending total of £22 million was less than the £31.5 million that Spender had fought so hard for in 1950, and points to some of the difficulties faced by Australian officials. Looking back in 1957 at the

[100] Creighton Burns, "Progress Report on the Colombo Plan," *Australia's Neighbours*, January 1954. This article is found in NAA: A1838, 2020/1/12 PART 1.

[101] Economic and Technical Assistance Section, "The Colombo Plan—Present Status of the Australian Effort."

[102] J.K. Waller to A.H. Tange, March 21, 1957, NAA: A1838, 2020/1/2 PART 1.

plan to spend £8,950,000 in 1950, Foreign Aid Branch official, David Dexter, commented, "It seems fantastic that we should ever have hoped to spend these amounts in such a brief period."[103] Nevertheless, by 1957 Australia had played a central role in establishing a vital component of the international system of developmental assistance in Southeast Asia.

The Colombo Plan: More Than Just Engagement

In his reflections on Australian foreign policy written after a long career of public service, Arthur Tange claimed that 1950 was the most significant year in Australia's brief foreign affairs history. This year saw the start of the Korean War, the establishment of the Colombo Plan and the consolidation of the new Menzies Government.[104] While pinpointing single moments (or even individual years) as causing monumental shifts in policy can be problematic, 1950 was indeed an important year for Australian aid policy, as it was marked by the establishment of the Colombo Plan, the second component of Australia's involvement in the age of international development. By the end of the Plan's first term in 1957, the Colombo Plan and PNG were established as the dominant spheres of Australian development assistance. Developmental ideas had clearly established themselves within the Commonwealth bureaucracy, albeit in diverse ways. While the Colombo Plan served important diplomatic purposes, it was also a product of the increased international attention being paid to development. The enthusiasm of Australian officials for development, demonstrated in this chapter, was a major driving force behind the establishment of the Plan.

The Colombo Plan was not marked by a great deal of interaction with Australian aid to PNG in its early years. Nevertheless, it was clear that both the New Deal for PNG and the Colombo Plan were products of very similar international intellectual forces. Both emerged out of intensified calls by development experts to incorporate their ideas into government policy. In Canberra, bureaucrats with academic expertise promoted both policies. In External Affairs, academically trained officials,

[103] D. Dexter draft memorandum, April 15, 1957, NAA: A1838, 2020/1/2 PART 1.

[104] A.H. Tange, "Notes for Memoir," n.d. Tange Papers, NLA, MS 9847, Box 25.

such as Arthur Tange and John Burton, were central to the establishment of the Colombo Plan.[105] These figures played a similar role to that of DORCA in the New Deal. As the 1950s progressed, the similarities between the Colombo Plan and Australian colonial policy would become more pronounced, leading Australian officials to make explicit links between the two policies.

[105] Joan Beaumont et al., eds., *Ministers, Mandarins and Diplomats: Australian Foreign Policy Making, 1941–1969* (Melbourne: Melbourne University Press, 2003).

CHAPTER 4

"New Codes and a New Order": Papua New Guinean Development in the Hasluck Era, 1951–1963

On October 26, 1961, Paul Hasluck spoke about PNG's economic development at the New South Wales branch of the Economic Society of Australia.[1] For over a decade, from 1951 to 1963, Hasluck served as Minister for Territories in the Menzies Coalition government. During this time, he and his department exerted almost complete control over the administration and development of PNG. In his speech, Hasluck discussed the major features of Australian colonial policy of the 1950s and early 1960s. Laden with the rhetoric of modernisation theory, his comments reflected the influence of the evolving understanding of development on Australian policy:

> In Papua and New Guinea economic change means a transition from the primitive life to the more demanding routine of commerce and industry; from sharing one's wealth within the village and family to the life of individual enterprise and individual saving and spending; from the security and protection of the group to a competitive unpredictable world of rising and falling prices and fluctuating employment. Primitive beliefs and codes must

[1] Drafts of the speech are located at NAA: A452, 1961/6694. The finished copy of the address was published the following year: Paul Hasluck, "The Economic Development of Papua and New Guinea," *Australian Outlook* 16, no. 1 (1962).

N. Ferns, *Australia in the Age of International Development, 1945–1975*, Security, Conflict and Cooperation in the Contemporary World, https://doi.org/10.1007/978-3-030-50228-7_4

> gradually give way to new codes and a new order and social adjustments must be made.[2]

This characterisation of the developmental process in PNG was typical of the attitudes of the Hasluck period. The Australian colonial administration brought profound and irreversible changes, which would see the 'primitive' lifestyles of the Indigenous population replaced with 'modern' practices. There was also a note of concern in Hasluck's address, as the upheaval associated with the modernisation process clearly occupied his mind. His ministerial tenure was marked by weighty considerations on how best to balance the forces of development with the maintenance of social and political stability.

This chapter examines Australian developmental policy in PNG throughout Hasluck's tenure as Minister for Territories. While he was Minister, Australian aid policy assumed many of its dominant characteristics, which derived from both international and Australian developmental thought. By the end of the 1950s, modernisation theory became formalised and consolidated in the United States. While American theorists concentrated on the economic and social development of Latin American, African and Asian countries, many Australian academics focused on PNG. Nevertheless, American scholarship proved useful to Australian experts and policymakers in their analysis of 'primitive' PNG. Australia's colonial development policy under Hasluck was shaped by the adaptation of international ideas to the 'unique' situation of PNG. This adaptation combined with Hasluck's belief that PNG's development would be a gradual process, with self-independence still many decades away.

The Hasluck era in PNG was a time when developmental imperatives began to take precedence over political goals in Australian colonial policy. As the strategic rationale behind strengthening PNG dissipated throughout the 1950s, Australia's trusteeship responsibilities became the dominant driver of colonial development.[3] While there was political pressure associated with UN oversight, the notion of trusteeship was permeated with humanitarian concern for the improvement in living

[2] Hasluck, "The Economic Development of Papua and New Guinea," 19.

[3] MacWilliam, *Securing Village Life*, 116.

standards of dependent peoples. The evolution of Australian developmental policy in PNG throughout Hasluck's tenure was associated with the greater level of attention that Australian policymakers paid to the strengthening orthodoxy of the modernisation paradigm. Agricultural improvement and educational assistance were the dominant features of Australian development policy. These features had guided the Australian experience of development, which was perceived as being a product of the country's increasingly efficient production of primary exports. In the Colombo Plan, agricultural improvement was promoted through the provision of economic and technical assistance, while the scholarship program provided educational opportunities to Asian students. These characteristics were also a central component of Hasluck's PNG policy. At a time when developmental imperatives took precedence over politics, the Hasluck era is a vital period in the history of Australian aid.

The period is generally presented by historians as one of consistency, both in administrative and policy terms. Ian Downs and Scott MacWilliam employ the term 'uniform development' to describe Hasluck's policy, which was essentially aimed at slowly 'improving' the lives of the entire Indigenous population without creating an elite who experienced more rapid development.[4] In his biography of Hasluck, Geoffrey Bolton depicts the Minister's Western Australian upbringing as guiding his faith in a "yeoman myth of rural productivity," which explains his attitude towards agricultural development in PNG.[5] Hasluck's conception of uniform development was the product of a broader intellectual context. My analysis builds on the work of historians such as Joseph Hodge, Suzanne Moon and Frederick Cooper, who have demonstrated that colonial development policies should be seen as a component of the post-war system of international development.[6] During the same period, American aid policy became driven by the dominant modernisation paradigm, as outlined by Nick Cullather, David Ekbladh and David Engerman.[7] Australian colonial

[4] Downs, *The Australian Trusteeship Papua New Guinea, 1945–75*, 94, 116; MacWilliam, *Securing Village Life*, 93, 116.

[5] Bolton, *Paul Hasluck*, 88.

[6] Hodge, *Triumph of the Expert*, 2; Cooper, "Writing the History of Development," 10; Moon, *Technology and Ethical Idealism*, 149–150.

[7] Cullather, *The Hungry World*, 150; Ekbladh, *The Great American Mission*, 149–150; Engerman, "West Meets East," 202.

development policy in PNG was a part of this international process, and Hasluck drew upon international influences for guidance.

Modernisation Theory

Paul Hasluck's tenure as Minister for Territories coincided with the emergence of modernisation theory as the orthodox conception of development. As Gilbert Rist explains:

> The general framework for the 'development' adventure was in place by the early sixties. The core of the doctrine had been clearly stated, the international organizations had managed to arouse widespread interest and to mobilize growing resources, decolonization was well under way, and the rulers of the new Third World States had discovered ways in which they could themselves benefit from offers of international aid.[8]

The consolidation of developmental theory went hand in hand with the evolution of developmental policies throughout the Western world. After almost a decade, post-war aid policies had moved beyond the experimental phases of the late 1940s and early 1950s. Australian aid programs in PNG and Southeast Asia were part of this international trend.

The modernisation paradigm was vital to the increased formalisation of developmental economics throughout the 1950s. W. Arthur Lewis' 1955 *The Theory of Economic Growth* became a central text in development studies.[9] According to his biographers, Barbara Ingham and Paul Mosley, this book was the central achievement of Lewis' "exceptional" creative moment from 1952 to 1955. Working at the University of Manchester, Lewis was able to bring together his experiences working in the Colonial Office, the UN and academia in his pursuit of achieving a "better and fairer world through social and economic reform."[10] In *Theory of Economic Growth*, Lewis treated 'growth' and 'development' as interchangeable, and he argued for the improvement of technical expertise (particularly in agriculture) as the key requirement in the developmental process.[11]

[8] Rist, *The History of Development*, 92.

[9] Arndt, "Economic Development," 465; Ekbladh, *The Great American Mission*, 164.

[10] Barbara Ingham and Paul Mosley, *Sir Arthur Lewis: A Biography* (London: Palgrave Macmillan, 2013), 1–2.

[11] Lewis, *The Theory of Economic Growth*, 10, 136.

Eugene Staley also produced important new work in the 1950s. His analysis underwent a shift in approach that saw his theoretical model become more closely informed by Cold War assumptions. In setting out the argument of *The Future of Underdeveloped Countries*, first published in 1954, Staley made his position clear: "Economic development of these areas in cooperation with the West is a necessary part of the conditions for Western survival and for the survival in the world of some of the West's most important contributions to human progress."[12] Lewis and Staley's work in the 1950s provided many of the features that became central to the modernisation paradigm most clearly expressed by Walt Rostow: an emphasis on economic growth along capitalist lines combined with the political imperatives of the Cold War. The orthodoxy established by these theorists had by the late 1950s produced a vision of development that informed policymakers.[13]

The most prominent exponent of modernisation theory was Walt Rostow. Rostow was a fascinating figure, someone who attracted both significant support from key figures, such as President John F. Kennedy, while also arousing the ire of others, such as the prominent American diplomat, W. Averell Harriman, who dubbed him "America's Rasputin."[14] A deeply intelligent person (he entered Yale at the age of fifteen in 1932), Rostow emerged as one of the dominant development theorists of the 1950s and 1960s. His intellectual significance is sometimes overshadowed by his role in the Kennedy and Johnson Administrations' waging of the Vietnam War, but it is important not to separate this from his developmental work.[15]

[12] Staley, *The Future of Underdeveloped Countries*, 3.

[13] Other examples of the rising modernisation paradigm in the 1950s and early 1960s include: Max Franklin Millikan and W.W. Rostow, *A Proposal: Key to an Effective Foreign Policy* (NY: Harper, 1957); Daniel Lerner, *The Passing of Traditional Society: Modernizing the Middle East* (Glencoe, Il: Free Press, 1958); Gabriel Almond and James S. Coleman, eds., *The Politics of Developing Areas* (Princeton: Princeton University Press, 1960); Lucian W. Pye, *Politics, Personality, and Nation Building: Burma's Search for Identity* (New Haven: Yale University Press, 1962).

[14] David Milne, *America's Rasputin: Walt Rostow and the Vietnam War* (New York: Hill and Wang, 2008), 7.

[15] Ekbladh, *The Great American Mission*, 208.

Working at the Massachusetts Institute of Technology (MIT) throughout the 1950s, Rostow spent the decade gradually refining his understanding of the developmental process.[16] His 1960 book, *The Stages of Economic Growth: A Non-Communist Manifesto*, was the defining statement of modernisation theory.[17] Rostow identified five stages through which traditional societies must go to fully complete the process of modernisation. These stages were: traditional society, preconditions for take-off, take-off, the drive to maturity and the age of high mass consumption.[18] This process was more or less the same for all traditional societies, and the ultimate aim, that of "high mass consumption," was typical of the United States-centric universalism of most modernisation theorists.[19] It was Rostow's emphasis on 'take-off' as the critical moment in the development of a society that set his work apart. According to Rostow, it was during this period that a country was in a state of flux, caught somewhere between 'traditional' and 'modern' institutions. The role of the state was very important during this phase, as a strong central authority would be required to harness the forces of nationalism in the interests of continued economic growth.[20] As Cullather writes, Rostow's idea of 'take-off' extended earlier theoretical approaches by identifying "more precisely when and where aid investments should go, and to whom."[21] The political impact of Rostow's ideas was further enhanced by his recruitment into the Administration of US President John F. Kennedy. With a clear sense of policy implementation in mind, Rostow's vision of modernisation also proved immensely useful to Australian policymakers. Whereas the establishment of the New Deal for PNG and the Colombo Plan in the late 1940s and early 1950s were marked by an atmosphere of experimentation in both developmental theory and policy, by the time

[16] Gilman, *Mandarins of the Future*, 56–58.

[17] Ekbladh, *The Great American Mission*, 185.

[18] Rostow, *Stages of Economic Growth*. Rostow's intellectual progress can be seen throughout the 1950s as he worked towards his concise presentation of the modernisation process. An earlier example of his views can be found in Millikan and Rostow, *A Proposal*.

[19] Ekbladh, *The Great American Mission*, 103.

[20] Rostow, *Stages of Economic Growth*, 30.

[21] Cullather, *The Hungry World*, 150.

of Hasluck's tenure as Minister for Territories there were "clearer ideas about what ought to be done" in PNG.[22]

This consolidation in developmental thought filtered through to Australia, revealing the international influence on Australian developmentalism. This is evident in the work of John Crawford, one of the central post-war scholar-bureaucrats. During the Hasluck period, Crawford was both a part of the policymaking bureaucracy and a leading academic. From 1950 to 1960, Crawford was head of two Commonwealth departments, Commerce and Agriculture (1950–1956) and Trade (1956–1960). He then left the Commonwealth Public Service to take up the position of Professor of Economics and Director of the Research School of Pacific Studies at the Australian National University (ANU).[23] Crawford therefore straddled the bureaucratic and academic worlds, placing him in an important position to guide the interaction of theory and policy.

The tenets of modernisation theory can be found in Crawford's comments on PNG in 1962. He stated that in PNG "there can be no reversion to the pre-European state of affairs; there can be no effective sealing off from the impact of the world external to Papua-New Guinea."[24] While Crawford was not one to blindly accept a theoretical approach, his work certainly fits into the broad category of modernisation thought. The belief that development was an irreversible process was central to the modernisation paradigm and would be one of the key assumptions of policymakers throughout the Hasluck period.[25] This idea can be seen as far back as 1952, in prominent anthropologist Cyril Belshaw's analysis of community development in PNG. Advocating industrial development and drawing a curious parallel with Australia's own development, Belshaw wrote: "Many people, arguing from our own

[22] Paul Hasluck, *A Time for Building: Australian Administration in Papua and New Guinea, 1951–1963* (Carlton, Vic: Melbourne University Press, 1976), 201.

[23] J.D.B. Miller, "Crawford, Sir John Grenfell (Jack) (1910–1984)", Australian Dictionary of Biography, National Centre of Biography, Australian National University, http://adb.anu.edu.au/biography/crawford-sir-john-grenfell-jack-1391/text22223, published first in hardcopy 2007.

[24] J.G. Crawford, "Emerging Issues in New Guinea," in *The Independence of Papua-New Guinea: What are the Pre-Requisites? Four Lectures Presented under the Auspices of the Public Lectures Committee of the Australian National University*, ed. David George Bettison, et al. (Sydney: Angus and Robertson, 1962), 63.

[25] Latham, *Modernization as Ideology*, 15.

unhappy industrial experience, view with alarm the tendency to introduce machinery and industry into primitive agricultural society. Such a view is far too pessimistic."[26] Here we see the components of Australian developmentalism in one place: the pervasiveness of Australian experience, the 'primitive' nature of PNG, and a faith in the positive effects of modern infrastructure. Several years later, in 1956, John Legge published *Australian Colonial Policy*. Legge, a political historian better known for his work on Indonesia, traced the history of Australian policy in PNG, giving close attention to the process of development. His commentary on Australian policy was revealing, as Legge observed that the "emphasis is on development rather than tradition – upon the evolution of a new machinery for local government rather than upon the adaptation of existing institutions."[27] Crawford, Belshaw and Legge, through the acceptance of the 'fact' that 'traditional' PNG society needed to be replaced with 'modern,' European features, provided the central features of the Australian conception of modernisation.

Australian Perceptions of PNG

As in the 1940s, the notion of PNG 'primitiveness' was ubiquitous amongst Australian observers into the 1960s. Just as this perception informed the New Deal for PNG, it also interacted with the emerging modernisation paradigm to provide an important intellectual foundation for Australian colonial policy under Hasluck. E.K. 'Fred' Fisk employed this conceptual framework in his analysis of PNG. Fisk joined Crawford's Research School of Pacific Studies in 1960. He had previously worked as a development expert in British Malaya, making him one of many examples of Australian scholars who investigated both Southeast Asia and PNG.[28] Commenting on PNG in 1962, Fisk observed, "it is questionable whether the term 'underdeveloped' should be applied to New Guinea at all. It would probably be more realistic to describe it by some other term,

[26] Cyril S. Belshaw, "Community Development in Papua," *Australian Outlook* 6, no. 1 (1952): 56.

[27] J.D. Legge, *Australian Colonial Policy: A Survey of Native Administration and European Development in Papua* (Sydney: Angus & Robertson, 1956), 222.

[28] Academy of the Social Sciences in Australia, "Dr Fred Fisk," http://www.assa.edu.au/fellowship/fellow/deceased/94.

perhaps as an 'undeveloped' or 'primitive' economy."[29] Once again, this shows the ubiquity of the notion of PNG 'primitiveness' in the Australian understanding of the modernisation process. American modernisation theorists largely examined 'underdeveloped' areas, such as Southeast Asia, and their models of development reflected this focus.[30] On the other hand, Australian scholars such as Fisk were of the opinion that PNG had not even reached the 'underdeveloped' stage of development. Consequently, Australian experts conceived of a developmental stage that existed prior to Rostow's 'traditional society.' This 'pre-traditional' stage can be considered an Australian contribution to 1950s and 1960s developmental theory and was important in guiding its colonial policy.

The idea of PNG as 'primitive' remained pervasive throughout the 1950s. In 1959, John Kerr, who had served as an early principal of ASOPA (and who would later go on to become Governor-General of Australia) wrote: "In Australia we have listened for years to speeches making the all-too-obvious point that New Guinea is primitive and the difficulties in bringing it to a modern standard of civilisation are practically insuperable. Let us take this for granted."[31] Numerous areas of Australian society, be they academia, the press or public service, agreed with Kerr's advice to simply take PNG 'primitiveness' for granted. A 1953 review in the Melbourne *Age* of Colin Simpson's travelogue *Adam with Arrows* presented PNG as "A Last Frontier of the Primitive World."[32] The *Canberra Times* reported in 1957 that a cancer survey in PNG would be the first of its kind "among an entirely primitive people."[33] A 1956 article in the *Age* on the construction of schools in the isolated town of Telefomin observed: "Thirty-one primitive school children who

[29] E.K. Fisk, "The Economy of Papua-New Guinea," in *The Independence of Papua-New Guinea: What Are the Pre-requisites? Four Lectures Presented under the Auspices of the Public Lectures Committee of the Australian National University*, eds. David George Bettison, E.K. Fisk, F.J. West, and J.G. Crawford (Sydney: Angus and Robertson, 1962), 26.

[30] Staley, *The Future of Underdeveloped Countries.*

[31] J.R. Kerr, "The Political Future of New Guinea," *Australian Outlook* 13, no. 3 (1959): 185.

[32] *The Age*, October 31, 1953.

[33] *Canberra Times*, October 30, 1957.

frightened their teachers five months ago are now cleaning their fingernails."[34] Indeed, education policy was a particularly fruitful field for the identification of the Indigenous population as 'primitive.' A 1960 Territories Department paper that suggested revisions to teacher standards in PNG justified the recommendation on the observation that the pupils comprised of "primitive children who have never been subjected to the strains or sophistications of a modern society."[35] The assumption of PNG's primitiveness guided Australian experts as they adapted and applied the modernisation paradigm to local conditions.

Anthropologists, who had long taken an interest in the island of New Guinea, also incorporated the notion of the PNG 'primitive' into their analysis of cultural change in PNG. These experts were acquainted with the field of developmental theory. Prominent Australian anthropologist and former DORCA member W.E.H. Stanner observed the substantial interest in development throughout the world. Writing in *Australian Outlook*, he highlighted the value of development for places such as PNG and observed that in the broad field of development, "something like a body of stable, if still intermediate, doctrine is starting to emerge."[36] Throughout the 1950s, anthropologists investigated various elements of PNG society, consolidating the image of the population as amongst the most 'primitive' in the world. A 1952 article by Belshaw featured analysis of Papua's "primitive agricultural society."[37] Belshaw, who had been educated under prominent Australasian anthropologist Raymond Firth at the LSE, wrote the article while involved in a government-sponsored study of PNG with geographer Oskar Spate and economist Trevor Swan.[38] Belshaw emphasised the need for policies that resembled

[34] *The Age*, August 16, 1956, located in NAA: A452, 1957/3985.

[35] Territories Department, "Education—Papua and New Guinea," August 5, 1960, NAA: A452, 1960/4427.

[36] W.E.H Stanner, review of *Costa Rica: A Study in Economic Development*, by Stacy May, et al., *Australian Outlook* 9, no. 4 (1955): 251–252.

[37] Belshaw, "Community Development in Papua," 56.

[38] O.H.K. Spate, C.S. Belshaw, T.W. Swan, *Some Problems of Development in New Guinea: Report of a Working Committee of the Australian National University* (Canberra: Australian National University, 1953); Association for Social Anthropology in Oceania, "Cyril S. Belshaw," http://www.soc.hawaii.edu/asao/pacific/honoraryf/belshaw.htm, accessed July 31, 2016. MacWilliam, *Securing Village Life*, 92–93. Swan would later go on to become involved with the Massachusetts Institute of Technology's study

those seen in Australia many decades earlier. It highlighted the contrast between 'primitive' Papua and 'developed' Australia.

The Australian conception of PNG as particularly 'primitive' distinguished Australia's PNG policy from the Colombo Plan. As a supposedly 'pre-traditional' society, the Australian developmental task was made more difficult. This was in contrast to the Colombo Plan, where it was suggested that many of the recipient countries were 'underdeveloped' and fitted neatly into Rostow's stages of development. The term 'primitive' was widespread in Australian depictions of PNG, while the phrase 'underdeveloped' was pervasive in External Affairs' discussions of Colombo Plan countries.[39] These developmental differences resulted in different policy approaches. Alongside the 'unique' nature of the developmental challenge in PNG—as compared to Southeast Asia—Australian officials had greater control over the implementation of development programs, given the nature of the colonial relationship. Territories officials also had greater resources at their disposal, and because of their long-term vision for Australian colonial policy, they encouraged slow, gradual development.

Paul Hasluck and Development

Given the length of his tenure as Minister for Territories and his subsequent move to the External Affairs portfolio in 1964, Paul Hasluck's attitude towards development was of immense importance to the evolution of Australian aid policy. A domineering minister, Hasluck was personally involved in many of the developmental programs that were implemented under his watch. In the words of the official historian of the Australian colonial administration in PNG, Ian Downs: "In a country in which there was so much to be done before it could become a nation,

of Indian development. Arndt, *A Course Through Life*, 44. Raymond Firth was influential in the establishment of the Australian National University, mentored a number of DORCA members and advised Hasluck. Robert Porter, *Paul Hasluck: A Political Biography* (Nedlands: University of Western Australia Press, 1993), 100.

[39] R.G. Casey, "The Colombo Plan: Report Presented to the Australian Parliament on 9th April, 1954," NAA: A1838, 740/4/5 PART 1; Australian Embassy, Washington to Department of External Affairs, February 4, 1960, NAA: A3092, 221/1/4/7/6; Department of External Affairs, "Australian Aid for Under-Developed Countries," n.d. [written in early 1962], NAA: A1838, 2020/1/2 PART 3.

Paul Hasluck had done more than anyone else."[40] Hasluck's attitude towards colonial development was dictated by his classical liberal worldview and could best be termed gradualist. He recognised the need for development, and it formed a central component of his policies for PNG, but there was always an underlying expectation that progress would be slow because of the 'primitive' level of PNG's development. Historians of the period, such as Donald Denoon, have referred to the "glacial" pace of development under Hasluck.[41] This vision of uniform development was embedded into Australian colonial policy after 1951.

Hasluck's academic and bureaucratic experience provided fertile ground for scholarly understandings of development to find their way into colonial policy. An early associate of 'Nugget' Coombs in Perth, he briefly lectured in history at the University of Western Australia (UWA) between 1939 and 1940, working with John Legge, before being brought into the Department of External Affairs at the behest of another Western Australian, Prime Minister John Curtin.[42] Hasluck quickly rose through the ranks of External Affairs and worked closely with the members of PWR. After falling out with External Affairs Minister H.V. Evatt in the late 1940s, Hasluck resigned from the Commonwealth bureaucracy, but soon returned to public affairs as the victorious Liberal candidate for Curtin in 1949.[43]

After reluctantly assuming the relatively unimportant Cabinet position of Minister for Territories in late 1951, Hasluck took some time to familiarise himself with the Australian responsibility for PNG. In his memoir, he reflected on the fact that he had "read the relevant textbooks" on colonial policy as an undergraduate student at UWA, which exposed him to

[40] Downs, *The Australian Trusteeship Papua New Guinea, 1945–75*, 256.

[41] Denoon, *A Trial Separation*, 28.

[42] Bolton, *Paul Hasluck*, 29, 108, 186.

[43] Hasluck was not the only scholar who made the transition between bureaucracy and Parliament. Leslie Bury, who served as Treasurer and Minister for External Affairs in the late 1960s and early 1970s, also played a role in post-war reconstruction following the Second World War. Indeed, Bury served under Alf Conlon as a part of the Directorate of Research and Civil Affairs. Donald Boadle, "Bury, Leslie Harry Ernest (1913–1986)", Australian Dictionary of Biography, National Centre of Biography, Australian National University, http://adb.anu.edu.au/biography/bury-leslie-harry-ernest-12270/text22027, published first in hardcopy 2007.

the ideas of Lugard and other British experts, and enabled him to incorporate the notion of trusteeship into colonial policy.[44] Indeed, Hasluck had played a role in drafting the trusteeship provisions in the UN Charter, which provided the layer of international oversight for Australian developmental policy in PNG.[45] His ministerial style ensured that he would dominate policy in PNG. As Rachel Cleland, wife of long-time Administrator Donald Cleland reflected: "he could not bare [sic] people to disagree with him in conversation, and if you did, you never knew when his face would suddenly suffuse and with clenched teeth he would put you down in a most shattering manner."[46] This sometimes confrontational style of leadership also had the effect of slowing down the implementation of development programs in PNG.

Perhaps one of the clearest statements of Hasluck's attitude towards the Australian role in PNG was presented to Parliament on September 1, 1954. Responding to his own question as to what "points of interest" Australia had in PNG, Hasluck began with familiar references to security and economics. The Second World War had demonstrated the strategic importance of PNG, and there was a clear economic imperative for the Territory to "produce enough to meet both Australian and world needs."[47] But for Hasluck, the duty of Australia to the Indigenous population of PNG transcended these considerations. Having accepted the role of trustee, Australia's responsibility was profound. Speaking to his fellow members of Parliament, Hasluck explained his vision:

> I think that what we do as a nation in the development of this Territory is something that we do in order to live up to our own standards, and in order to live up to our own ideas of national responsibility. I suggest that that is a national reason, far more compelling than any of the other reasons, strategic and economic, which might be argued very persuasively.[48]

[44] Hasluck, *A Time for Building*, 5.

[45] Hasluck, *A Time for Building*, 5.

[46] Rachel Cleland, *Pathways to Independence: Story of Official and Family Life in Papua New Guinea from 1951 to 1975* (Cottesloe: R. Cleland, 1985), 90.

[47] *CPD*, House of Representatives, no. 35, 1954, September 1, 1954, 847.

[48] *CPD*, September 1, 1954, 848.

This developmentalist and paternalistic justification for the Australian mission to develop PNG guided Hasluck throughout his long tenure as Minister for Territories.

Driven by his gradualist approach, Hasluck sought to avoid the social, political and economic instability that often accompanied the development process.[49] Uniform development was marked by a firm opposition towards the establishment of an educated Indigenous elite that would lead the development of PNG. Although this can be seen as an egalitarian approach to development, it also limited the speed with which change could take place. In the field of education policy, for example, the colonial administration expanded primary education but stalled the development of secondary and tertiary education. This had the effect of delaying Indigenous self-rule by preventing the rise of educated political leadership. In a way, this policy was a response to the work of Australian scholars, who presented the transition from 'traditional' to 'modern' as "creating social maladjustment or even hostility" towards the Australian administration.[50] Hasluck was wary of the effects of development on the Indigenous population of PNG, and this conditioned his attitude towards the pace at which progress should be encouraged. In 1955 Hasluck drew these considerations together, examining the dual forces of material and social progress:

> If these two things get out of balance — if we push ahead in a ruthless and altogether careless fashion, merely exploiting the resources of the country – we could easily find ourselves facing great problems which, perhaps, might even destroy our administration there. We could also set up conditions which would be contrary to the welfare of the indigenous people.[51]

The balance between material and social progress was vital to Hasluck's emphasis on uniform development.

Hasluck justified his advocacy of uniform development by invoking the 'primitive' image of PNG. As he noted in October 1955, Australia's administrative and developmental "problem is much more complex and

[49] Cullather, *The Hungry World*, 244.

[50] Legge, *Australian Colonial Policy*; Bettison, "The People of Papua-New Guinea," 18.

[51] *CPD*, House of Representatives, no. 40, 1955, October 6, 1955, 1330.

made more difficult by the circumstance of having a dependent, primitive population."[52] Hasluck maintained that significant proportions of the Indigenous population were "still living a life only one or two stages above that of the primitive savage."[53] Indeed, Hasluck persisted with the image of the 'primitive' PNG population through the entirety of his tenure as minister, with references in 1962 to "primitive people – people who, until a matter of only four, five, six or ten years ago, were headhunters or cannibals, engaged in a perpetual state of belligerence."[54] Because of the large developmental gap between the 'primitive' population of PNG and the 'developed' world, Hasluck indicated that development should be slow and under the close control of Australian officials.

Over time, however, the principles of uniform development became more difficult to maintain. By the early 1960s, the emergence of a "more advanced" section of the Indigenous population served to undermine Hasluck's vision of gradual progress towards self-government, as well as the broader vision of 'primitive' Papua New Guineans. This shift coincided with the zenith of the modernisation paradigm in the early 1960s, as scholars such as Rostow argued for the centrality of an educated, entrepreneurial elite in the developmental process.[55] The Colombo Plan also provided a guide, as the scholarship program was seemingly doing an effective job of establishing a Western-educated elite throughout Southeast Asia. Of course, in PNG the expatriate community was already providing that role, which Hasluck reflected on in his memoir, where he commented that even in 1960 "white investment and management were needed for economic development."[56] In spite of Hasluck's policy of uniform development, an Indigenous elite emerged.

In his memoir, Hasluck presents the second half of his tenure as Minister for Territories as featuring a "growing sense of urgency."[57] The

[52] *CPD*, October 6, 1955, 1329.

[53] Hasluck, *Australian Policy in Papua and New Guinea*, 6.

[54] *CPD*, House of Representatives, no. 8, 1962, February 21, 1962, 97.

[55] Rostow, *Stages of Economic Growth*, 51.

[56] Hasluck, *A Time for Building*, 255.

[57] Hasluck, *A Time for Building*, 201.

emergence of an Indigenous elite resulted in calls for increased representation in the Legislative Assembly and higher educational facilities. Reflecting on his policies, Hasluck accepted that:

> The inequalities of opportunity for the Territory population both by reason of the uneven distribution of the natural resources of the country and the wide disparities in the advancement of the people, presented the prospect that economic progress would be uneven.[58]

This was partly a product of developmental policy throughout the 'underdeveloped' world, as the benefits of increased living standards and educational opportunities were rarely evenly spread.[59] According to the head of the ANU's New Guinea Research Unit, David Bettison, the elite emerged most clearly in "major towns and their hinterlands," which were areas that were more exposed to Australian development policy than the isolated highland regions.[60] This corresponded with orthodox development theory. Hasluck's delayed recognition of the "unevenness" of development forced a reluctant acknowledgement of the need for more urgent developmental policy.

Writing in 1962, which Hasluck identified as a "turning point" in PNG, Bettison identified the emergence of an Indigenous elite.[61] He acknowledged the appearance of a "class of Indigenous person who is looking to the future with ambitious eyes, a rapidly growing competence and a willingness to experiment with new and modern forms of organisation."[62] Hasluck also recognised the increased complexity of the Australian developmental task in the early 1960s, with the arrival of "a younger generation of articulate and knowledgeable [Indigenous] men and women" who were "taking an increasing part in public life."[63] While the emergence of this elite 'class' might have caused him some concern,

[58] Hasluck, *A Time for Building*, 326.

[59] Gilman, *Mandarins of the Future*, 30.

[60] Bettison, "The People of Papua-New Guinea," 5.

[61] Hasluck's reference to 1962 as a "turning point" can be found in Hasluck, *A Time for Building*, 374.

[62] Bettison, "The People of Papua-New Guinea," 10.

[63] *CPD*, House of Representatives, no. 19, 1963, May 7, 1963, 1074.

their arrival was an unavoidable consequence of the uniform development approach. Hasluck's broader vision of development for PNG, which revolved around uniform development and slow progress towards self-government, was challenged by the inevitable rise of Indigenous leaders.

Development: A Prerequisite for Self-Government

The preparation of PNG for self-government was the core component of Australia's trusteeship agreement with the UN. The eventual granting of independence was built into the trusteeship framework. For historian, Camilla Boisen, one of the central tenets of the trusteeship idea was that Europeans were to "hold the land in trust for the indigenous peoples, until they had reached a stage of civilisation at which self-determination was appropriate."[64] This was manifested in the UN Trusteeship Council, which oversaw the preparation of trust territories for self-government. In her analysis of the Council, Neta Crawford commends this supervisory role, writing that "the twin practices of development assistance alongside international assistance in the transition to independent self-government became a model for increasing autonomy in other non-self-governing territories."[65] In his memoir, published shortly after PNG gained its independence, Hasluck claimed that the end goal of his vision for PNG's development was a form of self-government, with "the emergence of a society that lived on the highest standards of civilized man."[66] However, his comments during his time as Minister for Territories give a different impression, as he frequently presented self-government as something that would not occur for some time. The lack of development in PNG was presented as the key obstacle. In effect, through their policy of uniform development, which slowed the rate of change in PNG, Hasluck and the Australian administration were obstructing the path to self-government.

Throughout the 1950s and 1960s, the UN Trusteeship Council underwent significant change as increasing numbers of Asian and African countries gained their independence. Officials in the Territories Department saw this as a source of concern for Australia, as:

[64] Boisen, "The Changing Moral Justification of Empire," 336.

[65] Crawford, "Decolonization through Trusteeship," 104.

[66] Hasluck, *A Time for Building*, 73.

> The increase in the membership of the United Nations, which is resulting from the independence of new African nations, is likely to create problems for Australia. Some of these nations will tend to take an extreme 'anti-colonial' stand on matters relating to trusteeship and non-self-governing territories.[67]

This changing context manifested itself in calls by the Council for more intensified development, which was expected to speed up the timetable for PNG's self-government.[68] Some Australian experts joined in these calls. In 1962, John Crawford called for the Commonwealth to "proceed quite rapidly" in the preparation of the Indigenous population for self-government.[69] The pressure for self-government intensified further throughout the 1960s.

In spite of this growing international pressure, Hasluck held firm to his belief that self-government could not be provided in PNG until development had reached a point where the country could "stand on their own feet."[70] Crucially, Hasluck was the central figure in driving the speed of development. The Minister continued to cite the lack of development in PNG as a reason for continued Australian administration. In 1959, Hasluck explained: "There can never be any real and lasting advancement of the native people, and certainly no reality of self-government for the country until the country develops an economy that frees it from dependence on outside support to finance its own services."[71] This viewpoint meant that the Australian Government was reluctant to set a date for PNG's independence. In a 1956 response to UN Trusteeship Council pressure for target dates, the Australian representative claimed that because the "inhabitants are in all stages of advancement from primitive tribesman to civilized life," it would be "inappropriate" to look

[67] Territories Department notes on Questions Connected with Trusteeship and Non-Self-Governing Territories in the UN, June 27, 1960, NAA: A452, 1960/2803.

[68] "Extract from Conclusions and Recommendations of the Twenty-Fourth Session of the Trusteeship Council Relating to the Territory of New Guinea," 1959, NAA: A452, 1958/4106.

[69] Crawford, "Emerging Issues in New Guinea," 71.

[70] *CPD*, House of Representatives, no. 38, 1954, September 29, 1954, 1470.

[71] *CPD*, House of Representatives, no. 40, 1959, September 30, 1959, 1576.

towards a particular date for independence.[72] Even more decisive was Hasluck's 1960 comment that he foresaw continued Australian administration "for at least another 20 or 30 years."[73] These comments reveal the contradictory position of development within Australian colonial policy, as development served to both justify continued Australian administration, while also being presented as the key element that would ensure PNG's independence.

In order to satisfy the ultimate objective of trusteeship and grant independence to PNG, Hasluck eventually began to call for increased resources to promote development. Commenting on the connection between development and self-government in 1962, Hasluck explained: "Papua and New Guinea cannot reach and maintain self-government in any adequate sense without considerable further expenditure on basic facilities for economic development, such as roads, wharves, bridges, drainage, power supplies, marketing organisation."[74] The Commonwealth grant to PNG had risen significantly during the Hasluck period, from around £5.5 million in 1951–1952 to £23.6 million in 1962–1963.[75] In contrast, annual Australian Colombo Plan spending hovered between the £3–5 million mark during the same period. With the apparent lack of development providing the central obstacle to the end of Australian colonial rule, economic assistance to PNG assumed a dominant position within the overall system of Australian aid. As a consequence, the increase in Commonwealth funding to PNG brought increased ministerial scrutiny over the implementation of developmental programs. This was particularly the case with regard to agricultural improvement and educational expansion.

[72] Excerpt from 1955 to 1956 Australian report on New Guinea to UN Trusteeship Council, NAA: A452, 1960/374.

[73] *CPD*, House of Representatives, no. 41, 1960, October 13, 1960, 1990.

[74] Hasluck, "The Economic Development of Papua and New Guinea," 23.

[75] Annex to Department of External Affairs, "Papua/New Guinea: The Australian Effort," n.d. [Written at some point in the middle of 1964], Tange Papers, NLA, MS 9847, Box 6.

Colonial Development Policy: Education and Agriculture

As the 1950s progressed, Australia's colonial development policy coalesced under Hasluck's principles of uniform development. Speaking at the University of Sydney in 1956, Hasluck explained the aims of colonial development in PNG:

> In general, when we turn attention to these economic activities, we have in mind the idea that the resources of the Territory should be developed in order to sustain the higher standard of living and the wider range of public services which are being established in the Territory, and partly in order to make available to the outside world commodities which the Territory can produce.[76]

Australian policymakers focused on two key areas to achieve these aims. Hasluck and officials in Canberra and Port Moresby believed that improved educational facilities would enable a rise in the standard of living, while an expanded agricultural sector would allow for increased production of commodities for export. This was an orthodox developmental approach, in keeping with both American modernisation practices, as well as British colonial development strategies in their remaining African possessions.[77] Agricultural improvement and educational assistance were also at the heart of Australia's contribution to the Colombo Plan. Despite the fact that policymakers in Territories and External Affairs were conscious of the differences between PNG and Southeast Asia, there were clear areas of symmetry between the two strands of Australian aid policy, as orthodox concepts of development became more established.

Aside from Hasluck, two key figures drove the implementation of developmental policy in PNG. Departmental secretary Cecil 'Eski' Lambert was appointed in the middle of 1951 to replace previous permanent head J.R. Halligan. Hasluck valued Lambert's "practical" attitude, which had been honed in his earlier work for the Rural Bank of New South Wales, where he worked closely with John Crawford, and the Commonwealth Rural Reconstruction Commission.[78] The other

[76] Hasluck, *Australian Policy in Papua and New Guinea*, 27.

[77] Cullather, *The Hungry World*, 3–4; Hodge, *Triumph of the Expert*, 231.

[78] Peter C. Grundy, "Lambert, Cecil Ralph (Eski) (1899–1971)", Australian Dictionary of Biography, National Centre of Biography, Australian National University,

person was Donald Cleland, the Administrator of PNG from 1953 to 1967. A career army officer, Cleland was amongst the leadership of the wartime Australian New Guinea Administrative Unit (ANGAU), which worked alongside DORCA in planning the post-war administration and development of PNG. Appointed as the replacement for Keith Murray, Cleland's significance in Australian post-war colonial administration of PNG is perhaps second only to that of Hasluck.[79] The Minister was deeply reliant on Cleland for the efficient and prompt implementation of his vision for PNG's development.

The Australian emphasis on agricultural development in PNG was a product of the combination of international developmental ideas alongside Australia's own historical development. A central component of post-war developmental theories was that while Western investment was seen as crucial to the development of 'underdeveloped' economies, the ultimate goal was to establish a self-sustaining economy, fuelled by Indigenous enterprise.[80] The Australian administration of PNG was no exception to this. Thus, while Hasluck placed great importance on the role of Australian private investment, it was to be conditional on the growth of Indigenous enterprise. Given the 'primitive' nature of PNG's Indigenous economy, along with the fact that "the advice on mineral resources was not encouraging," it was little surprise that the first improvements would come in agriculture.[81] Hasluck commented on the progress being made in this field in 1957. He emphasised the government's policy of "advancement of native agriculture" through "better land use in village gardens and improved agricultural methods."[82] This was textbook developmental

http://adb.anu.edu.au/biography/lambert-cecil-ralph-eski-10774/text19105, published first in hardcopy 2000. Lambert's nickname 'Eski' supposedly came from his resemblance to an 'Eskimo'. The link between Lambert and Crawford is mentioned in Macintyre, *Australia's Boldest Experiment*, 169.

[79] H.N. Nelson, "Cleland, Sir Donald Mackinnon (Don) (1901–1975)", Australian Dictionary of Biography, National Centre of Biography, Australian National University, http://adb.anu.edu.au/biography/cleland-sir-donald-mackinnon-don-9762/text17247, published first in hardcopy 1993.

[80] Staley, *World Economic Development*, 45; Lewis, *The Theory of Economic Growth*, 244–249.

[81] Hasluck, *A Time for Building*, 292.

[82] Hasluck, "Developments in Papua and New Guinea," *Canberra Comments*, June 15, 1957, NAA: A452, 1957/950.

policy, as seen in Rostow's claim that much of the funding for modernisation would "come from rapid increases in output achieved by higher productivity in agriculture and the extractive industries."[83]

Agricultural development in PNG revolved around improving the production of older crops, such as copra and rubber, while introducing new ones, particularly cocoa and coffee. In addition to expanding cash crop production, the Administration was instructed to increase food production. Hasluck suggested that "this agricultural work among natives to ensure their food supply and to promote the advancement of their welfare is one of the basic requirements in our work in the Territory."[84] By producing more agricultural goods for both export and domestic consumption, Hasluck expected that the people of PNG would be able to enjoy a higher standard of living. He expressed a level of pride in achievements with regard to coffee and cocoa, which had grown by "nearly 2,000 per cent" during his tenure.[85] Reflecting on agricultural growth in his memoir, Hasluck was so satisfied as to provide statistics, indicating that "in 1950–1 only 317 tons of cocoa beans and 33 tons of coffee beans were exported and by 1961–2 the figures were 10,014 and 3444."[86]

Australian expertise was called upon to provide guidance to villagers who sought to expand their agricultural production. At a basic level, all district officers were a part of the system, as fundamental lessons were conducted from the first encounter between a patrol officer and the Indigenous population. As Hasluck reflected, "from the day it opened, a patrol post commenced a course of education in economics."[87] More significantly, the agricultural extension program, which was driven by the Agriculture Department of the PNG Administration, had trained 3000 Indigenous farmers by 1960, with "137 European officers and 300 native agricultural assistants."[88] These officers provided a colonial technical assistance function. W. Cottrell-Dormer, who in 1954 was an agricultural extension officer based on the south-eastern tip of Papua, spent much

[83] Rostow, *Stages of Economic Growth*, 22.

[84] P.M. Hasluck to D.M. Cleland, January 11, 1954, NAA: A518, C2/1/1.

[85] *CPD*, House of Representatives, no. 40, 1959, September 30, 1959, 1575.

[86] Hasluck, *A Time for Building*, 139.

[87] Hasluck, *A Time for Building*, 80.

[88] Hasluck, *A Time for Building*, 193.

of his time explaining why it was necessary to plant coffee beans, thereby starting "new businesses":

> People who have no money cannot pay tax to the Council. If the Council does not have enough money it cannot do things to help people. We all want better roads and good schools and good hospitals. But if the Council has not got enough money it can do very little to help us get these things. So we must all do our best to get all the money we can from our copra business and we must also start new businesses. Then everyone will have money and be able to help pay for the good roads and other things we must have to make our country a good place to live in.[89]

This was the Australian experience of development transplanted onto its colonial possession. Improved agricultural production was expected to facilitate increased revenue, which would then pay for new public infrastructure.

Education was another major area of Australian interest and was also the clearest demonstration of Hasluck's idea of uniform development. The Minister emphasised investment in primary schooling for much of his tenure, in the belief that it could reach a much broader base of the Indigenous population than the smaller proportion that were ready for higher education. Hasluck explained that "there is an urgent and immediate demand in the Territory for boys and girls with a primary education so that we can turn them into something better."[90] The emphasis on primary schooling was shown in enrolment numbers in Administration schools between 1954 and 1960. In the year 1954–1955, there were 5201 primary pupils and 906 intermediate (a step between primary and secondary schooling) pupils, but by 1959–1960 the number of primary pupils had risen to 17,895, while the intermediate number had dropped to 853.[91]

However, by the early 1960s policymakers began to discuss the need for increased investment in secondary teaching, along with suggestions of

[89] W. Cottrell-Dormer, "Talk to Ealeaba Council at Gwalili," October 7, 1954, NAA: A518, C2/1/1. Cottrell-Dormer also displayed a paternalism that was reasonably common in PNG at this time, as seen through his repeated references to his 'boys' in his reports: W. Cottrell-Dormer to D.M. Cleland, January 16, 1955, NAA: A518, C2/1/1.

[90] Hasluck, *Australian Policy in Papua and New Guinea*, 15.

[91] Territories Department, "Education—Papua and New Guinea," August 5, 1960, NAA: A452, 1960/4427.

a tertiary institution. This was both due to, and in spite of, the principles of uniform development. Hasluck's investment in primary education had set the foundation for higher schooling, as students progressed through the system. The result for Hasluck was that "by 1961 the schools system was beginning to produce candidates for higher education in sufficient numbers for us to be able to turn more purposefully towards tertiary education in the Territory."[92] He enlisted the services of George Currie who had been a colleague of Hasluck's at UWA in 1939 and who had enjoyed a distinguished academic career in both Australia and New Zealand.[93] Currie's report, which was not published until after Hasluck left the Territories portfolio, served as the blueprint for the establishment of the University of Papua New Guinea in 1965. The progression towards tertiary education in PNG happened in spite of Hasluck's firm belief in uniform development.

Australian attitudes to education policy within PNG also demonstrated Australia's understanding of its own developmental status. In a 1960 policy paper, the Territories Department, recognising some of the limitations in its investment in education, sought to increase educational opportunities in a way that was less financially demanding. The key solution was to have Indigenous, Australian-trained teachers doing the work that was previously done by expatriate teachers. The fundamental assumption driving this policy could have come straight from the work of E.K. Fisk (in an Australian context), or Walt Rostow. Territories officials believed that:

> The educational and cultural climate in the Territory is not equivalent with our own; that it will be a great number of years before there will be natives with Australian-equivalent tertiary training to staff Territory Services; that the natives are at a lower stage of development than we are, and the immediate need is simply to provide basic primary education to upward of 200,000 native children of school age.[94]

[92] Hasluck, *A Time for Building*, 386.

[93] D.E. Hutchison, "Currie, Sir George Alexander (1896–1984)", Australian Dictionary of Biography, National Centre of Biography, Australian National University, http://adb.anu.edu.au/biography/currie-sir-george-alexander-12384/text22257, published first in hardcopy 2007; Hasluck, *A Time for Building*, 388.

[94] Territories Department, "Education - Papua and New Guinea," August 5, 1960, NAA: A452, 1960/4427.

By drawing a distinction between the Australian and Papua New Guinean stages of development, the Department had found a way to justify a more efficient education policy. Further, they employed an idea used in the Colombo Plan, by suggesting that Indigenous teachers come to Australia to receive the benefits of 'Western' training. The convergence between the two theatres of Australian aid was becoming more pronounced.

Port Moresby Versus Canberra

Just as during Eddie Ward's New Deal, tensions between Canberra and Port Moresby created obstacles for development policy. It was one thing to have a broad vision of the best way to improve the standard of living of the Indigenous population, but implementation was another matter entirely. Hasluck's penchant for maintaining firm control over the work of his department produced friction between the department and the Administration. Hasluck kept a tight rein on the work of the Administration and frequently expressed his frustration at the lack of progress made on the ground. He reflected in his memoir that "there is no area in which I have a greater sense of failure than in my inability to get the Territory Administration to work harder and do its job better."[95]

Constant delays were exacerbated by criticism from expatriate private interests in PNG, which although not as vitriolic as against Ward, still constituted a challenge to Hasluck's developmental objectives. In the *Pacific Islands Monthly*, the mouthpiece of the expatriate community, references to the "Canberra Czars" demonstrated disapproval of Hasluck's development policy. This was often in the context of discussing land policy, as there was a clear tension between Canberra's "preoccupation with native welfare" and expatriate desires for fewer obstructions to European-led development.[96] Expatriate interests were also actively opposed to Hasluck's vision for gradual development, as seen in a 1956 editorial that referred to Hasluck's objectives as "sheer dreaming."[97] As had been the case in the late 1940s and early 1950s in both the New Deal and the Colombo Plan, local complications revealed the fragility of

[95] Hasluck, *A Time for Building*, 207.

[96] "New Guinea Progress Is Shackled by Canberra," *Pacific Islands Monthly* 25, no. 2 (1954): 13–14.

[97] "Minister Hasluck's Papua-New Guinea," *Pacific Islands Monthly* 27, no. 2 (1956): 18.

the Australian commitment to promoting development through coherent and effective policy.

Throughout his time as Minister, Hasluck suggested that Australian private enterprise would supplement Administration attempts to assist in the promotion of PNG's economic development. This was a clear step away from the New Deal. Early on in his tenure, Hasluck made it clear that "the European settlement will increase, and development of that territory will be mainly the result of European enterprise in the years immediately ahead."[98] However, as the criticism from the *Pacific Islands Monthly* indicated, Hasluck's advocacy of this was not universally admired. By 1960, Hasluck claimed some success in the developmental tutelage provided by Australian businesses in PNG, explaining that:

> Many remarkable instances exist throughout the Territory of very great achievement by the exceptional man who, seeing what the European can do, has decided that he can do it too, and, with various forms of assistance, both as technical instruction from the Department of Agriculture and guidance from extension officers, and with some credit assistance, has been able to enter into production in quite a substantial way.[99]

Hasluck's belief in the centrality of Australian private enterprise persisted through to 1963 when he commented on the links between expatriate interests and increased Indigenous political representation. He maintained his belief in the role of Australian settlers, explaining:

> It would be fatal for the Territory and for the people of the Territory if we in this Parliament were to do anything or if the Territory itself were to choose a path which meant a frightening of investment or an exodus of those who are ready to give and who can give so much to the Territory.[100]

In order to maintain the interest of potential Australian investors, Hasluck and the Administration established land reform policies that would make investment appear more attractive. However, Hasluck remained interested in ensuring that Indigenous farmers would have access to land, which resulted in the need for a fine balance between protecting Indigenous

[98] *CPD*, House of Representatives, no. 36, 1952, September 5, 1952, 1090.

[99] *CPD*, House of Representatives, no. 13, 1960, March 29, 1960, 689.

[100] *CPD*, House of Representatives, no. 20, 1963, May 15, 1963, 1405.

interests and opening up new land to Australian expatriates. This caused some tension between Port Moresby and Canberra, with Administration officials favouring expatriate investors with better land. Hasluck was critical in his observation of this process, indicating that he had an "uneasy feeling that, while the Administration is now doing more to carry out this policy, it still does not fully grasp the ideas behind the policy."[101] In attempting to strike a balance between Indigenous and European enterprise, Hasluck generated an area of contention between Canberra and Port Moresby.

The conflict between Hasluck's desire for control over developmental policy and his reliance on the Administration for its implementation often led to Ministerial criticism of Cleland and his staff. For instance, in 1955, Hasluck was frustrated at the lack of progress with regard to agricultural development. He noted that:

> When a clear instruction has been given, I regard it as the personal responsibility of the Administrator to ensure that every possible effort is being made to make the Government policy effective. The Government relies on the Administrator to ensure that there is an effective execution of its policy decision and this is still one field in which, in spite of the large measure of good work already done, I feel that the Administration still has to go a long way in order to meet the wishes of the Government.[102]

Hasluck was sharp in his criticism and clearly saw limitations in the implementation of his developmental program. Hasluck's frustration at the lack of progress found its way into criticism of both the Administration and the Department in 1960. Responding to comments by Lambert that Port Moresby should continue to pursue the drafting of plans, rather than implement policies that had already been decided upon, Hasluck was scathing:

> Pursue? Pursue? Is this some illusory thing that we chase with a butterfly net? If the Administration and the Department could not immediately, on a chance request by Cabinet, place on my table an exact statement of what we are going to try to do in the next three years in any major field of

[101] P.M. Hasluck handwritten comment, October 31, 1955 on C.R. Lambert to P.M. Hasluck, October 4, 1955, NAA: A518, C2/1/1.

[102] Hasluck to C.R. Lambert, May 20, 1955, NAA: A518, C2/1/1.

> activity in Papua and New Guinea then I think they have fallen down on the job.[103]

Hasluck's prickly character can be understood from his treatment of his departmental secretary. The increasing urgency associated with developmental policy was undermined by a hesitant and conservative department and an inefficient administration.

Another complicating factor in Hasluck's plans for colonial development was his observation of "colonialist attitudes" amongst both the administration and expatriate population of PNG.[104] In his memoir, Hasluck commented on the beginning of his ministerial tenure, citing a speech he gave in November 1951:

> One early point that I made was that in Papua and New Guinea the colonizing process was taking place after the colonial age had ended. Any nation administering such a territory today must place in the forefront of its thinking the conception that the people had rights of their own. Colonial days had passed and the Territory could never be treated as a colony in the old meaning of the term.[105]

Relations between Port Moresby and Canberra were influenced by Hasluck's pressure to move away from the "old meaning" of colonialism. Ultimately, while Hasluck's criticism suggested a more equal partnership between Indigenous and expatriate communities, this was undermined by the persistence of colonialist attitudes. This raises questions about whether or not Hasluck genuinely sought to redefine the attitudes underpinning Australian colonial administration.

The subordinate role of Indigenous development can be seen in the recommendations of representatives from the Lutheran missions, who suggested in 1958 that "the more the Native people's economic and political destiny is interwoven with European led movements the better it will be for the political stability of the country."[106] In contrast to Hasluck's publicly expressed desire for a balance between Indigenous

[103] Hasluck to C.R. Lambert, January 29, 1960, NAA: A452, 1960/374.

[104] Hasluck, *A Time for Building*, 197–198.

[105] Hasluck, *A Time for Building*, 69.

[106] Lutheran Mission Memorandum, attached to John Kuder to D.M. Cleland, August 27, 1958, NAA: A452, 1958/3188.

and European development, the Mission representatives called for European interests to be prioritised. Attitudes such as these ran counter to Hasluck's rhetoric of gradual development and caused tensions within PNG. Ultimately, Hasluck felt that such attitudes were reminiscent of earlier Lugardian notions of colonial rule, which he felt were a "device by which colonial rule could be assisted and perpetuated rather than a path towards the development of Indigenous political institutions."[107] Nevertheless, Hasluck's repeated rhetoric of a slow path to independence for PNG may have encouraged the self-interested attitudes of some expatriates who challenged Australian colonial policy by undermining a more significant focus on Indigenous interests.

PNG and Australian Developmentalism

The Hasluck period in PNG consolidated the dominant characteristics of post-war Australian developmental assistance. In his memoir, Hasluck reflected on the place of economic theories in shaping his policies towards PNG. He was sceptical of their effectiveness, claiming: "It seemed to me that the economic doctrinaires were always likely to act so that the means to an end became an end in itself."[108] For Hasluck, this was a critique of how developmental theory could emphasise the centrality of a process like agricultural improvement without really conceiving of why this improvement was necessary. Through this reflection, it is possible to draw an important conclusion regarding the Hasluck period of Australian colonial policy in PNG. For the Minister, the specific components of developmental theory were troublesome, as he felt they emphasised the means rather than the ends of policy. But, by incorporating them into his notion of uniform development—a theory in its own right—Hasluck co-opted developmentalism in a way that suited his goal of promoting a gradual trajectory towards self-government. Hasluck's rhetoric and policy were synonymous with the attitudes of the age of international development.

The fundamental trajectory of Australian colonial policy in PNG was to impose an Australian model of economic and political life on the Indigenous population. Politically, Hasluck saw the Australian progression towards independence as a model for PNG, claiming in 1963 that

[107] Hasluck, *A Time for Building*, 165.

[108] Hasluck, *A Time for Building*, 154.

"we have ourselves risen to nationhood from the status of colonial dependencies ruled from overseas."[109] Despite Hasluck's clear disregard for the different colonial experiences of Australia and PNG, he expected that PNG's progress towards representative government would follow a similar pattern to Australia.[110] Before that could happen, Hasluck felt that more extensive economic advancement was required. He argued that exposing the Indigenous population to more advanced economic concepts would facilitate the shift towards political independence.[111] In making this case, Hasluck's attitude towards development shared many characteristics with the broader international developmental system, which also involved a close connection between economic, political and social development. Further, by taking an Australian model as his basis, Hasluck's policies correspond with the process of 'convergence,' identified by Nick Cullather as the conviction that "there is one best form of political economy and that all states are moving toward it."[112] The Australian policy of encouraging educational and agricultural development using the Australian experience as a guide provides the clearest example of this process during the Hasluck period.

Of course, PNG was not the only place receiving developmental assistance from Australia during the Hasluck era. The assumptions that drove Australian scholarship on the development of PNG filtered through to work on Southeast Asia. Consequently, various aspects of Australian policy in PNG bore a striking resemblance to Australian aid policy for Southeast Asia. Aside from the broad emphasis on 'development' through the provision of Australian experts, more specific parallels can be drawn. One of the most prominent examples involved young Papua New Guinean children coming to study in Australian schools. In a process that resembled the Colombo Plan, small numbers of Indigenous students spent time in Australian schools (particularly in Queensland), where they were expected to learn Australian techniques and gain a greater understanding of the 'modern' way of life. Policymakers, employing international developmentalist logic, expected that these students would then return to

[109] "Notes for Minister's Use in Drafting Second Reading Speech on Papua and New Guinea Bill", attached to Lambert to Hasluck, April 1963, NAA: A452, 1962/5561.

[110] Hasluck, *A Time for Building*, 170.

[111] Hasluck, *A Time for Building*, 326.

[112] Nick Cullather, "Research Note: Development? It's History," *Diplomatic History* 24, no. 4 (2000): 642.

their homes ready to lead the way along the development process.[113] In accordance with the accepted Australian view regarding Indigenous 'primitiveness,' only a very small number of Papua New Guinean children were sent to Australia. Nevertheless, many of these people would go on to assume leadership positions as PNG became more politically autonomous, thereby fulfilling the apparent goals of Australian developmental policy.[114]

In 1961, External Affairs officials suggested a kind of Colombo Plan in the South Pacific.[115] These officials presented the idea that the Colombo Plan and the South Pacific Commission had the same goals, "to help the peoples of under-developed countries to raise their standards of living and thus become better equipped to take their place in the highly-competitive world of today."[116] While this early attempt to connect colonial and foreign aid policy did not eventuate, it is revealing of the ways that Australian attitudes towards 'underdeveloped' peoples were converging. Suggestions such as this reflected the growing acceptance within the policymaking bureaucracy in Canberra that the Australian grant to PNG was a form of foreign aid, a key point which will be discussed in more detail in the next two chapters.

[113] The link between modernisation theory and the training of experts in 'developed' countries for return to 'underdeveloped' countries is examined in Bradley R. Simpson, *Economists with Guns: Authoritarian Development and U.S.-Indonesian Relations, 1960–1968* (Stanford, CA: Stanford University Press, 2008), 20.

[114] Prominent early leaders who studied in Australia include Julius Chan, Josephine Abaijah, and John Kaputin. Downs, *The Australian Trusteeship Papua New Guinea, 1945–75*, 413–414.

[115] Department of External Affairs, Draft Memorandum, "Aid Plan for the Pacific Islands," attached to D.W. McNicol to C.H. Cox, June 15, 1961, NAA: A452, 1960/5670.

[116] Department of External Affairs, "The Colombo Plan and the South Pacific Commission," n.d. [end of 1960], NAA: A452, 1960/5670.

CHAPTER 5

"Developed, Developing or Midway?" Australia at the United Nations Conference on Trade and Development, 1964

On January 28, 1965, Peter Samuel, the young economics editor at the *Canberra Times,* published the second article in his five-part "Aspects of Australian Aid" series.[1] Titled "The Midway Doctrine: An Exercise in Deceit", Samuel's article was deeply critical of the Australian Middle Zone policy presented at the United Nations Conference on Trade and Development (UNCTAD), held in Geneva.[2] This policy was most closely associated with Deputy Prime Minister and leader of the Country Party, John McEwen, and his Department of Trade and Industry. The Middle Zone posited that Australia did not belong in either of the two blocs represented at UNCTAD, those of the 'developed' and 'developing' countries. Instead, owing to its reliance on primary exports (like the developing countries) and its high standard of living (like the developed countries), it had elements of both. This approach built on earlier attempts to distance Australia from the rich countries, such as those

[1] The other articles examined Australian aid to India, the link between manufacturing and development, voluntary organisations and the value of multilateral assistance to Papua New Guinea.

[2] Peter Samuel, "The Midway Doctrine: An Exercise in Deceit," *Canberra Times*, January 28, 1965, NAA: A1313, 1964/2380 PART 1.

N. Ferns, *Australia in the Age of International Development, 1945–1975*, Security, Conflict and Cooperation in the Contemporary World, https://doi.org/10.1007/978-3-030-50228-7_5

outlined by 'Nugget' Coombs in the late 1940s.[3] Samuel rejected the central premise of the Middle Zone, directing his ire at the misleading uses of the words 'developed' and 'developing.' He observed the slippages in terminology applied to "less fortunate countries." According to Samuel: "Once they were plain 'backward'; then 'undeveloped'; then 'underdeveloped'; then 'emerging' and now they are 'developing'."[4] This terminology was important. As Samuel noted:

> Our midway doctrine only makes any sense because of the use of words 'developed' and 'developing.' In fact, these words are merely polite modern equivalents of the now indecent words 'rich' and 'poor,' and if these were more commonly used the deceit of our position would be obvious.[5]

This criticism suggested that the developmental arguments in the Middle Zone policy were merely a cover for the self-interested aim of protecting Australian trade interests. While self-interest was one motivation behind the Middle Zone, the fact that Trade and Industry officials employed developmental arguments to support their position reveals the ongoing intersection between development as an ideal and the practical application of Australian foreign policy.

This chapter will examine Australia's Middle Zone policy at the 1964 UNCTAD. The Middle Zone extended the Australian contribution to the age of international development beyond economic assistance to PNG and the Colombo Plan. Emerging out of long-standing bureaucratic differences within the Commonwealth Government over the meaning of development, the Middle Zone challenged the dichotomy at the heart of post-war international developmentalism. However, these internal tensions also undermined the Middle Zone's international appeal. As a conference brought about by pressure from the growing number of independent developing countries, UNCTAD aimed to resolve the perceived trade imbalance that favoured the rich, industrial, developed countries.

International aid policy was also on the agenda at UNCTAD, as almost two decades of developmental assistance had seemingly failed to

[3] H.C. Coombs, *Trial Balance* (South Melbourne: Macmillan, 1981), 59–65; Ann Capling, *Australia and the Global Trade System: From Havana to Seattle* (Cambridge; Melbourne: Cambridge University Press, 2001), 23.

[4] Samuel, "The Midway Doctrine."

[5] Samuel, "The Midway Doctrine."

solve the 'problem' of development. McEwen and his department were concerned that the outcomes of this conference would threaten Australian export earnings, which were vital to Australia's overall economic position. He and his department devised the Middle Zone, which presented Australia as neither developed nor developing. Australia would therefore be excluded from the trade concessions expected of the developed countries. Aside from the clear self-interest inherent to the Middle Zone, this approach was an explicit attempt to complicate the political classifications that had emerged out of international development practice since the end of the Second World War. Due to international scepticism from both developed and developing countries about Australia's claim and the inherent contradictions within the policy, the Middle Zone approach failed. Nevertheless, it was an important moment of intersection between the Australian conception of its own development and its political engagement with international developmentalism. McEwen's approach at UNCTAD marks an important phase in Australia's engagement with international development in the decades after 1945. The developing countries' challenge to the status quo forced Australian experts and policymakers to explicitly present their own conceptions of Australia's developmental status. The Middle Zone was the culmination of almost two decades of debates over whether or not Australia was truly 'developed.' This debate, which often revolved around the ability of Australia to promote development overseas, had rarely been explicitly presented to the rest of the world. In conceiving the Middle Zone, Australian policymakers connected developmental ideas and foreign policy in a new and provocative way.

International scholarship on UNCTAD generally places the Conference in the context of rising co-operation amongst the countries of the developing world. Marc Williams and Vijay Prashad both frame the Conference as the first successful attempt by what became known as the Global South to convene an international conference dedicated to examining economic problems peculiar to them.[6] Prashad refers to UNCTAD as "the economic arm of the Third World project."[7] Scholars such as Nils Gilman present the first UNCTAD in 1964 as a key moment in the

[6] Prashad, *The Poorer Nations*; Marc Williams, *Third World Cooperation: The Group of 77 in UNCTAD* (London: Pinter Publishers, 1991).

[7] Prashad, *The Poorer Nations*, 2–3.

establishment of the New International Economic Order (NIEO), which emerged as an international force in the 1970s.[8] Numerous historians of the institution itself accept the view that UNCTAD was the site of the considerable economic conflict between the developing and developed countries.[9] UNCTAD reflected a growing North–South divide in international affairs, which challenged the East–West divide of the Cold War. Furthering the understanding of this divide, David Ekbladh argues that UNCTAD undermined the acceptance of modernisation theory as a basis for development policy.[10] Nils Gilman presents UNCTAD's challenge to the modernisation paradigm in the context of the rise of dependency theory, which was associated most closely in the early 1960s with Raul Prebisch, the inaugural Secretary-General of UNCTAD.[11] Whether examining UNCTAD from the perspective of the developing or developed countries, it was a vital moment in post-war developmentalism.

In the Australian context, the developmental considerations behind the Middle Zone have largely been ignored. As a result, the historical understanding of Australia's participation at UNCTAD is limited. When it has been addressed, the Middle Zone is generally presented as either an example of Australian identification with the difficulties of developing countries, or as a means by which Trade Minister McEwen sought to protect Australian exports. Daniel Oakman mentions UNCTAD in passing in his history of the Colombo Plan, touching on how the Conference illustrated the links between Australian trade and aid policies, while largely ignoring the Middle Zone concept.[12] In his biography of John McEwen, Peter Golding asserts that the Minister was a strong supporter of the developing countries at UNCTAD, but provides little evidence

[8] Gilman, "The New International Economic Order." Gilman's article introduced a special issue of *Humanity* that was devoted to the history of the NIEO in 2015.

[9] Ian Taylor and Karen Smith, *United Nations Conference on Trade and Development (UNCTAD)* (New York: Routledge, 2007), 10–13; Williams, *Third World Cooperation*, 43; Sidney Dell, "The Origins of UNCTAD," in *UNCTAD and the South-North Dialogue: The First Twenty Years, Essays in Memory of W.R. Malinowski*, ed. Michael Zammit Cutajar (New York: Pergamon Press, 1985), 31.

[10] Ekbladh, *The Great American Mission*, 247.

[11] Edgar J. Dosman, *The Life and Times of Raul Prebisch, 1901–1986* (Montreal: McGill-Queen's University Press, 2008); Rist, *The History of Development*, 113; Gilman, *Mandarins of the Future*, 234.

[12] Oakman, *Facing Asia*, 253–254.

to support this claim.[13] More recently, Clinton Fernandes has explored the Middle Zone as part of Australia's reaction to the NIEO, arguing that "in many respects, the middle zone illustrated just why Australia – although a former British colony – was very different to other former colonies."[14] Historians of Australian trade relations touch on the Middle Zone when discussing the Australian delegation's strategies at UNCTAD and the Kennedy Round of the General Agreement on Tariffs and Trade (GATT). Ann Capling explains that the Middle Zone was a product of Australian products being vulnerable to international competition, which meant that McEwen and his representatives were more likely to identify with the developing countries that also relied upon primary exports.[15] Whether approaching the Middle Zone from an aid or trade perspective, Australian scholars have generally presented it as a result of an Australian desire to protect its own trade interests. While this was clearly a major consideration, it is also vital to understand the Middle Zone as a pivotal moment in Australia's engagement with international development, both conceptually and politically.

Dependency Theory: A Challenge to the Orthodoxy

Raul Prebisch, who served as head of the UN Economic Commission for Latin America (ECLA) and was the first Secretary-General of UNCTAD, presented an early challenge to the orthodox view that developing countries' terms of trade in agriculture would improve relative to that of manufacturing. Writing in 1949, he theorised that the reverse was the case, devising what would become known as the Prebisch-Singer Thesis.[16] Throughout the 1950s and early 1960s, Prebisch continued to observe that in spite of continued economic and technical assistance, developing

[13] Peter Golding, *Black Jack McEwen: Political Gladiator* (Carlton South, VIC: Melbourne University Press, 1996), 150.

[14] Clinton Fernandes, *Island of the Coast of Asia: Instruments of Statecraft in Australian Foreign Policy* (Clayton: Monash University Publishing, 2018), 137.

[15] Capling, *Australia and the Global Trade System*, 73–75.

[16] Hans Singer, a German-born British economist, reached similar views at around the same time. John Toye and Richard Toye, "The Origins and Interpretation of the Prebisch-Singer Thesis," *History of Political Economy* 35, no. 3 (2003); Economic Commission for Latin America, *The Economic Development of Latin America and Its Principal Problems.*

countries (referred to by Prebisch as the 'periphery') relied on primary exports and were falling further behind their developed counterparts (the 'centre').[17] This notion ran counter to orthodox developmental theory, which argued that economic growth in 'underdeveloped' economies would be enhanced by assistance from the richer parts of the world. By the mid-1960s, Prebisch's analysis was adopted and built upon by Andre Gunder Frank, and became known as dependency theory.[18] Nevertheless, as Nick Cullather identifies, while the ideas of dependency challenged those of the modernisation paradigm, "they agree on fundamental assumptions encoded on the terms *development* and *modernization*."[19] While modernisation theorists held an intrinsically optimistic view of development, scholars like Prebisch and Frank emphasised the inequities within the international capitalist system.[20] Development was still the goal for dependency theorists; they just sought to revise the structural terms by which the process would take place. Given their focus on resolving deep inequities in the international economic system, these ideas received an understandably positive response throughout the developing world.

Dependency theory emerged in the mid-1960s as the modernisation paradigm was at the peak of its influence over developmental thinking. While Prebisch's observations of the declining position of the developing countries appealed to the leaders of newly independent countries, much of the international development system continued to be informed by modernisation. Nevertheless, there was growing awareness within the developed world of the lack of progress being achieved by development policy. The dominant complaint from the Global North revolved around the concern that despite almost two decades of economic and technical assistance, the need for continued aid appeared more necessary than ever. In the United States, this concern was best represented by the 1963 Clay Committee on Foreign Aid, which had the task of investigating the efficiency of American aid spending. One of the key

[17] Robert O'Brien and Marc Williams, *Global Political Economy: Evolution and Dynamics*, 3rd ed. (New York: Palgrave Macmillan, 2010), 317.

[18] Frank, *Capitalism and Underdevelopment in Latin America*.

[19] Cullather, "Research Note: Development? It's History," 643 [Emphasis in original]. A similar point is made by Daniel Immerwahr in *Thinking Small*, 172.

[20] Rist, *History of Development*, 110–111.

complaints noted by the Committee was the feeling amongst many American politicians that the United States was bearing too much of the burden of economic and technical assistance throughout the world.[21] According to observers of the Clay Committee, "congressional and public support for foreign aid had been sapped by the all-too-frequent readiness of the American government to give aid that could not be justified by economic criteria."[22] Similar questions regarding the use of aid funding drove the 1964–1965 Australian Inter-Departmental External Aid Review, which will be examined in the next chapter. These concerns over the effectiveness of foreign aid challenged two decades of assertions by development theorists who had confidently argued that economic and technical assistance would enable poorer countries to progress through the stages of economic development.

The challenge to the modernisation paradigm eventually filtered through to Australia. Dependency attracted an Australian following, but this did not really take place until the late 1960s and early 1970s, as will be discussed in Chapter 7.[23] In the first half of the 1960s, the work of W. Arthur Lewis and Walt Rostow continued to exert an influence in Australia and was regarded as "required reading" for scholars interested in economic growth.[24] However, their orthodox views were not the only inspiration to Australian experts. One of the most prominent and influential international development experts during the 1950s and 1960s was the Swedish economist Gunnar Myrdal. A close companion of 'Nugget' Coombs, Myrdal's Keynesian credentials, combined with his innovative work on developmental theory, informed Australian attitudes towards development.[25] Myrdal visited Australia in 1957 to present the Dyason Lectures for the Australian Institute of International Affairs. Speaking

[21] Jacob Viner, George Meany, Fowler Hamilton, Otto Passman and Paul Hoffman, "The Report of the Clay Committee on Foreign Aid: A Symposium," *Political Science Quarterly* 78, no. 3 (1963): 322–323.

[22] Viner, Meany, Hamilton, Passman and Hoffman, "Report of the Clay Committee on Foreign Aid," 324.

[23] Mortimer, *Showcase State*; Amarshi, Good and Mortimer, *Development and Dependency*. Jemma Purdey briefly touches on Herb Feith's flirtation with dependency theory in the early 1970s. Purdey, *From Vienna to Yogyakarta*, 374.

[24] C.A. Blyth, review of *The Economics of Take-off into Sustained Growth*, ed. W.W. Rostow, *Australian Outlook* 40, no. 4 (1964).

[25] Coombs and Myrdal were regular correspondents, exchanging economic ideas from the end of the Second World War through to the end of the 1960s. Rowse, *Nugget*

on "Economic Nationalism in Under-Developed Countries", Myrdal presented a nuanced critique of the modernisation approach. He was particularly critical of the idea that understanding the process of development in developed countries provided a useful model to 'underdeveloped' economies:

> A large part of the literature on economic development in under-developed countries presently produced in the richer countries, which is making use of such historical analogies, entirely misses the point and remains therefore irrelevant to the real problems of these countries.[26]

Myrdal argued that the differences between 'developed' and 'developing' countries were so profound that the path to improved living standards would not be the same. As such, he proposed that radical institutional changes were necessary in these poorer countries.[27] Australian scholars' engagement with modernisation theory was tempered by scholars, such as Myrdal, whose views towards development provided a contrast to the prominence of Americans like Rostow.[28]

This intellectual diversity was reflected in Australian studies of development in the early 1960s. The orthodox modernisation paradigm could be seen in the work of some Australian economists, particularly Douglas Copland and John Crawford.[29] Heinz Arndt also emerged as a dominant figure in Australian developmental studies, best known for his work on Indonesian development throughout the 1960s.[30] Arndt's analysis

Coombs, 130; H.C. Coombs to Gunnar Myrdal, July 9, 1968, NLA, Coombs Papers, MS 802, Box 7.

[26] Gunnar Myrdal, "Economic Nationalism and Internationalism," *Australian Outlook* 11, no. 4 (1957): 21.

[27] Meier and Seers, *Pioneers in Development*, 154.

[28] Myrdal was regularly cited alongside Rostow and other modernisation theorists in Australian studies of economic development in the late 1950s and early 1960s. James P. Belshaw, review of *Possibilities of Economic Progress*, by A.J. Youngson, *Economic Record* 35, no. 3 (1959): 448; R.K. Hefford, "Foreign Aid—Australia's Contribution," *Economic Record* 38, no. 2 (1962): 246–247; Augustine H.H. Tan, "Special Development Problems of a Plural Society: The Malayan Example—A Comment," *Economic Record* 40, no. 1 (1964): 117.

[29] J.G. Crawford Draft Address, "Australia's Stake in Asia," November 21, 1961, NAA: A1838, 2020/1/2 PART 3; Copland, *The Changing Structure of the Western Economy*.

[30] Arndt, *A Course Through Life*, 52–63.

broadly adhered to the modernisation school and would come into conflict with the more radical approach of scholars, such as former communist Rex Mortimer, later in the decade. Another perspective was provided by economists Anthony Clunies Ross (who would become the founding Professor of Economics at the new University of PNG) and Richard Downing, who called for one per cent of Australian gross national product (GNP) to be devoted to foreign aid.[31] While they shared the modernisation school's belief in transfers of capital and expertise, there was a greater consideration of the recipients of foreign aid in their work. The one per cent target became a major demand of the developing countries at UNCTAD, and its avoidance by Australia was an important consideration in the Middle Zone policy. While the modernisation paradigm was dominant, there was room for debate within the developmental orthodoxy.[32]

The Establishment of UNCTAD

UNCTAD stemmed from the growing discontent amongst developing nations at the lack of progress being made in economic development. The crux of this discontent revolved around the perceived failures associated with the United Nations 'Decade of Development.' This movement, which emerged out of United States President John F. Kennedy's speech to the UN in September 1961, had as its basis a desire for developing countries to achieve economic growth levels of five per cent per capita throughout the 1960s.[33] The dominant modernisation paradigm was at the heart of the development decade. Kennedy and his advisors, such as Walt Rostow, expected that the conventional patterns of trade and increased aid would enable these targets to be met.[34] It did not take long for observers—particularly those in the developing countries—to realise

[31] Anthony Clunies Ross, *One Per Cent: The Case for Greater Australian Foreign Aid* (Melbourne: Melbourne University Press, 1963).

[32] Joseph Hodge presents a persuasive critique of the homogenising tendency in many of the histories of American modernisation theory. Joseph Morgan Hodge, "Writing the History of Development (Part 1: The First Wave)," *Humanity: An International Journal of Human Rights, Humanitarianism, and Development* 7, no. 1 (2015): 443.

[33] Address by John F. Kennedy to the UN General Assembly, September 25, 1961, US Department of State, http://www.state.gov/p/io/potusunga/207241.htm.

[34] Ekbladh, *The Great American Mission*, 190.

that these targets were unlikely to be met through the existing levels of aid and trade, and that even if they were met, much higher growth rates were required to bridge the gap between the developed and developing countries. Out of the increased recognition of the failings of conventional developmental theory, Prebisch's fledgling dependency school found a ready audience. Developing countries found the ideas of dependency, with its emphasis on the structural inequalities within the international economy, much more useful than the dominant modernisation paradigm.

Prior to UNCTAD, Prebisch and his secretariat produced *Towards a New Trade Policy for Development*, which outlined the perceived problems that the Conference would address, along with proposed solutions.[35] From the outset, Prebisch explained what he perceived as the key problem in the international economy:

> From the standpoint of the developing countries, the Conference will be particularly concerned with a phenomenon that was a subject of controversy until recently, but which is today a matter of understandable general concern: the persistent tendency towards external imbalance associated with the development process.[36]

Economic statistics supported this contention. Whereas the share of world exports of primary commodities for 'industrialised' countries increased from 47 per cent in 1950 to 55 per cent in 1961, the share for 'developing' countries fell from 41 per cent to 29 per cent.[37] This was the basic tenet of the Prebisch-Singer thesis, and the establishment of UNCTAD was aimed at rectifying the negative effects of modernisation-guided development.

For the purposes of the Conference, the primary means by which the international trade imbalance could be overcome was through the expansion of export opportunities for the developing countries.[38] In order to achieve this, the various barriers to trade within the developed countries would need to be removed or weakened. These barriers attracted particular ire within the developing world, as they were perceived as preventing

[35] Raul Prebisch, *Towards a New Trade Policy for Development* (New York: United Nations, 1964).

[36] Prebisch, *Towards a New Trade Policy for Development*, 3.

[37] Prebisch, *Towards a New Trade Policy for Development*, 18.

[38] The 'developing' countries also urged more effective and increased economic aid.

exports that were central to the development process. Indeed, Prebisch himself reflected on this point in the final section of *Towards a New Trade Policy for Development*:

> It is no good to preach the need for them [the 'developing' countries] to develop by their own efforts and at the same time to limit their possibilities of giving practical expression to that effort in the international field through the expansion of their exports.[39]

At UNCTAD, the developing countries placed pressure on the developed bloc to liberalise trade in order to achieve a more equitable international trade system. According to the Geneva Declaration—which was signed in June 1963 and was the clearest expression of the developing countries' viewpoint—the developing bloc demanded the "progressive reduction and early elimination of all barriers and restrictions impeding the exports of the developing countries, without reciprocal concessions on their [the developed countries] part."[40] Unsurprisingly, this provoked resistance from the developed countries, whose sustained economic growth was partly a product of their existing trade policies. For instance, the United States, despite being a strong public advocate of trade liberalisation, had established an extensive system of indirect obstacles to imports from the developing countries, and so was concerned at the possible implications of such demands.[41] These competing interests illustrated the emergence of the North–South divide as rising to challenge the dominant East–West division of the Cold War.

The establishment of UNCTAD was the first step in what became known by the 1970s as the NIEO. It came out of the Conference, when the developing bloc, in their assessment of UNCTAD, expressed their hope that it provided a "significant step towards creating a new and just world economic order."[42] As Gilman explains, the NIEO's fundamental

[39] Prebisch, *Towards a New Trade Policy for Development*, 124.

[40] "Joint Statement by Representatives of the Developing Countries," Second Session of the Preparatory Committee, UNCTAD, June 27, 1963, NAA: A452, 1963/7763.

[41] Stuart Ward, *Australia and the British Embrace: The Demise of the Imperial Ideal* (Carlton South, VIC: Melbourne University Press, 2001), 124.

[42] *Proceedings of the United Nations Conference on Trade and Development, Geneva, 23 March–16 June 1964*, 8 vols. (New York: United Nations, 1964), 66.

objective was to "*transform the governance of the global economy to redirect more of the benefits of transnational integration toward 'the developing nations'* – thus completing the geopolitical process of decolonization and creating a democratic global order of truly sovereign states."[43]

The Middle Zone

The Australian Middle Zone policy, which also sought to transform the international economy by challenging the dichotomy between developed and developing blocs, worked parallel to the NIEO. As scholar and public servant, Stuart Harris observed in 1978:

> Australia's position on the NIEO is that she has herself been arguing separately for major changes in the status quo but has tended to help the North defend the status quo against the South. Many of her interests are common with those of developing countries but she clearly has other interests which she is entitled to defend.[44]

This incisive critique of the Australian position with regard to the NIEO highlighted some of the key issues present in the Middle Zone. Policymakers in Canberra had long recognised Australia's dependence on primary exports and lack of industrial development, at least in contrast to the countries of North America and Western Europe.[45] Nevertheless, the subtleties of the Australian economy had often not been fully acknowledged in an international setting.

Attempts by Australian trade officials to present Australia as something different to the rich, industrialised, developed countries go back to the immediate post-war period and the London Negotiations of the International Trade Organisation (ITO) Charter in 1946. At this meeting, 'Nugget' Coombs, as head of the Australian delegation, sought to present Australia as different from the 'developed' countries. Coombs was supported by the American representative, Winthrop Brown, who

[43] Gilman, "The New International Economic Order," 1 [Italics in original].

[44] Stuart Harris, "Australia and the New International Economic Order," *Australian Outlook* 32, no. 1 (1978): 39.

[45] Capling, *Australia and the Global Trade System*, 74–75.

went so far as to identify Australia as the "leader of the underdeveloped countries."[46] As with the Middle Zone position almost twenty years later, Australia's position in London was driven by concerns over terms of trade that were heavily in favour of industrial countries. While the ITO never came into being, Australia continued to challenge the two-bloc system that was established as its successor, the GATT. Indeed, Australia had some success in the mid-1950s, managing to secure amendments that recognised its status as a country that was still reliant on primary exports.[47] While this recognition satisfied McEwen's concerns over Australia's trade position at that time, the increasingly vocal calls from the developing countries for preferential trade access in the first half of the 1960s prompted another attempt to explain Australia's apparently peculiar position.

The policy that emerged out of Australia's reaction to this shifting international context became known as the Middle Zone. The most explicit explanation of the Middle Zone policy can be found in a Trade and Industry paper of January 1964. The paper's central argument can be discerned from its opening lines:

> In Preparatory Committee meetings for the United Nations Conference on Trade and Development (UNCTAD) only two groups of countries have been recognised – *developed* and *developing* (synonymous with under-developed). A few countries, particularly Australia and New Zealand, do not fit easily into either category.[48]

This institutional critique can also be read as a broader comment on the consequences of incorporating developmental theory into official policy. The vast body of literature that examined developmental issues in the years following the Second World War helped to crystallise the division of

[46] Winthrop Brown, quoted in Capling, *Australia and the Global Trade System*, 23; Rowse, *Nugget Coombs*, 133.

[47] H.W. Arndt, "Australia—Developed, Developing or Midway?" *Economic Record* 41, no. 95 (1965): 323–324.

[48] Department of Trade and Industry, "UNCTAD—'Middle Zone' Position," NAA: A1313, 1964/2380 PART 1 [Emphasis in original].

the world into 'developed' and 'developing' countries.[49] By suggesting that Australia did not fit into these categories, the Department of Trade and Industry was putting some of the dominant assumptions of post-war developmentalism to the test.

The bulk of the paper elaborated upon the characteristics that Australia shared with the developing and developed countries. Ten 'Features similar to Australia and the Developing Countries' were identified, ranging from the shared reliance on primary exports to the "dependence of capital inflow for rapid development."[50] The Trade and Industry Department also emphasised that Australia shared with developing countries the need "to diversify exports by increasing exports of manufactures."[51] This was crucial as it served as the dominant rationale behind Australia's attempt to avoid the American proposal at the Kennedy Round of GATT to cut tariffs "across the board" by fifty per cent.[52] The proposed cuts ran counter to McEwen's desire to protect some domestic secondary industries that would not be able to compete with cheaper international imports.[53] The Australian delegation emphasised these concerns at UNCTAD, and they served to allow McEwen to distance Australia's economic position from those of the major developed countries, such as the United States.[54] The intellectual argument surrounding Australia's developmental status was partly an attempt to obscure its ongoing reliance on protective tariffs.

The paper also recognised the similarities between Australia and countries like the United States, in its examination of the 'Features common to Australia and the developed countries.' They ranged from Australia's high standard of living to the fact that Australia was an aid donor. With

[49] Gilman, *Mandarins of the Future*, 141. Gilman reflects on the way that modernisation theorists drew a clear distinction between 'modern' and 'traditional' societies, which operated in the same way as the 'developed'/'developing' and 'advanced'/'backward' dichotomies.

[50] Department of Trade and Industry, "UNCTAD—'Middle Zone' Position."

[51] Department of Trade and Industry, "UNCTAD—'Middle Zone' Position."

[52] Capling, *Australia and the Global Trade System*, 71.

[53] John McEwen, "John McEwen: His Story," 58, NLA, Crawford Papers, MS 4514, Box 206.

[54] *UNCTAD Proceedings*, vol. 1, 122.

regard to Australia's living standards, the paper explained that the country's per capita GNP in 1961 was £679, which placed it in the world's top ten, between Sweden and the United Kingdom. The inference was that Australia fitted neatly amongst the richer countries of the world.[55] Observations such as these undermined the prospects for acceptance of the Middle Zone at UNCTAD, as it clashed with the worldview of the developing countries. While the majority of the Western countries divided the world into developed and developing countries, the developing bloc framed the system as a divide between the 'rich' and 'poor.'[56] This important difference set the stage for the ultimate rejection of the Middle Zone.

The Middle Zone was part of a transnational movement to establish a more complex political framework for international development. While at least partly motivated by self-interest and a desire to protect domestic industries, there was some validity to the argument that the existing dichotomy was overly simplistic. Even Heinz Arndt, who was critical of the Middle Zone, acknowledged that "McEwen was surely right when he criticized the new GATT chapter as being 'based on the premise that the countries of the world fall into two – and only two – economic categories'."[57] Other countries took a similar position to Australia. For instance, the New Zealand delegation argued:

> It is the view of the [New Zealand] delegation that there should have been explicit recognition by the Conference of the fact that countries are diverse in their stages of growth and in the size and structure of their economies.[58]

The attempt by these countries with 'midway' economies—that were also generally settler colonial societies—to challenge the dichotomy of UNCTAD and GATT possessed some validity. This was acknowledged by outside observers, including the Pakistani Delegate to the UN

[55] Department of Trade and Industry, "UNCTAD—'Middle Zone' Position."

[56] Gilman, "The New International Economic Order," 3–4.

[57] Arndt, "Australia—Developed, Developing or Midway?," 330.

[58] New Zealand Delegation at UNCTAD to Secretary of UNCTAD, June 16, 1964, in series United Nations Conference on Trade and Development (UNCTAD) and United Nations Industrial Development Organization (UNIDO), S-0552-0007-0005, United Nations Archives (Hereafter cited as UNA).

General Assembly, Ghulam Ali Allana. Commenting on Australia and New Zealand in the context of arguing for the improvement of the trade positions of developing nations, Allana observed: "Among the developing countries it was necessary to include those whose economy depended upon the export of a narrow range of primary commodities; Australia and New Zealand could be cited as examples of countries fitting that description."[59] This point was underlined by Trade and Industry officials, and suggested international support for the Middle Zone.

However, there was also international opposition to the Middle Zone, which was foreshadowed prior to UNCTAD. In a piece of analysis prepared for members of the Conference preparatory committee, Oxford economist Thomas Balogh examined the relationship between trade and aid. Maintaining the argument that aid considerations should not be forgotten in the trade negotiations, Balogh commented on the position of countries like Australia. In a direct critique of McEwen's position regarding Australia's terms of trade, Balogh remarked:

> The deterioration of the terms of trade has no doubt played an important part in the growing international inequality in income distribution. It should be noted, however, that the rich primary producing countries, notably Australia, have been able to offset and in some respects more than offset, the deterioration in the price of primary produce by increases in productivity.[60]

Commentary such as this, which corresponded with the views of Australian observers such as the journalist Samuel and economist Arndt, distinguished Australia from the developing countries, thereby undermining the Middle Zone. While Australia continued to be dependent on its primary exports, the challenges that it faced were not the same as the countries that were emerging from colonial rule.

[59] Seventeenth Session of the United Nations General Assembly, Agenda Item 36, "Question of Holding an International Conference on Trade Problems," October 31, 1962, NAA: A1313, 1964/2380 PART 1.

[60] Thomas Balogh, "Notes on the United Nations Conference on Trade and Development," attached to UN circular, January 24, 1964, series Commissions, Committees, and Conferences, Secretary-General U Thant fonds, S-0858-0003-02, UNA.

Bureaucratic Debate Over the Middle Zone: Trade and Industry vs. External Affairs

Inter-departmental debate regarding the Middle Zone highlighted the divergent developmental attitudes that existed within the Commonwealth bureaucracy. These different attitudes reflected both the intellectual diversity in the field of developmental theory and the ongoing vulnerability of developmental policy to political imperatives. They provide a clear demonstration of how development revealed the intersections of political and intellectual questions that were raised in Canberra. In the lead up to UNCTAD, the key debate was between the Departments of Trade and Industry and External Affairs. It is informative of the nature of Australia's contribution to the age of international development, as it centred on the interaction between trade and aid in the promotion of development. Informed by competing developmental ideas, the Trade and Industry and External Affairs' positions were a product of the previous two decades of Australian engagement with developmental thought and practice.

The Trade and Industry position was marked by a clear sense of self-interest, albeit with an awareness of the ongoing importance of international development. This position was heavily informed by the department's powerful minister, 'Black Jack' McEwen. A farmer from regional Victoria, McEwen has been presented as one of the most influential politicians in Australian history, with political commentator Paul Kelly suggesting that he defined the Australian economy well into the 1980s.[61] Referred to by biographers and historians as "the arch-protectionist of all time" and the "archetypal economic nationalist", McEwen's advocacy for the Middle Zone was a product of his recognition that Australia's manufacturing sector lagged far behind the developed countries of North America and Western Europe.[62] His dogged belief in the ongoing need for protectionist policy was inherently connected to his conception of Australia's development.

[61] Paul Kelly, quoted in Golding, *Black Jack McEwen*, 5–6; C.J. Lloyd, "McEwen, Sir John (1900–1980)," *Australian Dictionary of Biography*, National Centre of Biography, Australian National University, http://adb.anu.edu.au/biography/mcewen-sir-john-10948/text9455, published first in hardcopy 2000.

[62] Golding, *Black Jack McEwen*, 2; Capling, *Australia and the Global Trade System*, 72.

For McEwen and his departmental officials, international development needed to be synchronised with Australian development. This was particularly noticeable in McEwen's comments on the international trading system. Speaking to the House of Representatives in 1962 in the face of British attempts to enter the European Economic Community (EEC) and the continuing decline in the international terms of trade in primary products, McEwen exclaimed:

> Of course, it would be a travesty for the established industrial nations of the Western world to welcome the transition to political independence of the many under-developed countries, if there were not displayed concurrently an absolute determination to preserve for those new countries a basis of economic survival.[63]

When Australian interests were threatened by the policies of the industrialised, developed countries, McEwen was quick to identify Australia as 'developing.' His department supported this position by showing that the Australian terms of trade had declined by around 24 per cent between 1954 and 1962.[64] This decline was in keeping with the Prebisch-Singer thesis and was attributed by McEwen and his department to the discriminatory trading practices of the industrialised countries. For McEwen, Australian export markets were limited by what Capling refers to as the "hypocritical" attitudes of the EEC and United States, as they called for tariff liberalisation while maintaining non-tariff barriers to agricultural products.[65] The Trade and Industry position was therefore marked by an assertion of Australia's 'developing' status, at least in comparison with the rich countries of Western Europe and the United States.

In contrast, as we have already seen throughout this book, officials within External Affairs argued that Australia was part of the developed bloc. The External Affairs critique revolved around concerns that the Middle Zone approach would undermine Australia's foreign aid program.[66] Indeed, the External Affairs interpretation of the Middle

[63] *CPD*, House of Representatives, no. 18, 1962, May 3, 1962, 1974.

[64] Department of Trade and Industry, "UNCTAD—'Middle Zone' Position," January 22, 1964.

[65] Capling, *Australia and the Global Trade System*, 78.

[66] Department of External Affairs, "Future Australian External Economic Aid," April 1964, NAA: A1838, 2020/1/33.

Zone was closer to the analysis of Samuel and Arndt, who wrote that "to some of us in Australia this official 'midway' doctrine has had about it a distasteful ring of hypocritical special pleading."[67] In the middle of UNCTAD, External Affairs officials produced a paper examining "Future Australian External Economic Aid." Perhaps anticipating the foreign aid policy review that was to begin later in the year, this paper outlined projections for Australian aid objectives over the next ten years. At its heart was the assumption that Australia possessed the capacity to significantly increase its aid spending, providing there was no additional budgetary pressure applied by the grant to PNG or increases in defence spending.[68] However, the Middle Zone impinged on this view. In a section titled, "Should we do more in the Aid Field?" the following point was made:

> If Australia occupies a 'middle zone' position in the trade field, which implies that we cannot be expected to make a response to requests from the less developed countries for action to improve their trading position comparable to that which can be expected from the highly industrialised countries, it would follow that we occupy a similar 'middle zone' position among aid donors. The Australian aid effort should be one consistent with Australia's own developmental needs and appropriate to its special situation.[69]

The clear implication of the Middle Zone for aid policy was that it would lead Australia to assume fewer commitments than "the highly industrialised countries." Nevertheless, External Affairs officials claimed that in spite of the importance of Australia's own developmental position, Australian aid should submit to "the pressures which will be exerted on all donor countries over the next few years to increase their aid."[70] This position formed the basis of the External Affairs position in the 1965 aid review.

Ultimately, the Middle Zone magnified the competing intellectual forces operating in Australia with regard to international development. Trade and Industry felt that presenting Australia as a developing country promoted domestic development. On the other hand, the Department

[67] Arndt, "Australia—Developed, Developing or Midway?" 318.

[68] Department of External Affairs, "Future Australian External Economic Aid."

[69] Department of External Affairs, "Future Australian External Economic Aid."

[70] Department of External Affairs, "Future Australian External Economic Aid."

of External Affairs sought to increase Australia's foreign aid spending, and they were concerned about the increased international acceptance of Australia's 'special situation.' For External Affairs, providing aid to countries in Australia's region demonstrated that as "a white 'have' country on the rim of Asia... we accept an obligation to assist our less developed neighbours."[71] Following the inter-departmental debate, McEwen outlined Australia's 'special' position in his speech in the opening stages of the Conference in Geneva. Recognising the pre-eminence of the developing countries at UNCTAD, McEwen directed his focus towards their concerns, noting:

> Australia's own recent experiences in pursuing development, in fostering industrial expansion, of persistent balance of payments problem, of financing the heavy demand for imports, of capital equipment, of adverse trends in the terms of trade and of overcoming obstacles in export markets combine to give us a most vivid understanding of the problems facing the developing countries.[72]

This was consistent with both the Middle Zone analysis of early 1964 and the longer history of Australian identification with the trade concerns of developing countries.[73] McEwen then explicitly introduced the Middle Zone idea, explaining:

> So we live with the same problems that the developing countries face or will face, but we undoubtedly have made progress and achieved a high living standard. This, we feel, places us in something of a midway position between the developed and the developing countries.[74]

The scene was thus set for the testing of Australia's attempt to complicate the dominant categorisation of international development.

[71] Department of External Affairs, "Future Australian External Economic Aid."

[72] "Statement to the United Nations Conference on Trade and Development in Geneva by the Deputy Prime Minister and Minister for Trade and Industry, John McEwen, Thursday, March 26, 1964," NAA: A1313, 1964/2380 PART 1.

[73] Capling, *Australia and the Global Trade System*, 23.

[74] McEwen, "Statement to the United Nations Conference on Trade and Development."

UNCTAD

While Australian planning for UNCTAD largely revolved around the Middle Zone and its arguments regarding Australia's trade position, the Conference also fits into the broader history of Australian aid policy. Ironically, given that it was established with the primary goal of improving terms of trade for developing countries, the clearest achievement of UNCTAD was in the field of foreign aid. The Conference formally recognised the target of one per cent of GNP to be provided in financial assistance from developed to developing countries, which had emerged in the late 1950s.[75] During the Conference, one UN official identified this move, which was encouraged by the French delegation, as a "bombshell."[76] In keeping with the Middle Zone policy, the Australian delegation spoke against this proposal at the Conference.[77] The success in the field of foreign aid was a surprise to many involved in the conference, including Raul Prebisch.[78] Yet in many ways this made perfect sense, as aid had been the dominant means by which international development had been promoted since the end of the Second World War. Whereas international trade was a site of competition between countries, financial and technical assistance was generally perceived as a unifying process. For Australia, while the Middle Zone was established as a means of protecting export industries, it also achieved its principal success in the field of economic assistance. Indeed, the only formal recognition of the Middle Zone at UNCTAD was in regard to the one per cent target.

The recognition of the Middle Zone was found in the section of the Final Act that dealt with the provision of one per cent of GNP in economic assistance:

[75] Organisation for Economic Co-operation and Development, *Development Co-operation Report 1999: Efforts and Policies of the Members of the Development Assistance Committee* (Paris: Organisation for Economic Co-operation and Development, 2000), 45–46.

[76] Ismat Kattani to Philippe de Seynes, May 15, 1964, in file United Nations Conference on Trade and Development—institutional arrangements, in series Economic and Social Affairs—subject files, Office of the Chef de Cabinet fonds, S-0288-0021-05, UNA.

[77] "Main issues arising during week ended May 15," attached to G.P. Phillips to W.A. Westerman, May 22, 1964, NAA: A1313, 1964/2388.

[78] Raul Prebisch notes, attached to Raul Prebisch to C.V. Narasimhan, June 29, 1964, in file Conference on Trade and Development (UNCTAD), in series Commissions, Committees, and Conferences, Secretary-General U Thant fonds, S-0858-0003-01, UNA.

> Each economically advanced country should endeavour to supply, in light of the principles of Annex A.IV.1, financial resources to the developing countries of a minimum net amount approaching as nearly as possible to 1 per cent of its national income, *having regard, however, to the special position of certain countries which are net importers of capital.*[79]

This was a limited success for McEwen and his department, as it signified international recognition of one of the points that the Australian delegation argued placed Australia outside of the developed bloc.[80] Indeed, this clause fitted with the long-term claims of some Australian policymakers, particularly those in the Treasury, that Australian aid expenditure should be limited by the fact that it called upon resources that were required for national development. The 'success' of the Middle Zone position on aid provided impetus for some of the criticism by academic observers such as Heinz Arndt. He was particularly critical of the Government's link between Australia's status as a capital importing country and its inability to provide foreign aid. He expressed his view that this argument was "like saying that you cannot really afford to give money to your church because you are still paying off a mortgage on your house."[81] This analysis corresponded with the work of other academic observers, such as Anthony Clunies Ross and Ian Shannon, who felt that the Australian position as an importer of capital was not an impediment to reaching the one per cent of GNP aid target.[82] These analyses point to the ways that economic experts conceived of Australia as a rich, developed country, perfectly capable of providing greater amounts of foreign aid. This perspective guided much of the criticism of the Middle Zone as a self-interested attempt to protect Australian interests at the expense of poor, developing countries.

Apart from the one per cent concession, the Middle Zone approach largely went ignored at UNCTAD. Australian delegation head, Allen Fleming, reported back to Trade and Industry that he was still trying to secure recognition of the Middle Zone in May, almost two months after

[79] *UNCTAD Proceedings*, vol. 1, 44 [Emphasis added].

[80] McEwen, Draft Cabinet Submission, "United Nations Conference on Trade and Development," n.d. [Most likely written at the end of February, 1964], NAA: A1313, 1964/2380 PART 1.

[81] Arndt, "Australia—Developed, Developing or Midway?" 324.

[82] Clunies Ross, *One Per Cent*, 42; Ian Shannon, "Economic Aid," *Australian Outlook* 17, no. 3 (1963): 336.

meetings had begun.[83] As the Conference progressed, the prospects for the Middle Zone became increasingly bleak. Fleming noted that there was "some suspicion about Australian 'middle zone' position especially where no element of sacrifice is detected."[84] In this case, the self-interested aspects of the Middle Zone meant that other delegates at UNCTAD were unable to see the developmental claims being made by the Australian delegation. Australian officials did the Middle Zone no favours at UNCTAD, as they frequently voted with the Western group of 'developed' countries on recommendations, which alienated the 'developing' bloc.[85] The combination of lack of interest verging on suspicion on the part of other delegations with Australia's tactical inconsistency meant that the Middle Zone had little chance of success.

Despite the Middle Zone's evident failure, Fleming maintained its rhetoric throughout the entire conference. At the final plenary session, he expressed his criticism of the divide between developed and developing countries. In the context of expressing disappointment on behalf of countries reliant on the export of the primary commodities, he observed: "The tenor of most resolutions before us is to divide all countries into only two categories – developed and developing and not to recognise stages of development between these two extremes."[86] Similar complaints were made by the New Zealand and South African delegations. The New Zealanders lamented: "Just as there are differences in the needs of various countries for special protection and assistance, so also are there differences in the capacities of various countries to extend such protection and assistance."[87] Minor acknowledgements of the status of primary commodity exporting and capital importing countries were not enough to overcome the perception of these rich countries as being formally classified as developed.

[83] A.P. Fleming, "Main Issues Arising During Week ending May 9, 1964," NAA: A1313, 1964/2388.

[84] A.P. Fleming, "Main Issues Arising During Week ended May 23, 1964," NAA: A1313, 1964/2388.

[85] A.P. Fleming, "Main Issues Arising During Week ending 24 April, 1964," NAA: A1313, 1964/2388.

[86] Speech by A.P. Fleming to Final Plenary Session of UNCTAD, June 10, 1964, NAA: A1313, 1964/2380 PART 1.

[87] *UNCTAD Proceedings*, 77. The South African delegation made similar arguments, but their position was severely undermined by criticism of the *Apartheid* system.

Perhaps the clearest indication of Australia's inability to draw itself away from the rich, developed countries can be seen in the allocation of voting groups at UNCTAD. Four groups were established at the end of the Conference, divided by developmental stages and geographical areas. Group A contained the Afro-Asian developing countries; Group B the developed Western group, containing countries in Western Europe, the United States and the 'older' countries of the Commonwealth, such as Australia and New Zealand; Group C comprised the developing countries of Latin America and the Caribbean; and Group D was made up of the socialist countries of Eastern Europe and the USSR, who were considered to be developed.[88] This grouping reflected the division of the world into developing and developed camps and also served as a statement that Australia's status was as a rich, industrialised, developed country. In the Trade and Industry policy paper, one of the primary considerations for the Australian delegation was to avoid being too closely identified with either bloc:

> As a result of our conscious decision not to align ourselves fully with the developing countries, there is a need to counterbalance the effect of such action by an increased attention to the need not to appear to be placing ourselves in the 'developeds' camp.[89]

The incorporation of Australia into the same political group as the United States and other white, rich countries revealed that while Australia had gone some way towards distancing itself from the developed countries in economic terms, it was still perceived as such in political terms.

UNCTAD and PNG

The previous chapter showed that by the early 1960s there was increasing interaction between the two theatres of Australian aid policy, South and Southeast Asia and PNG. While this became more pronounced following the Inter-departmental Aid Review of late 1964–early 1965, Australian planning for UNCTAD also drew PNG more clearly into discussions

[88] Williams, *Third World Cooperation*, 61.

[89] Department of Trade and Industry, "UNCTAD—'Middle Zone' Position."

about aid and international development. Unfortunately for those interested in the promotion of development in PNG, the Middle Zone approach at UNCTAD did not result in strong Australian advocacy for PNG's interests. In their planning before the Conference, Territories Department and Administration officials in Port Moresby identified three principal objectives for PNG. They were:

> (a) looking for concessions to meet the special position of Papua and New Guinea among developing countries, (b) protecting both the favourable position for marketing Papua and New Guinea products in Australia and increasing Australian assistance for Papua and New Guinea, and (c) seeking special provisions for late developing countries such as Papua and New Guinea in any international commodity agreements.[90]

These goals did not quite mesh with the Trade and Industry position that sought to protect Australian trade interests. As the difficulties of the Australian delegation at UNCTAD demonstrated, looking for concessions for one country was difficult enough. Trying to secure concessions for both PNG and Australia was exceedingly difficult. In this case, the political importance of securing Australian trade interests took priority over achieving concessions for PNG.

Despite these complications, Trade and Industry did still engage with the development of PNG in their planning for UNCTAD. They identified four points on "accelerated development as an urgent need": the recent emergence of a cash crop economy; the incomplete reconstruction from wartime damage; the reliance on tropical products; and balancing advances in the "educational, medical, social and political" fields with broader economic progress.[91] Implicit in this analysis was a growing sense that PNG was to be treated as an independent developing country, rather than as a dependent colony. This was hinted at further in the strategic planning for UNCTAD, where Trade and Industry officials commented:

[90] C.R. Lambert to D.M. Cleland, n.d. [Early 1964], NAA: A452, 1964/2692.

[91] "Special Position of Papua and New Guinea," annexed to Department of Trade and Industry, "UNCTAD—'Middle Zone' Position," January 22, 1964, NAA: A1313, 1964/2380 PART 1.

> Care must be taken, however, that the interests of the bigger and older developing countries, do not submerge the interests of smaller developing countries just beginning to emerge to a cash economy, which have a long way to go even to reach an initial stage of development.[92]

Trade and Industry sought to maintain the 'special' status of PNG by keeping, or even extending trade concessions received by the territory.[93] Through the observation that PNG had yet to reach even "an initial stage of development", Trade and Industry officials engaged with the Australian perception of its colony as particularly 'primitive.' Further, we can see that PNG was to be considered a "smaller developing country." This suggestion, which sidestepped PNG's dependent status, would become a key feature in the increasing consideration that Australian assistance to PNG constituted 'overseas' aid. The pervasiveness of these ideas became increasingly influential on Australian aid policy in the mid-1960s.

Aware of the fact that Trade and Industry were trying to incorporate PNG into the Middle Zone, Lambert and his Territories officials expressed a sense of hope for PNG at UNCTAD. This made sense given the intellectual and political atmosphere of the Conference. Lambert observed that PNG stood to gain from increased developing country access to export markets, but was wary of accepting all of the developing bloc claims, as he felt that cheaper labour in these countries would intensify competition in tropical products. Lambert therefore advocated a tentative position, suggesting that "in short, we should, while exhibiting a spirit of friendly co-operation on some of the important common problems *not* tie ourselves too much in advance of the main conference."[94] Territories official, E.J. Wood, further demonstrated this compromise position in comments to Cleland, where he explained:

> The Administration of Papua and New Guinea tends to advocate a dynamic approach by Australia specifically to help LDC's generally. This seems at least partly to overlook the considerable benefit derived by the territory from concessional markets in Australia, particularly for rubber and coffee.[95]

[92] "Special Position of Papua and New Guinea."

[93] "Special Position of Papua and New Guinea."

[94] C.R. Lambert to D.M. Cleland, October 25, 1963, NAA: A452, 1963/7763 [Emphasis in original].

[95] E.J. Wood to D.M. Cleland, January 29, 1964, NAA: A452, 1963/7763.

This quote points to the contradictions that the Australian delegation had to grapple with at UNCTAD. Fleming was under pressure to secure special concessions for PNG, while also demonstrating solidarity with the rest of the developing bloc, whose trade would suffer from PNG being given preferential treatment. With the Middle Zone presenting a significant challenge of its own at UNCTAD, advocating the development of PNG simply added another level of negotiations for the Australian delegation. Given the layers of often-contradictory objectives, it is little surprise that the Australian delegation did not manage to either secure the recognition of the Middle Zone or argue forcefully for PNG's 'special' position.

The Conference's pledge that one per cent of GNP should be dedicated to each country's foreign aid would have meant increased economic assistance for PNG had Australia accepted it. As the next chapter will show, Australian officials were very keen to include Australian spending to PNG in order to demonstrate Australia's generosity in the provision of aid. However, by managing to avoid the one per cent obligation, Australia undermined its own claim that it provided significant amounts of aid. Ironically, McEwen presented Australia's responsibility for PNG as an impediment to making concessions. Speaking in Parliament almost a year after the conclusion of UNCTAD, he drew PNG into his justification for Australia's peculiar position:

> Our own development needs and policies, and our responsibilities for the development of Papua and New Guinea, set limits on our ability to help the less-developed countries in the particular ways they were seeking and which might well be the most appropriate ways for the mature industrial countries to contribute.[96]

From the mid-1960s, the Australian Government tried to have its cake and eat it too. It frequently presented its assistance to PNG as a sign of its high level of aid spending, yet also presented PNG as the key impediment to increased aid elsewhere. Despite the Australian delegation's half-hearted advocacy for PNG at UNCTAD, the promotion of colonial development persisted as a significant feature of Australian aid policy. In their planning for UNCTAD, Australian policymakers reached an understanding of Australian aid policy that would persist throughout the final decade of the age of international development.

[96] *CPD*, House of Representatives, no. 20, 1965, May 19, 1965, 1633.

The Middle Zone: Doomed to Fail?

Following UNCTAD, the weaknesses of the Middle Zone were examined in a variety of Australian contexts. The *Australian Financial Review* commented that the Middle Zone was "far from being accepted", while the *Sydney Morning Herald* expressed criticism of McEwen's conception of Australia as a developing country, explaining that "it is playing with words to apply it to Australia in some contexts, and this is one of them."[97] This commentary on the Middle Zone took the same view as Peter Samuel that in the international setting developing countries were equivalent to the poor countries of the world, and that for Australia to claim this status was "deceitful."[98] Academic observers also commented on the limitations of the Australian approach. Arndt stated that "while one must of course grant some latitude in the choice of arguments to official negotiators engaged in tough trade bargaining, it does little good to Australia's international standing to have her case associated with untenable and hypocritical propositions."[99] John Crawford, who had spent many years working closely with McEwen, was less hostile towards the policy, but still acknowledged that "words like 'midway' or 'middle zone' do not properly describe the Australian position."[100] The final word is perhaps best expressed by McEwen himself, who reflected on the fact that "we were never able to shake off the image of a rich country that was able to look after itself."[101] In the face of the overwhelming evidence that Australia was a rich country, it was unsurprising that the Middle Zone approach was not given the international acceptance that McEwen sought.

The failure of the Middle Zone was a result of the inherent contradictions within Australia's attempt to present the case that it was neither 'developed' nor 'developing.' Perhaps the key weakness in the Middle Zone was that it revolved around arguments of what Australia *was not* rather than what it was. Driven by McEwen's self-interested attempt to protect Australian export industries and to distance Australia from the

[97] *Australian Financial Review*, February 2, 1965; *Sydney Morning Herald*, February 10, 1965.

[98] Samuel, "The Midway Doctrine: An Exercise in Deceit."

[99] Arndt, "Australia—Developed, Developing or Midway?" 321.

[100] John Crawford, *Australian Trade Policy 1942–1966: A Documentary History* (Canberra: Australian National University Press, 1968), 609.

[101] McEwen, "John McEwen: His Story," 61.

concessions expected of developed countries, the Middle Zone was a product of Australian policymakers' close engagement with the country's developmental status. As the nature of Australia's development was interrogated on a global stage, the contradictions in the Middle Zone policy became evident. Nevertheless, while the Middle Zone policy failed to achieve international recognition, the lack of results does not take away from its broader significance, the attempt to challenge the stark division between developed and developing countries. It was also a vital moment where the intellectual and political underpinnings of Australian engagement with development intersected.

The position of PNG within Australian planning for UNCTAD highlighted and exacerbated the numerous complexities within Australia's conception of development in the mid-1960s. The ambiguity in Australia's public handling of PNG as at times a separate entity, while at other times an important Australian responsibility, reflected broader issues surrounding the inclusion of PNG within foreign aid calculations. Generally, the status of PNG as a foreign country was only promoted when it served Australian claims of generosity or when dealing with newly independent countries. This was further compounded by the fact that Australia's advocacy for PNG was due to the colonial relationship between the two, which drew the political ire of a number of new postcolonial countries. For instance, recommendation XIV of UNCTAD stated: "Complete decolonization ... and the liquidation of the remnants of colonialism in all its forms is a necessary condition for economic development and the exercise of sovereign rights over natural resources."[102] This went against the dominant Australian notion that economic development was a prerequisite for self-government, which had exerted such power during the Hasluck era in PNG. These factors demonstrate the complex intersection of factors at the heart of Australian developmental policy for PNG. On a more immediate level, they undermined the strength of the Middle Zone at UNCTAD.

Finally, the Middle Zone was undermined by a lack of agreement amongst policymaking officials over the connection between the idea of development and development policy. While there was agreement that Australia had a role to play in assisting the developing countries of the

[102] United Nations Office of Public Information, "UNCTAD," July 1964, in file Conference on Trade and Development (UNCTAD), in series Commissions, Committees, and Conferences, Secretary-General U Thant fonds, S-0858-0003-01, UNA.

world, the means of providing this assistance attracted debate. Trade and Industry officials, in conjunction with their counterparts in Treasury, held a vision of international development that put Australian growth first. As such, these departments tended towards the vision of Australia as 'developing.' Opposing this view were External Affairs and Territories, whose policies were generally aimed at promoting development overseas. Officials in these departments also engaged most closely with international developmental theories that called for large transfers of capital and expertise from developed to developing countries. This belief, combined with their greater exposure to developing societies through the provision of developmental assistance, convinced them that Australia belonged firmly in the developed camp. In many ways, this recognition was confirmed by 1971, when Australia joined the Organisation for Economic Co-operation and Development (OECD).[103] The policy decision to join the 'rich countries club' demonstrated the ultimate decline of the Middle Zone idea in Australia. While these political differences undermined the coherence of the Australian approach to the age of international development, they did not dampen the interest of policymakers in the ways that development could inform policy. In fact, these debates continued into the mid-1960s, with their clearest expression being found in the 1964–1965 Inter-departmental Review of Australian Aid Policy.

[103] Australia joined the Development Assistance Committee (DAC) of the OECD in 1966.

CHAPTER 6

"We Should Be Doing More Than We Are": The Colombo Plan, Papua New Guinea and the Australian External Aid Review, 1957–1965

In September 1964, the Minister for External Affairs, Paul Hasluck, wrote to Prime Minister Sir Robert Menzies giving his thoughts on the current state of Australian foreign aid policy. Hasluck had moved from the portfolio of Territories to External Affairs, via a brief four-month stint in the Defence portfolio. In making this move, Hasluck took over the second theatre of Australian aid, the Colombo Plan. Throughout the second half of the 1950s and first half of the 1960s, the Plan continued to operate broadly under the same objectives that guided its creation in 1950. During this period, however, a number of competing attitudes towards Australian developmental assistance had emerged within the Commonwealth bureaucracy. After lamenting the ad hoc nature of Australian aid spending, Hasluck commented:

> My own immediate difficulty arises from the fact that when I turned my attention to the question whether or not our contribution in foreign aid was adequate – and my own disposition is to suggest that we should be doing more than we are – I found that I would be unwilling to make any definite recommendations to Cabinet because, at this stage, I could

N. Ferns, *Australia in the Age of International Development, 1945–1975*, Security, Conflict and Cooperation in the Contemporary World, https://doi.org/10.1007/978-3-030-50228-7_6

> not feel any certainty that the additional contribution to be recommended would be the best one to make in Australian interests.[1]

From the enthusiasm surrounding the establishment of the Colombo Plan in the early 1950s, by the 1960s Australian aid had become inefficient and was a target for criticism both within and outside government circles. Hasluck indicated a personal preference for increasing Australian aid spending, but was troubled by the unfocused nature of aid policy. His letter spurred the establishment of the Inter-Departmental Committee to Review Australian External Aid, which marked the first comprehensive effort to revise Australian aid policy since 1950.

This chapter provides the first in-depth historical analysis of the 1964–1965 Australian foreign aid policy review. The review offered yet another demonstration that Australian aid policy transcended questions of national interest and engagement with Asia. The inter-departmental debates that were a feature of the policy review were rooted in the divergent developmental approaches that had emerged in the two decades following the Second World War. The External Affairs position was marked by a belief in both the developmental and political arguments for increased aid spending; Treasury and the Trade and Industry department sought to ensure that overseas developmental assistance was in harmony with Australian economic growth; and Territories argued that the trusteeship system put Australian aid to PNG in a category of its own. At the heart of the aid review was an ideological debate over the nature of Australian engagement with international development.

The decision to initiate the review can be attributed to a series of causes, ranging from the perceived stagnation of the Colombo Plan to the international shifts in the field of developmental ideas and practice of the mid-1960s. It was also connected to the ongoing growth of the PNG grant, which totalled over £65 million by 1964–1965.[2] The aid review's most significant result was to bring the different developmental positions within the Commonwealth bureaucracy to light. Prior to 1964, competing departmental attitudes were expressed at key moments in policy formation, such as in the creation of the Colombo Plan or in

[1] P.M.C. Hasluck to R.G. Menzies, September 17, 1964, NAA: A1838, 2020/1/24 PART 3.

[2] *Official Year Book of the Commonwealth of Australia* (Canberra: Commonwealth Bureau of Census and Statistics, 1966), 1117, 1124.

the planning for UNCTAD. Differences between External Affairs, Treasury and Territories were tacitly acknowledged in departmental planning, but there was no opportunity for the debates to be brought into the open. The 1964–1965 aid review provided this opportunity, enabling policymakers to share their understandings of the development process. While this led to little immediate policy change, it created an environment whereby Australian aid would have a more rigorous intellectual basis. The full results of these debates would emerge in the decade following the review.

The Australian aid policy review fits into a broader international pattern of developmental policy shifts in the early to mid-1960s. The arrival of the Kennedy Administration in the United States, which was closely linked to modernisation theorists such as Walt Rostow, saw the introduction of numerous aid initiatives, including the Peace Corps and the Strategic Hamlet program in South Vietnam.[3] Yet, as David Ekbladh has shown, by the mid-1960s American policies guided by modernisation theory were coming under increased scrutiny.[4] Bradley Simpson argues that the 1963 Clay Committee into American overseas assistance challenged many of the dominant assumptions that guided earlier aid programs, such as Point Four.[5] Similar shifts were taking place in the United Kingdom, as the independence of former British colonies instigated a re-examination of British aid policy. Gordon Cumming has shown that increasing perceptions of inefficiency within British aid resulted in the establishment of the Overseas Development Ministry in 1964.[6] Other scholars of British aid, such as Jim Tomlinson, show that the reforms of the mid-1960s marked a shift away from the earlier provision of colonial development.[7]

[3] Latham, *Modernization as Ideology*.

[4] Ekbladh, *The Great American Mission*, 221.

[5] Simpson, *Economists with Guns*, 95–96.

[6] Gordon Cumming, *Aid to Africa: French and British Policies from the Cold War to the New Millennium* (Aldershot: Ashgate, 2001), 71–72; D.J. Morgan, *Changes in British Aid Policy, 1951–1970* (London: Macmillan, 1980), 20–30.

[7] Jim Tomlinson, "The Commonwealth, the Balance of Payments and the Politics of International Poverty: British Aid Policy, 1958–1971," *Contemporary European History* 12, no. 4 (2003): 423; Hodge, *Triumph of the Expert*, 20; Joseph M. Hodge, Gerard Hodl, and Martina Kopf, eds., *Developing Africa: Concepts and Practices in Twentieth-Century Colonialism* (Manchester, MA: Manchester University Press, 2014).

The Australian aid review fits within this broader process, as international demands for a reconsideration of aid policy made an impact in Australia.

Australian scholarship on foreign aid pays scant attention to the 1964–1965 aid review. Jack Corbett briefly mentions the review in the context of discussing Australia's involvement in the First Development Decade.[8] Daniel Oakman touches on the review in his study of the Colombo Plan, arguing that it was evidence of continuing Australian interest in the "Western effort to resist regional aggression and subversion."[9] For Oakman, this External Affairs argument had not changed since the establishment of the Colombo Plan in 1950, thereby demonstrating the consistency in the Department's attitude towards international development. In contrast to Oakman's emphasis on the link between the Colombo Plan, the Cold War and Asian engagement, this chapter will examine the developmental arguments that were made throughout the aid review. It will demonstrate that Australian aid policy continued to be underpinned by a desire to promote development for its own sake, in keeping with international theoretical and policy norms, and not merely for strategic interests. While Commonwealth departments disagreed over the best way to encourage development in the poorer regions to Australia's north, their commitment to development in its broad terms continued to be strong. By examining the aid review in this light, it emerges as a pivotal moment in Australia's participation in the age of international development.

Stagnant Aid Policy

As was discussed at the end of Chapter 3, Australian officials were coming to terms with the challenges in providing economic assistance to Asian countries by the late 1950s. One of the consequences of these perceived difficulties was to increase the emphasis on technical assistance in the Colombo Plan. David Hay, at this stage Assistant Secretary in the Department of External Affairs (he would go on to become the Administrator of PNG in the late 1960s[10]), gave voice to this shift in a memorandum to External Affairs Minister, Richard Casey. Commenting

[8] Corbett, *Australia's Foreign Aid Dilemma*, 20.

[9] Oakman, *Facing Asia*, 250.

[10] John Farquharson, "Hay, Sir David Osborne (1916–2009)," Obituaries Australia, National Centre of Biography, Australian National University, http://oa.anu.edu.au/obituary/hay-sir-david-osborne-474/text475.

on the technical assistance component of the Colombo Plan, Hay wrote: "Training is probably our most valuable Colombo Plan exercise ... [I]t may be possible to increase our training intake in all fields to something between 800 and 1,000 at any one time costing between £800,000 and £1,000,000 per year."[11] As the cheaper and supposedly more successful component of the Colombo Plan, there was logic to External Affairs' turn to technical assistance. In spite of this shift, economic assistance continued to receive the vast majority of Colombo Plan funding. Australian Colombo Plan spending to the end of 1963 had totalled almost £50 million. Of this figure, almost £37 million had been spent on economic assistance, compared to less than £13 million on training and experts.[12] Despite External Affairs' emphasis on the effectiveness of scholarships and experts through the Plan, the pattern of Australian aid spending had consistently been dominated by the economic assistance component. This demonstrated a level of continuity in Australian aid spending.

By the 1960s, the Foreign Aid Branch had evolved into the Economic and Technical Assistance (ETA) Branch within External Affairs. In 1960, it was a small office, with eighteen staff working under G.N. Upton. Upton had risen from being a diplomatic cadet and would later serve as High Commissioner in Sri Lanka and India. While the branch possessed some discretion with regard to training matters, much of its activity required Ministerial approval.[13] The heavy administrative duties associated with directing existing projects made it difficult for the ETA Branch to come up with new approaches to developmental policy, thereby contributing to the sense of stagnation in the Colombo Plan. This lack of momentum can be seen in the 1961 progress report of Australia's involvement in the Plan, which indicated recognition of the "urgent need for more rapid development and for efforts to be directed towards that end."[14] This language, which is almost identical to that used at the time of the creation of the Colombo Plan in 1950, suggests that while

[11] D.O. Hay to R.G. Casey, January 31, 1958, NAA: A1838, 2020/1/2 PART 1.

[12] Department of External Affairs, "Australia in the Colombo Plan—Progress Report to December 31, 1963," NAA: A1838, 2020/1/2 PART 4.

[13] C.T. Moodie to J.G. Gorton, March 30, 1960, NAA: A1838, 2020/1/2 PART 3.

[14] Department of External Affairs, "Australia's Part in the Colombo Plan—Progress Report to December 31, 1961," NAA: 2020/1/12 PART 3.

foreign aid programs were bringing developmental issues to international attention, solving them was another matter altogether.

In the late 1950s, the Department of External Affairs, at Casey's urging, enlisted the services of Osmar White, a prominent writer and journalist for the *Herald and Weekly Times*, to travel through recipient countries in an effort to promote the work of the Colombo Plan. Travelling through Asia in 1959, White returned to Australia with stories of waste and inefficiency, which presented a challenge to External Affairs officials who had sought to use the trip for publicity purposes.[15] Eventually, a toned down version of White's observations was published in 1960, but there remained a lingering sense in the department that the Colombo Plan was not being run as effectively as possible. In a memorandum written by Upton, it was remarked that "Osmar White's writings ... toned down as they were, have left an aftermath of public doubt about the value of many Colombo Plan activities."[16] Upton acknowledged many of White's criticisms, which mainly focused on poor Australian supervision of local projects, with the resulting waste of resources undermining the developmental effectiveness of Colombo Plan aid. While Upton did not agree with all of White's criticisms, he admitted that:

> For our part we have learned some lessons from the Osmar White exercise, the most valuable being to reinforce our views on the desirability of close expert supervision of projects and of not undertaking projects unless we are satisfied the local governments can make use of aid provided.[17]

Following White's criticisms, there was increasing acceptance within External Affairs that policy changes were needed.

Exacerbating this situation, the administration of the Colombo Plan was coming under increased academic scrutiny. In a 1962 speech to the Royal Institute of Public Administration, prominent Australian economist, Dr. P.W.E. 'Pike' Curtin, argued that poor administration was diminishing the Colombo Plan's popularity throughout Asia. He thought that the small amount of Australia's Colombo Plan contribution (0.09

[15] Lowe and Oakman have examined White's trip in substantial detail, see Oakman, *Facing Asia*, 154–168; Lowe, "Journalists and the Stirring of Australian Public Diplomacy," 185.

[16] G.N. Upton to A.J. Eastman, April 20, 1960, NAA: A1838, 2020/1/2 PART 3.

[17] G.N. Upton to A.J. Eastman, April 20, 1960.

per cent of Australia's GNP) was regarded as a kind of 'charity' offering, which caused resentment amongst Asian countries.[18] These figures posed a problem for policymakers, particularly given the increasing volume of Australian and international calls for aid to be targeted at one per cent of GNP.[19] The *Canberra Times* report on the speech emphasised Curtin's comparison between American and Australian aid programs in Asia. According to Curtin: "The American plan was organised in such an efficient and professional way that it sometimes made the loosely-framed Colombo Plan look amateurish."[20] The way to overcome this issue, Curtin suggested, was to incorporate Colombo Plan aid into larger international aid programs. This proposal was in keeping with the External Affairs vision of Australia's role in the international development system, which would attract debate during the aid review.

Australian assistance to PNG was also coming under increased international scrutiny in the first half of the 1960s. A visit by UN Trusteeship Council observers, led by former British colonial administrator, diplomat and future peer, Sir Hugh Foot, demonstrated increasing international interest in the development of PNG. In discussions with officials from Territories and External Affairs, Foot reported that the Australian administration of PNG lacked direction, and it was "urgently necessary for Australia to decide what it was doing in New Guinea."[21] The UN visit led to suggestions of an International Bank for Reconstruction and Development (IBRD) mission to propose detailed plans for the development of PNG, which took place in 1965. In the planning for the IBRD's visit, Australian officials discussed UN recommendations that "unless the tempo of economic development is increased the rate of progress will fall far short of future needs. More opportunity for more people is the

[18] *The Canberra Times*, May 25, 1962. A clipping of this article can be found in NAA: A1838, 2020/1/2 PART 3.

[19] Oakman, *Facing Asia*, 253–254. Douglas Copland also called for the West to provide one per cent of its GNP as foreign aid, Copland, *The Changing Structure of the Western Economy*, 55.

[20] *The Canberra Times*, May 25, 1962.

[21] Minutes of Discussion with Sir Hugh Foot, involving Territories and External Affairs staff, March 30, 1962, NAA: A1838, 909/8/1/5.

fundamental and urgent need."[22] This international critique of Australian policy in PNG exacerbated the increasing sense that Australian aid policy was in need of review.

Paul Hasluck and the Australian External Aid Policy Review

Paul Hasluck's previous role as Minister for Territories is vital to understanding his involvement in the foreign aid review. His work in promoting development in PNG demonstrated his engagement with developmental theory and practice throughout the 1950s and early 1960s. This experience informed his attitude towards foreign aid as Minister for External Affairs, a position he assumed in April 1964. In *A Time for Building*, Hasluck wrote that his experience as Minister for Territories "helped me to increase the effectiveness of our Colombo Plan aid in Asia and our civil aid during the war in Vietnam."[23] Hasluck's experience with policy in both PNG and Southeast Asia provided the continuity between colonialism and development that existed in other international contexts.[24] Hasluck's active ministerial style was vital to the instigation of the Australian External Aid Policy Review. More significantly, similarities in the issues he confronted as Minister for Territories and Minister for External Affairs encouraged his belief that Australian policy in PNG and Southeast Asia should be more closely associated with one another.

The decision to conduct a review of Australian aid policy can be traced to the September 17, 1964, letter from Hasluck to Menzies quoted at the beginning of this chapter. Hasluck called for an investigation into the purposes of Australian external aid, looking for any "duplication, overlapping or ineffectiveness", along with a re-evaluation of the distribution

[22] Territories Department, "Proposed Economic Survey of Papua and New Guinea by the International Bank for Reconstruction and Development," September 7, 1962, NAA: A452, 1961/928.

[23] Hasluck, *A Time for Building*, 109.

[24] Joseph M. Hodge and Gerard Hodl, "Introduction," in *Developing Africa: Concepts and Practices in Twentieth-Century Colonialism*, ed. Joseph M. Hodge, Gerard Hodl, and Martina Kopf (Manchester, MA: Manchester University Press, 2014), 21; Frey, "Control, Legitimacy, and the Securing of Interests"; Dimier, *The Invention of a European Development Aid Bureaucracy*.

of foreign aid expenditure.[25] In a rare moment of active involvement in aid policy, Prime Minister Menzies set the review into action almost two months later. He sent a letter to Acting External Affairs Minister John Gorton, accepting many of Hasluck's points. The Prime Minister set out the terms of reference for the review, explaining that "the philosophy and practice of Australia's foreign aid might be put to study and a report prepared including recommendations about the pattern and administration of aid programmes in future, which could then be considered in Cabinet."[26]

In order for Cabinet to be adequately briefed for such an examination, Hasluck argued the necessity of establishing an inter-departmental committee, headed by Arthur Tange, the Secretary of the Department of External Affairs. In addition to External Affairs, representatives of the Treasury and Prime Minister's Department were involved in all parts of the review. Given the wide range of Commonwealth departments interested in Australian aid policy, representatives from Defence, Trade and Industry and Territories attended occasional meetings.[27] The involvement of the Territories Department reflected the increasing acknowledgement that Australia's grant to PNG should be considered as a form of external aid.[28] This was in keeping with the recommendations of economists such as Clunies Ross and Downing.[29] The involvement of a diverse range of departments pointed to the disparate nature of Australian foreign aid policy, which was identified as an impediment to effective aid spending.[30]

[25] P.M.C. Hasluck to R.G. Menzies, September 17, 1964, NAA: A1838, 2020/1/24 PART 3.

[26] R.G. Menzies to J.G. Gorton, November 3, 1964, NAA: A1838, 2020 /1/24 PART 3.

[27] The number of departments involved in aid spending is highlighted in A.H. Tange, "Australian External Aid Policy," December 22, 1964, NAA: A1838, 2020 /1/24 PART 2.

[28] Record of Fourth Meeting of Committee to Review Australian Aid, December 18, 1964, NAA: A1838, 2020/1/24 PART 2.

[29] Clunies Ross, *One Per Cent*, 12.

[30] "Australian External Aid," Report to the Minister for External Affairs by the Inter-Departmental Committee to Review Australian External Aid, March 25, 1965, 109, NAA: A4311, 147/1.

The aid review took place at a time when international ideas of development were entering a state of flux. As previously noted, Australia's developmental policy in PNG acquired a sense of urgency in the first half of the 1960s, spurred on by the visits of experts from both the UN and the IBRD. Also, several months prior to the establishment of the inter-departmental committee Australia put forward its Middle Zone policy at UNCTAD. These key moments, in conjunction with a number of other shifts in both theory and policy, served to make 1964 and 1965 pivotal years in Australia's interaction with international development. The aid review brought many of the key institutions and ideas together in one place, producing an explicit engagement with the different developmental attitudes within the Commonwealth bureaucracy. In satisfying Hasluck's goal of defining "the purposes of external aid in relation to our general external policies", the aid review set the scene for a close examination of exactly how development fitted into Australian aid policy.[31]

The work of the inter-departmental committee lasted roughly four months, which indicates just how comprehensive the review was. Australian diplomatic missions around the world submitted observations on Australian aid, and all interested Commonwealth departments contributed to the aid review. Given the breadth of its terms of reference and the diverse range of opinions, the report was produced a month behind schedule, ultimately being completed on March 25, 1965. The report of the inter-departmental committee was then incorporated into a Cabinet Submission written by the External Affairs Department and submitted to Cabinet in May 1965. PNG was included in Australian aid considerations. The introductory section of the submission explained that "Australian expenditure in Papua and New Guinea is presented internationally as part of Australia's aid effort and was thus included in the Committee's report."[32] As we have already seen, the developmental basis of Australian assistance to PNG and the Colombo Plan justified the inclusion of PNG. This also reflected the political argument that including PNG in aid totals supported Australia's claim that it was a generous aid donor. Cabinet endorsed the findings of the aid review in June, taking

[31] P.M.C. Hasluck to R.G. Menzies, September 17, 1964, NAA: A1838, 2020/1/24 PART 3.

[32] Department of External Affairs draft Cabinet submission, "Australian External Aid," May 3, 1965, NAA: A1838, 2020/1/24 PART 3.

particular note of the potential for Australian involvement in an Asian Development Bank, as well as the unique position of Australian assistance to PNG.[33] The report was expected to guide Australian aid spending for at least the rest of the 1960s.

Inter-Departmental Debates

Three key debates took place during the aid review: the degree to which aid should be incorporated into a broader international effort; the integration of Australian assistance to PNG; and the competition for resources between Australian and international development. These debates had existed since the establishment of Australian aid following the Second World War, but the aid review brought them out into the open. Whereas the first two decades of the age of international development were marked by tacit acknowledgement of the different developmental ideas in Canberra, the debates of December 1964 and January 1965 forced each of the departments to consider their understanding of development. The debates revealed that there was a diverse set of attitudes within the Commonwealth bureaucracy and brought out into the open the ideological divisions regarding Australian aid. Just as important, the debates provided policymakers with a more rigorous understanding of the different intellectual forces at work in Australian aid policy, which provided an impetus for reform following the conclusion of the review.

As the review committee got to work at the end of 1964, the ideological differences between the departments quickly became apparent. Hasluck and External Affairs emphasised the importance of a strong Australian commitment to international developmental programs for both political and developmental reasons, and as such sought an increase in Australia's financial support. On the other hand, officials from Treasury emphasised the limited contribution that Australia could make to the development of poorer countries and therefore urged a policy that prioritised Australian development. This was a strategy that Treasury had employed since the establishment of the Colombo Plan, and they would continue to do so following the review. Territories sought to maintain the autonomy of Australian assistance to PNG, due to the special requirements associated with the principles of trusteeship. Trade and

[33] Cabinet Minute, Decision No. 1002, "Australian External Aid," June 9, 1965, A1838, 2020/1/24 PART 3.

Industry were interested in international development to the extent that it promoted Australian trade opportunities. The Prime Minister's Department often played a mediating role, siding on different occasions with either External Affairs or Treasury.

The principal disagreement was between External Affairs and Treasury. In a memorandum to Assistant Secretary, Colin Moodie, Tange anticipated potential Treasury criticisms regarding the effectiveness of aid programs, writing, "It is tactically very important for External Affairs to demonstrate that we are capable of detecting ineffectiveness, etc."[34] Such comments demonstrate Tange's awareness of the difference in approach with Treasury, as well as the political rivalries within the Commonwealth bureaucracy, which Joan Beaumont has examined in detail.[35] More than this, however, Tange's defensive tone illustrates the threat posed by Treasury towards Australian aid funding. Tange was justified in his defensive stance, for Treasury officials sought to use the review as an opportunity to challenge the existing foreign aid policy framework.[36] As historian Greg Whitwell has shown, throughout the 1950s and early 1960s Treasury was concerned with keeping Commonwealth spending within firm (and Treasury-defined) limits.[37] Yet, despite their desire to limit Australian aid spending, Treasury supported the idea that Australia should appear to be a generous aid donor in international terms. Thus, while the developmental approaches differed, the debates within the aid review revealed the ongoing acceptance within the Commonwealth bureaucracy that Australia had a role to play in the age of international development.

[34] Memorandum, A.H. Tange to C.T. Moodie, December 9, 1964, NAA: A1838, 2020/1/24 PART 2.

[35] Joan Beaumont, "Making Australian Foreign Policy, 1941–69," in *Ministers, Mandarins and Diplomats: Australian Foreign Policy Making, 1941–1969*, ed. Joan Beaumont, Christopher Waters, David Lowe, and Garry Woodard (Melbourne: Melbourne University Press, 2003), 18.

[36] A.H. Tange, "Australian External Aid Policy," December 22, 1964, NAA: A1838, 2020/1/24 PART 2.

[37] Whitwell, *The Treasury Line*, 122–123.

Australia's Place in the International Foreign Aid System

Since the establishment of the Colombo Plan in 1950, Australian foreign aid expenditure was strongly influenced by the policies of other major aid donors. Tange and his department sought to use the aid review to develop a clear sense of the place of Australian aid within the broader international developmental system. The External Affairs line can be seen in an early meeting of the inter-departmental committee. Responding to a query from a Prime Minister's Department official regarding Australian aid to India, Tange's response was noted:

> The Chairman [Tange] commented that Australian aid alone was unlikely to have any appreciable effect; but Australia's efforts should not be looked at in isolation from those of others: a doubling of our aid could stimulate an increase in other countries' aid and the combined effect on India's rate of growth could be significant.[38]

This argument revealed one of the developmental imperatives behind Australian aid. The Department of External Affairs admitted that Australian spending on aid was much lower than other donor countries (particularly the United States), but argued that Australian policy could exert some influence over international attempts to promote development.

This argument was a direct response to Treasury's opposition. M.W. O'Donnell, the Acting Secretary of the Treasury, expressed his scepticism of the External Affairs position. The minutes of the seventh committee meeting note that "Mr O'Donnell queried the implication in the first paragraph that Australian aid was economically effective if combined with that of others."[39] O'Donnell's view was demonstrative of the Treasury conception of international development. For Treasury officials, the relative insignificance of Australian aid meant that it had very little effect on economic growth in Southeast Asia. Instead, O'Donnell highlighted the political objectives of aid assistance, arguing that "the purpose of our

[38] Record of the Third Meeting of the Committee to Review Australian External Aid, December 11, 1964, NAA: A1838, 2020/1/24 PART 2.

[39] Record of the Seventh Meeting of the Committee to Review Australian External Aid, January 8, 1965, NAA: A1838, 2020/1/24 PART 2.

assistance to the countries of South and South East Asia is principally political."[40] If aid was used for political purposes, then it was enough to provide a token amount that demonstrated Australian goodwill. It also reflected a vision of aid that saw Australia outside of international debates on theory, implementation and effectiveness. Put together, this supported Treasury's viewpoint that aid spending should not be increased.

Ultimately, the Department of External Affairs managed to have their viewpoint presented in the final report. The final draft explained that "Australian international aid is only a small part of a wider Western, and in particular United States, effort, and generally its effectiveness has to be assessed in this context."[41] This underpinned aid policy for the next decade, as international forces drove major changes to Australian aid policy between 1965 and 1975, as examined in the next chapter. In the immediate context, the External Affairs victory ensured that Australian aid would be considered in relation to the programs of other countries, thereby making it more difficult for Treasury to argue that Australian aid had little developmental effect. In the light of this, the international developmental discourse becomes more relevant.

In the ferment of developmental ideas of the 1960s, modernisation theory continued to exert influence.[42] In one of the policy papers prepared for the inter-departmental committee, External Affairs officials placed their work in the explicit terms of Rostovian modernisation. According to the Department:

> The economic objective of international aid to developing countries is to assist in accelerating their development to a point where a satisfactory rate of growth can be achieved on a self-sustaining basis. No country can arrive at the 'take-off' point purely through foreign aid and domestic effort is vital to any economic development programme.[43]

[40] M.W. O'Donnell to A.H. Tange, January 4, 1965, NAA: A1838, 2020/1/24 PART 2.

[41] "Australian External Aid," 40.

[42] Rist, *The History of Development*, 94–102.

[43] Department of External Affairs, "Economic Significance of Australian Bilateral Aid to Asian Countries," December 29, 1964, NAA: A1838, 2020/1/24/23.

This analysis could have come straight from the texts of the dominant developmental economists of the time and reveals the influence of orthodox theory in the External Affairs conception of aid.

Australian overseas representatives presented developmental ideas in their submissions for the review. Some of these representatives had economic training, and their comments reflected their academic backgrounds. While a number of responses emphasised political considerations for Australian aid, developmental imperatives were also frequently addressed.[44] From the donor countries, the most theoretically aware response came from James Cumes, the Ambassador in Brussels. Prior to entering the public service, Cumes had received his doctorate in economics from the University of London, and so was especially qualified to examine foreign aid policy in the context of developmental theory.[45] Employing language taken straight from the most ardent modernisation theorists of the time, Cumes wrote: "The ultimate *economic* objective of aid is presumably to achieve self-sustaining economic growth, that is, to set recipient countries on the same road as the industrialised or highly developed countries of Europe, North America, Australia and Japan."[46] He also cited Gunnar Myrdal's work on development, further demonstrating the up-to-date nature of his analysis.

Similarly, responses from recipient countries also revealed a clear engagement with the terminology of developmental economics. The High Commissioner in Kuala Lumpur, Thomas Critchley, argued for increased assistance to Malaysia based on the idea that it was "a fast developing country on the threshold of self-sustained economic growth."[47] Both of these responses presented the key Rostovian goal of reaching self-sustained growth as an objective of Australian aid. A.H. Loomes, the Ambassador in Bangkok, also emphasised developmental objectives, writing: "Aid undertaken for political reasons, and not for the intrinsic

[44] Examples of emphasis on political considerations can be found in T.K. Critchley to A.H. Tange, November 26, 1964; F.J. Blakeney to A.H. Tange, December 8, 1964. These letters are in NAA: A1838, 2020/1/24/1 PART 1 and 2.

[45] "Dr James Cumes," University of Queensland Faculty of Business, Economics and Law, http://bel.uq.edu.au/james-cumes.

[46] J.W.C. Cumes to Tange, December 7, 1964, NAA: A1838, 2020/1/24/1 PART 1. [Emphasis in original].

[47] T.K. Critchley to A.H. Tange, November 26, 1964, NAA: A1838, 2020/1/24/1 PART 1.

soundness of individual projects, is apt to run into difficulties and subsequent irritations, frustrations, disappointments and recriminations are likely to undo the political ends which were the original object of the exercise."[48] The ease with which these representatives employed developmentalist terminology speaks to the depth of theoretical knowledge at External Affairs' disposal.

The debate over the international dimensions of Australian aid produced a more explicit understanding of the broader context within which Australia's economic assistance operated. In arguing for the need to place Australian aid into its broader international context, External Affairs emphasised the developmental effects of Australian aid in conjunction with other countries. This was in keeping with American attempts to establish a Western developmental system guided by modernisation theory, which has been examined by historians such as Latham and Cullather.[49] Further, it was useful as an attempt to counter Treasury arguments that Australian assistance had no real economic significance. International considerations would also become important to the second major area of debate in the aid review, which revolved around the incorporation of PNG into Australian foreign aid calculations.

Australian Assistance to PNG as Foreign Aid

In the two decades following the Second World War, Australian assistance to both Southeast Asia and PNG was informed by the post-war conception of international development. However, while the ideas underpinning colonial and foreign aid policy were similar, the bureaucratic machinery was kept separate. The Territories Department (along with its long-time Minister, Paul Hasluck) had almost complete control over development in PNG. The only time External Affairs was involved in Australian colonial policy was in the UN, when the Trusteeship Council examined the annual reports, which were prepared by Territories officials. This division was weakening by the mid-1960s, as both domestic and international pressures drew Australian policy towards PNG and the developing countries of Asia closer together. Chapter 4 concluded

[48] A.H. Loomes to A.H. Tange, December 14, 1964, NAA: A1838, 2020/1/24/1 PART 2.

[49] Latham, *Modernization as Ideology*, 12–13; Cullather, "Research Note: Development? It's History," 651.

with a brief discussion of how External Affairs officials began to identify connections between its Colombo Plan aid and the work of Territories in promoting development in PNG. By the time of the aid review, the status of Australian economic assistance to PNG was the subject of debate between Territories, External Affairs and Treasury. The debate between the representatives of these departments marked an important moment where the nature and purpose of Australian colonial policy was overtly examined by Australian policymakers.

Curiously, this was one area of the aid review that found Treasury and External Affairs arguing for a similar outcome. Both departments felt that PNG should be more closely linked to foreign aid but for different reasons. Treasury was the firmest in pressing the case for PNG to be considered external aid. It produced a paper for the review, which countered claims of colonial exploitation by arguing that PNG "constitutes a customs area quite separate and independent of the Australian customs system."[50] As a result, Treasury argued that the economy of PNG should be considered separate from that of Australia, and therefore, the Australian grant should be considered foreign aid. If that economic argument was not enough, Treasury went on to argue that "expenditure on economic development of overseas Territories is always included as external aid by donor countries in international comparisons made by the United Nations."[51] This was somewhat true, as grants to dependent territories were often counted as overseas assistance for UN surveys. However, the official historian of British colonial development policy, D.J. Morgan, explains that British policymakers made a clear distinction between international aid and colonial development.[52] Nevertheless, this turned out to be the most persuasive argument for the inclusion of PNG, given External Affairs also sought to present Australia as a generous aid donor.[53]

This political argument had the effect of making Australia seem more generous than it would otherwise appear. In the two decades following the Second World War, the grant to PNG comprised 80 per cent of

[50] Treasury Department, "Inclusion of Official Expenditure in Papua/New Guinea in Australian External Aid," January 13, 1965, NAA: A1838, 2020/1/24/23.

[51] Treasury, "Inclusion of Official Expenditure in Papua/New Guinea in Australian External Aid."

[52] Morgan, *Changes in British Aid Policy, 1951–1970*, 2.

[53] Report of the Third Meeting of the Committee to Review Australian External Aid, December 11, 1964, NAA: A1838, 2020/1/24 PART 2.

Australian official developmental assistance.[54] The inclusion of the grant to PNG in official aid figures brought Australia's aid spending to 0.62 per cent of GNP, which placed Australia fifth amongst aid donors.[55] Including PNG in Australian aid figures brought Australia much closer to the UNCTAD target of one per cent of GNP.

Treasury's handling of PNG employed a combination of political and developmental considerations. Once Treasury officials established their position that funding to PNG was a form of aid, they then integrated it into their argument that overseas developmental assistance made it more difficult to promote Australia's own development. For instance, in their submission to the committee, Treasury argued: "No one could deny that Australian Government expenditure in Papua/New Guinea involves a transfer of resources that otherwise would be available for use in Australia."[56] For the Treasury Department, the inclusion of PNG into foreign aid calculations was necessary, both because of the domestic developmental implications of the grant and because it demonstrated Australian generosity to an international audience.

In contrast to Treasury's emphasis on the sacrifices made to fund PNG, External Affairs officials used political and developmental arguments in a different way. For the ETA Branch, development was the link that brought PNG into foreign aid considerations. Acknowledging the link between foreign aid and colonial development, they observed: "Expenditure in Papua-New Guinea must necessarily be included in any international aid comparisons but only a proportion of such expenditure is aid in the true sense (i.e. developmental)."[57] Despite the recognition that parts of the Commonwealth grant to PNG were not developmental, the connection between PNG and foreign aid was acknowledged. This was in keeping with Hasluck's view, as set out in his letter to Menzies,

[54] "Australian External Aid," 21.

[55] Treasury Department, "Comparative Aid Disbursements by Australia and Other Donor Countries," December 21, 1964, NAA: A1838, 2020/1/24 PART 2.

[56] Treasury, "Inclusion of Official Expenditure in Papua/New Guinea in Australian External Aid."

[57] Department of External Affairs, Comments on Treasury Paper on "Comparative Aid Disbursements by Australia and Other Donor Countries," December 29, 1964, NAA: A1838, 2020/1/24 PART 2.

where he explicitly included "the annual grant made by the Commonwealth Parliament for Papua and New Guinea" in his consideration of external aid.[58]

While Treasury and External Affairs both acknowledged the place of PNG in foreign aid calculations, Territories sought to maintain the autonomy it had enjoyed since the end of the Second World War. The clearest expression of the Territories position came after the review had been drafted, when Cabinet met to discuss the report. At this time, Territories officials managed to obtain acknowledgement of PNG as "an Australian responsibility and the determination of its grant is to be treated as a separate matter."[59] This reflected the notion of trusteeship that had been the dominant principle in post-war Australian assistance to PNG. For Territories, Australia's Colombo Plan aid was the result of an Australian and Commonwealth initiative, but the grant to PNG was needed to satisfy the requirements of UN oversight.

The idea of 'responsibility' was co-opted by the other departments to support their own developmental perspectives. In the Treasury case, M.W. O'Donnell argued against an increase to Australian aid citing PNG as an important reason. At the eighth meeting of the committee, O'Donnell explained: "The Government had to choose among competing demands for resources ... The first call upon aid was for Papua and New Guinea – this was a responsibility which could not be passed to anyone else."[60] This argument worked its way into the final report, which noted: "Because we are likely to continue to have the sole responsibility for its development the Territory must have a very high priority amongst our external aid expenditures."[61] Ironically, the Territories conception had been twisted around to confirm the incorporation of PNG into Australian foreign aid.

The debate over the status of Australia's grant to PNG was amongst the most important of the aid policy review. It brought three different positions out into the open: Treasury emphasised the separateness of the PNG economy, which did not bring benefits to Australia and therefore served

[58] P.M.C. Hasluck to R.G. Menzies, September 17, 1964, NAA: A1838, 2020/1/24 PART 3.

[59] Cabinet Minute, Decision No. 1002, "Australian External Aid," June 9, 1965, A1838, 2020/1/24 PART 3.

[60] Report of the Eighth Meeting of the Committee to Review Australian External Aid, January 12, 1965, NAA: A1838, 2020/1/24 PART 2.

[61] "Australian External Aid," 64.

as a drain on domestic Australian resources; External Affairs concentrated on the developmental nature of Australia's assistance to PNG; and Territories' focus was on maintaining the 'special' position of PNG through repeated assertions of Australia's trusteeship responsibilities. The place of PNG in the final report was a compromise between these competing positions. This compromise position could only be found after all of the different positions had been brought out into the open. Aside from the notion of responsibility quoted above, PNG found its way into the report's definition of 'external aid':

> Australian expenditure in Papua and New Guinea is different in some respects but similar in others to our aid expenditure abroad. It is, however, substantial, and for international purposes is presented as part of Australia's aid effort and we have therefore included it in this report.[62]

The reference to "international purposes" was a gesture to the political advantage that came from the inclusion of PNG in aid figures. The incorporation of PNG was further indicated by its position at the head of all tables of Australian foreign aid, rather than in the separate position sought after by the Territories Department.[63] The inclusion of colonial spending in foreign aid calculations presented Australia as more generous than it actually was, given the international obligations associated with the PNG grant. Nevertheless, once the integration of PNG into Australian foreign aid had begun, the process would not be reversed.

Australia as a 'Developing' Country

The third and final area of difference amongst the inter-departmental committee revolved around the competition between Australian development and the promotion of development in the developing countries to its north. This had been an ongoing debate since the end of the Second World War, and its prominence in 1964–1965 was informative of the nature of Australian engagement with developmentalism. Indeed, this is a question that has persisted through to the twenty-first century. Once again the debate mainly took place between External Affairs and Treasury

[62] "Australian External Aid," 6.

[63] "Australian External Aid," 21.

officials, although the Department of Trade and Industry also made reference to its Middle Zone policy. While experts, such as Anthony Clunies Ross and Ian Shannon, contended that Australia's status as a developing country did not operate as an impediment to increased aid funding, the arguments of Treasury officials that the reverse was the case eventually carried the day.[64] This debate, in conjunction with the Middle Zone policy that Australia had asserted at UNCTAD around the same time as the aid review, marked the zenith of the Australian attempt to present itself as a developing country in order to avoid providing additional assistance to the developing countries.

We have already seen in this chapter that Treasury officials emphasised the drain on Australian resources posed by aid. M.W. O'Donnell persisted with this argument at the eighth meeting of the committee, where he explained: "The Government had to choose among competing demands for resources; in conditions of full employment external aid did not promote economic growth."[65] This point was made in the context of promises made by Menzies to increase Australian GNP by 25 per cent over the next five years. O'Donnell then claimed that "it had to be made clear there was a choice between aid, defence and economic growth. Throughout the 1950s the government accepted as its first task the development of Australia's resources."[66] This was one of the central tenets of what Whitwell has referred to as the 'Treasury line.'[67] In the context of the review, it supported the conclusion that foreign aid expenditure should be kept to a minimum, and the focus on Australian development maintained.

Trade and Industry Department officials also emphasised Australia's status as a developing country, in keeping with their approach at UNCTAD earlier in 1964. This was quickly recognised by Tange, who observed that "the point of view displayed by the Department of Trade seems to acquiesce in Treasury objections to aid or lending policies which

[64] Clunies Ross, *One Per Cent*, 42; Shannon, "Economic Aid," 336.

[65] Record of the Eighth Meeting of the Committee to Review Australian External Aid, January 12, 1965, NAA: A1838, 2020/1/24 PART 2.

[66] Record of the Eighth Meeting of the Committee to Review Australian External Aid.

[67] Whitwell, *The Treasury Line*, 122–123.

cover the export of inefficient Australian secondary industry."[68] As with the Middle Zone policy, the Trade and Industry position towards aid was primarily directed to ensuring that Australian interests were protected. According to M.M. Summers, the First Assistant Secretary of Trade and Industry and the department's representative at the sixth meeting of the committee: "Trade and Industry saw the question of Australia's attitude on commodity aid, UNCTAD and Australia's middle zone position, GATT and the model chapter concept, as all being tied together."[69] While this position acknowledged that there was a place for Australian aid in commodities to poorer parts of the world (particularly India), this needed to be considered in conjunction with Australia's status as a country that was still in the process of development.

The Department of External Affairs responded to these arguments in a number of ways, which represented the intersection of politics and theory that underpinned their attitude to aid policy. In developmental terms, they presented the view that Australia was a developed country and that it should provide a substantial amount of foreign aid in keeping with the "duties associated with being an 'advanced' country."[70] This observation fitted with External Affairs' broader ideological position that Australia should be considered a 'developed' nation. For External Affairs, the first "policy purpose" of Australian aid was "to reduce disparities in living standards and social welfare between the less developed and the highly developed countries."[71] Implicit in this statement was the view that Australia was amongst the 'highly developed countries', a categorisation supported by an External Affairs reference to Australia's "relative wealth" in comparison with the recipients of Australian aid.[72] For officials in External Affairs, a simple examination of the developmental differences

[68] A.H. Tange, "Australian External Aid Policy," December 22, 1964, NAA: A1838, 2020/1/24 PART 2.

[69] Record of the Sixth Meeting of the Committee to Review Australian External Aid, December 30, 1964, NAA: A1838, 2020/1/24 PART 2.

[70] Department of External Affairs, "The United Nations Expanded Programme of Technical Assistance—Origin and Purpose of Australian Participation," November 25, 1964, NAA: A1838, 2020/1/24/20.

[71] Department of External Affairs, "General Evaluation of Australian Aid—Relations with Recipients, Major Allies and Multilateral Institutions," December 15, 1964, NAA: A1838, 2020/1/24/23.

[72] External Affairs, "General Evaluation of Australian Aid."

between Australia and the recipients of its aid proved Australia's status as a developed country, with all of the associated international responsibilities that came with that label.

External Affairs also argued that the provision of aid would bring long-term benefits to the Australian economy. In a policy paper prepared for the committee, the views of the former Minister for External Affairs, Richard Casey, were noted:

> [Casey] also said that on a broader view, it can be said that in the long run success of the Plan in raising the living standards in Asia will have a considerable promotional effect on our marketing possibilities. In the short run, the supply of Australian goods and equipment to the area creates a knowledge of our capacities and sometimes a direct and immediate trade follow up.[73]

In contrast to Treasury and Trade and Industry, External Affairs used the logic of self-interest to call for *more* aid.

These arguments were in keeping with the work of Australian economists, such as Douglas Copland, who in 1963 published *The Changing Structure of the Western Economy*, in which he outlined his long-held view that countries like Australia were still in the process of development. For Copland, development in a country like Australia should be:

> Not merely a matter of developing resources on the basis of rapid technological advances, but of blending this higher return for economic effort with the broader and more subtle objective of improving the social structure of the nation as a community.[74]

This corresponds with his earlier recommendations for the 'developing' Australian economy, as deeper social factors needed to be taken into account as well. The 'Milk Bar Economy' only demonstrated the superficial results of development. However, Copland was also clear that increased amounts of international foreign aid were required, as his work was linked closely to the 'One Per Cent Group.' He described

[73] Department of External Affairs, "Colombo Plan—Origins and Purposes of the Plan and Australian Participation," December 9, 1964, NAA: A1838, 2020/1/24/20.

[74] Copland, *The Changing Structure of the Western Economy*, 38.

the Colombo Plan as an "imaginative" initiative, but was more positive towards American aid, which was provided on a "grander scale."[75] Copland's work, which drew on the ideas of Myrdal and American modernisation theorists, fitted reasonably well with the overall recommendations of External Affairs. While he differed from External Affairs in his conviction that Australia was best understood as a developing country, he nonetheless advocated an increase in Australian foreign aid to countries in Southeast Asia.

The aid review's final report equivocated on whether or not Australia was a developed or developing country. On one side, it explained: "With one of the world's highest per capita national incomes, Australia will be subject to pressure to give substantial assistance to all the multilateral programmes of aid."[76] This was clearly an acceptance that Australia was a rich country, which suggested it belonged with the developed bloc. However, the report also stated:

> We continue to be faced with a situation in which the level of domestic demand is placing heavy pressure on supplies of labour and other factors of production. In these circumstances transfers of resources abroad must add to the pressures on the economy.[77]

Here, Treasury presented their central argument, acknowledging the supposedly detrimental impact of foreign aid on the Australian economy. In keeping with many other aspects of the aid review, the committee was unable to establish a decisive position. This debate continues to go unresolved.

Policy Recommendations and the Consequences of the Aid Review

The mid-1960s were a time of political and theoretical introspection in the field of development, and this was reflected in the results of the aid review. After several months of debate and negotiation, the interdepartmental committee produced a number of policy recommendations

[75] Copland, *The Changing Structure of the Western Economy*, 51.

[76] "Australian External Aid," 83.

[77] "Australian External Aid," 101.

that were expected to guide Australian aid for at least the rest of the 1960s. While most tended towards the maintenance of the status quo, such as the continued prioritisation of Australian aid to Southeast Asia and PNG, the explicit inclusion of the PNG grant as a form of external aid was an important new policy feature. The committee's proposals can be seen as a product of the tension between developmental and political considerations in aid policy. Developmental arguments brought PNG and the Colombo Plan closer together, as well as providing impetus for the focus on Southeast Asia and PNG. Political differences undermined the possibilities of significant reform, particularly with regard to the debate over increases in Australia's aid spending. While there was little immediate change in aid policy, the reforms of the late 1960s and early 1970s, discussed in the final chapter, can be traced to the inter-departmental committee's observations of Australian aid.

PNG and the Colombo Plan countries of South and Southeast Asia were maintained as the primary targets for Australian developmental assistance. In developmental terms, External Affairs argued that "while in most of these [Asian] countries Australian aid is only a small proportion of the total aid received, it nevertheless helps in promoting economic growth and is therefore economically valuable."[78] As a result, External Affairs saw no reason to shift away from aid to Asia. On a political level, the geographic focus can be linked to Hasluck's objective of placing foreign aid within the context of broader Australian foreign policy. This objective filtered through External Affairs. In a memorandum, the Ambassador to South Vietnam argued that "Australian aid should not be diffused over too large a group of countries or areas and particularly where Australia has relatively marginal political interests, e.g. Africa and South America."[79] In contrast to the more common tension between developmental and political imperatives, on this occasion both pointed to maintaining the emphasis on the Colombo Plan and PNG. This was manifested in the External Affairs submission to Cabinet, which stated: "As a general rule, priority should be given to meeting our responsibilities in Papua and New Guinea and to providing bilateral aid to those countries in South and

[78] Department of External Affairs, "Economic Significance of Australian Bilateral Aid to Asian Countries," December 29, 1964, NAA: A1838, 2020/1/24/23.

[79] Memorandum attached to H.D. Anderson to A.H. Tange, December 9, 1964, NAA: A1838, 2020/1/24/1 PART 2.

South East Asia which are of immediate strategic importance to us."[80] As it had for the two decades before the aid review, Australian developmental assistance was to be directed to those developing areas to its immediate north.

The inclusion of PNG in the submission demonstrated the closer links between colonial development and foreign aid that emerged out of the aid review. This was one area of explicit change and was a product of Treasury and External Affairs holding similar views. In the days before the completion of the committee's report, Tange rejected a Territories Department suggestion that would reinforce the separateness of developmental assistance in PNG:

> The level of Australian expenditure in the Territory of Papua and New Guinea is a separate and different question from the level of external aid programmes. Australia has the direct obligation of administering the Territory of Papua and the Trust Territory of New Guinea. The objective of Australian policy in New Guinea may be stated as to build up a self-governing nation that will be politically stable, responsive to Australian influence when Australian interests are concerned and prepared to resist Indonesian or other undesirable penetration.[81]

By declining to include this passage in the final report, Tange and the Department of External Affairs ensured the inclusion of PNG as a recipient of Australian foreign aid. In many ways, this confirmed the international process whereby colonial powers presented their assistance to dependent territories as aid, which had been happening in the United Kingdom for decades.[82] While there was still an acknowledgement of Australia's special 'responsibility' in PNG, which it did not have elsewhere, the review demonstrated the increasing Australian understanding of the connections between its two principal areas of aid spending. The explicit statements of developmental ideas that were made by officials from External Affairs, Treasury, and Territories facilitated this understanding.

[80] Department of External Affairs Draft Cabinet Submission, "Australian External Aid," May 3, 1965, NAA: A1838, 2020/1/24 PART 3.

[81] G. Warwick Smith to A.H. Tange, March 22, 1965, NAA: A1838, 2020/1/24/2.

[82] Michael Ashley Havinden and David Meredith, *Colonialism and Development: Britain and Its Tropical Colonies, 1850–1960* (London: Routledge, 1993).

Administratively, the interaction of the Territories Department and External Affairs also had some long-term ramifications. Acknowledging that Territories would continue to direct development in PNG, the report stated:

> Although Papua and New Guinea is sui generis and the policies for its government and development lie within the jurisdiction of the Minister for Territories, the proceedings of this Committee have demonstrated the value of consultation also between the Department of Territories and other departments administering aid programmes.[83]

This statement was made in the context of increased recognition of the need for consultation between departments that had an interest in foreign aid policy. In the immediate aftermath of the aid review, an interdepartmental committee was established that met twice a year to discuss developmental assistance. Over time, however, this committee gave way to the establishment of the Australian Development Assistance Agency (ADAA) in 1974. The establishment of the ADAA would complete the integration of PNG into the foreign aid policy machinery. Once again, this placed Australia slightly behind its Western counterparts, with the United States Agency for International Development (USAID) being established in 1961 and the British Ministry of Overseas Development formed in 1964.[84]

Another major component of the aid review revolved around the size of Australia's aid commitment. We have already seen that Treasury sought to commit a minimal amount of resources to foreign aid, while External Affairs felt that more needed to be done. This was arguably one area of debate that had been overt since the early 1950s. Nevertheless, the negotiations within the inter-departmental committee produced more concrete and specific recommendations. In the final report, these minimums and maximums were set, with projections cast forward to possible expenditure in 1968–1969. Taking the minimum level of increase, which was based on steady Colombo Plan spending and preliminary IBRD recommendations for PNG, the figure of £65 million was reached.[85] In contrast,

[83] "Australian External Aid," 110.

[84] Ekbladh, *The Great American Mission*, 192; Morgan, *Changes in British Aid Policy, 1951–1970*, 13–29.

[85] "Australian External Aid," 79.

it was suggested if External Affairs and Territories had their way and more considerable increases to spending in Southeast Asia and PNG were provided, then Australia could be contributing £85 million in developmental assistance in 1968–1969.[86] As it was, by 1968–1969, Australia contributed just over $150 million (following the introduction of decimal currency in 1966) in foreign aid, which included PNG in the calculation of official aid spending. This represented 0.55 per cent of GNP, which was a reduction on the 0.62 per figure at the time of the review.[87] Indeed, the mid-1960s marked the peak of aid spending as a percentage of GNP, as it reached a high of 0.67 per cent.[88] The aid review, conducted in the shadow of modernisation theory and in the midst of the 'decade of development', foresaw a greater investment in governmental aid spending than would eventuate.

The inter-departmental review of Australian foreign aid, which took place at a time of challenges to aid theory and practice in the United States and United Kingdom, provided a forum for departmental officials to discuss the different developmental notions that existed in the Commonwealth bureaucracy. While ideological differences had been a component of Australian aid policy formation since the 1940s, officials had rarely been able to debate and investigate the different departmental attitudes. By opening up a discussion over the different meanings of development, the aid review enabled a more critical understanding of the intellectual foundations of Australian aid. Once these ideas were out in the open, aid policy became more intellectually sound than it had been before the review. Thus, while the immediate outcomes tended towards the status quo, the review provided the foundation for more significant reform in subsequent years.

[86] "Australian External Aid," 98.

[87] *Official Year Book of the Commonwealth of Australia* (Canberra: Commonwealth Bureau of Census and Statistics, 1970), 113.

[88] Jarrett, *The Evolution of Australia's Aid Program*, 6–7.

CHAPTER 7

Taking Up the "Latest Fashions": International Development in Flux and the Australian Response, 1965–1975

The final decade of the age of international development was marked by the rise of new ideas. Three constituent elements provide insight into the forces at work on Australian aid policy between 1965 and 1975. The rapid move towards independence in PNG forced policymakers to come to terms with the limits of the modernisation paradigm and introduced ideas of self-reliance to Indigenous leaders. The creation of the Australian Council for Overseas Aid (ACFOA) as an umbrella organisation for development non-governmental organisations (NGOs) facilitated the rise of the 'basic needs' paradigm in Australia. Finally, the establishment of the Australian Development Assistance Agency (ADAA) provided a new bureaucratic environment for development policy. Formed in 1974, the ADAA was marked by a complex interaction between orthodox modernisation ideas and the new theoretical approaches, as developmental imperatives briefly moved to the forefront of Australian aid policy. These elements reveal that international trends, both intellectual and political, continued to guide Australian policymakers in their attempts to promote development in poorer parts of the world.

The changes in Australian aid between 1965 and 1975 were a product of the proliferation of new approaches to development, which originated overseas and were co-opted by Australian experts and policymakers. Around the world, the authority of the orthodox modernisation paradigm, with its emphasis on national economic growth, was under

N. Ferns, *Australia in the Age of International Development, 1945–1975*, Security, Conflict and Cooperation in the Contemporary World, https://doi.org/10.1007/978-3-030-50228-7_7

serious challenge. The driving force for much of the new discourse on development was the rising voice of the Global South, which was increasingly critical of the orthodox Western-led and conceived modernisation paradigm. A conception of a 'basic needs' approach to international foreign aid policy arose and in some ways competed with the arguments of dependency theorists and the New International Economic Order (NIEO), that post-war developmental programs had done little to alleviate poverty throughout the developing world.[1] Where the modernisation paradigm emphasised economic growth through the establishment of large infrastructure programs, the 'basic needs' view emphasised small-scale assistance to the most poverty-stricken people in developing countries.[2] A key consequence of this approach was the greater influence of NGOs in the global development system. Their authority arose from the perception that while governments were well suited to providing assistance to other countries in establishing large projects, NGOs were more effective in establishing connections on a grass-roots level, to tackle poverty where it was being experienced.

UNCTAD served as an early sign that the Global South was coming to question the effectiveness of aid and trade systems based around the ideas of Rostow and his contemporaries. While external critique challenged the dominant understandings of development, internal economic crises linked to the global energy shortage provided an impetus to changes in the Global North that would reshape policy approaches to the 'problem' of development. Australia was no exception to this phenomenon. The late 1960s and early 1970s were marked by important intellectual challenges to Australian aid policy. These challenges reflected both the shifts in theoretical understandings of development and political changes taking place within Australia. A key political shift in Australia was the election of the Whitlam Labor Government in 1972, marking the end of twenty-three years of Liberal Coalition rule. This new progressive government sought to recast almost all aspects of Australian society and politics and

[1] Ekbladh, *The Great American Mission*, 224; Rist, *The History of Development*, 165. Samuel Moyn presents the rise of 'basic needs' as an attempt to "ethically outflank" the post-colonial claims of the NIEO. Samuel Moyn, *Not Enough: Human Rights in an Unequal World* (Cambridge: Belknap Press, 2018), 121.

[2] Katrin Lederer, Johan Galtung, and David Antal, *Human Needs: A Contribution to the Current Debate* (Koenigstein/Ts.: Oelgeschlager, 1980).

brought a fresh new approach to foreign policy.[3] In this environment, new actors emerged in the field of Australian aid, particularly the ADAA and ACFOA. Importantly, the rise of NGOs and a stand-alone aid agency like the ADAA replicated processes that had taken place earlier in countries like the United States and UK.[4] As had been the case since 1945, international forces exerted an influence on Australian policy.

These international forces guided Australian policymakers through the intellectual changes in international development between 1965 and 1975. Nevertheless, there was a degree of continuity with earlier Australian aid policy. Rostovian modernisation theory was in decline, through its associations with the Vietnam War and the rise of authoritarian regimes throughout the Global South.[5] Yet the ongoing prominence of economists like Heinz Arndt ensured that the developmental orthodoxy remained part of Australian developmental policies. PNG and Asia continued to receive the vast majority of Australian aid, and developmental debates between External Affairs (renamed Foreign Affairs in 1970) and Treasury persisted through to 1975. In the final decade of the age of international development, forces for change competed with a tendency towards continuity in Australian aid policy. Change and continuity occurred simultaneously, and both reflected the ongoing influence of international trends in developmental thought and practice on Australian academia and policy. As development took precedence over politics as the guiding force in Australian aid, new ideas and institutions emerged.

[3] Neville Meaney, "The United States," in *Australia in World Affairs, 1971–75*, ed. W.J. Hudson (Sydney: George Allen & Unwin for the Australian Institute of International Affairs, 1980), 180.

[4] Ekbladh, *The Great American Mission*, 188; Matthew Hilton, ed. *The Politics of Expertise: How NGOs Shaped Modern Britain* (Oxford: Oxford University Press, 2013).

[5] Ekbladh examines how modernisation theory was damaged by its associations with the Vietnam War, Ekbladh, *The Great American Mission*, 10. Bradley Simpson makes the connection between modernisation theory and the rise of authoritarian government in Indonesia, in *Economists with Guns*.

Developmental Debates: New Ideas Challenge the Orthodoxy

The evolution of international development theory and practice was mirrored in Australia both in academia and within the Commonwealth bureaucracy. Throughout this book, the discussion of developmental theory has been largely limited to the dominant modernisation paradigm and the mid-1960s rise of the dependency school. These ideas continued to exert an influence over the field of developmental economics into the mid-1960s and early 1970s. However, they faced major challenges. In the Global North, the 1973 Arab oil embargo and economic decline posed a threat to the ongoing provision of developmental assistance. In the Global South, political upheaval in places like Indonesia and Vietnam threatened many of the assumptions that were inherent to post-war developmental theory. By the late 1960s and early 1970s dependency theorists, such as Andre Gunder Frank, employed a 'neo-Marxist' approach, bringing a much more strident critique by arguing that development served the interests of the Global North (or 'centre' to use the terminology of dependency theory).[6] Modernisation theorists, perhaps compelled to take note of the rise of right-wing authoritarian regimes in countries that had received large amounts of Western aid, became less concerned with the idea that democracy was a prerequisite for development. Bradley Simpson examines this process in the Indonesian context. He demonstrates that experts, such as Rostow, continued to advocate increased aid to Indonesia, despite the clear absence of democratic institutions following the establishment of the New Order government in 1965.[7]

Adding even more intellectual complexity, Gunnar Myrdal published *Asian Drama* in 1968. This detailed critique of "modernisation ideals" built on his earlier scepticism of the effectiveness of Western economic models in a South Asian context.[8] While not going as far as the dependency theorists in his critique on modernisation, Myrdal still argued that Asian 'underdeveloped' countries needed to reject Western developmental models and devise their own programs of development. Treasurer William McMahon made an explicit reference to *Asian Drama* in 1969,

[6] Frank, *Capitalism and Underdevelopment in Latin America.*

[7] Simpson, *Economists with Guns*, 238–239, 246.

[8] Myrdal, *Asian Drama.*

in support of his claim that "irrational attitudes and outmoded institutions are primarily responsible for the low levels of living in Asia."[9] In spite of these changes, the orthodoxy's lingering influence was felt through to the 1970s. During a 1970 visit to PNG, Prime Minister John Gorton quoted W. Arthur Lewis in identifying educational reform as the "spearhead of development."[10] By taking Lewis as his intellectual inspiration, and emphasising economic growth as the driver of development, Gorton engaged with developmental ideas that had been dominant since the 1950s.

The modernisation versus dependency debate manifested itself in the early 1970s through two prominent experts on Indonesian development. Heinz Arndt and Rex Mortimer emerged as the respective voices of the 'orthodox' (modernisation) school and the 'critical' (dependency) school. The personal histories of these two scholars serve to inform an understanding of their intellectual approaches. Arndt, whose family had escaped Nazi Germany in the 1930s, steadily moved towards what could be considered a conservative understanding of economic development.[11] By the late 1960s, he was involved in the Australian National University's Indonesian Economy Project, which placed him in a position to assist the Department of External Affairs in their provision of aid to Indonesia.[12]

Rex Mortimer provided an interesting contrast. A young communist who unlike Arndt never really lost his radicalism, Mortimer was a late entrant into academia. Studying under Indonesia expert (and Volunteer Graduate Scheme pioneer) Herb Feith at Monash University, Mortimer was drawn to the radical ideas of development scholars, such as Andre Gunder Frank and Dudley Seers.[13] In much the same way that the dependency school emerged to provide a critique of the dominant

[9] Speech by William McMahon at a Seminar held by ACFOA, April 14, 1969, NLA, ACFOA Papers, MS 9347, Box 2.

[10] Department of External Territories, "Prime Minister's Speech—Goroka Teachers College," July 1970, NAA: A452, 1970/3068. Lewis' most prominent work was his 1955 study of economic growth, which places him firmly in the 'modernisation' school of development, Lewis, *The Theory of Economic Growth*.

[11] Arndt, *A Course Through Life*.

[12] Department of External Affairs to Australian Embassy, Jakarta, July 19, 1966, NAA: A1838, 2036/5 PART 9.

[13] Irving, "Mortimer, Rex Alfred (1926–1979)."

modernisation theory, Mortimer's work was directed towards identifying problems with Arndt's scholarship.

Nowhere was this more obvious than in Mortimer's *Showcase State*. Emerging out of a symposium held at Monash University in 1972, this book examined the economic policies of the Suharto regime in Indonesia.[14] In one key chapter, however, Mortimer examined the development of the social sciences in Australia. He touched on the influence of American approaches, such as the 'end of ideology' school, in Australia. These ideas were closely associated with Rostow and modernisation theory.[15] He linked Arndt to this school of thought and argued that "to a greater degree than most Indonesianists in Australia, and most Indonesian intellectuals outside the governmental in-group, he is highly optimistic about the progress of Indonesia's Western-conceived development effort."[16] In contrast, Mortimer suggested:

> The division of the world into countries that are growing relatively richer and countries that are growing relatively poorer is not simply the product of some historical accident... but constitutes a network of interactions which is systematically enforced by the wealthy club.[17]

This was a clear engagement with the conception of development presented by dependency scholars such as Frank, who suggested that the entire process perpetuated the phenomenon of 'underdevelopment.'[18] Through the intellectual disagreements between Arndt and Mortimer, international discourse made its way into Australian thinking.

[14] Mortimer, *Showcase State*; Mortimer would go on to produce similar analysis of the development of Papua New Guinea, Amarshi, Good, and Mortimer, *Development and Dependency*.

[15] Rex Mortimer, "From Ball to Arndt: The Liberal Impasses in Australian Scholarship on Southeast Asia," in *Showcase State: The Illusion of Indonesia's "Accelerated Modernisation"*, ed. Rex Mortimer (Sydney: Angus & Robertson, 1973). Nils Gilman, *Mandarins of the Future: Modernization Theory in Cold War America* (Baltimore: Johns Hopkins University Press, 2003), 16.

[16] Mortimer, "From Ball to Arndt," 121.

[17] Mortimer, "From Ball to Arndt," 129.

[18] Frank, *Capitalism and Underdevelopment in Latin America*, 27.

Other ideas emerged out of the intellectual debate between followers of the modernisation and dependency paradigms. The 'basic needs' concept emerged out of the increased recognition of the continued prevalence of poverty throughout the world, even after decades of development assistance.[19] By the late 1960s, the World Bank, under former US Secretary of Defense Robert McNamara, advocated a basic needs approach that, according to Nick Cullather, led to it becoming much more active in the field of alleviating poverty.[20] While some scholars, such as Matthias Schmelzer, see the shift to basic needs as more discursive than evident in development practice, it was clear that the modernisation paradigm had lost its international appeal.[21]

Another critique of development arose amongst scholars and politicians in developing countries who were concerned with the negative effects of foreign aid. Many of the leaders of these countries were concerned at the social effect of modernisation programs. The notion of developmental 'self-reliance' emerged out of this context. Most closely associated with Tanzanian President Julius Nyerere, these ideas exerted a large amount of influence throughout the developing world in the early 1970s.[22] At the heart of this approach was the view that traditional society should adapt to development, rather than simply be replaced. In the words of Nyerere: "We must take our traditional system, correct its shortcomings, and adapt to its service the things we can learn from the technologically developed societies of other continents."[23] The emphasis on self-reliance found a ready audience in PNG, with inaugural Prime Minister Michael Somare's Eight Aims (which are explained later in this chapter) sharing numerous characteristics with many of Nyerere's ideas. As Gilbert Rist explains, the self-reliance approach, along with the notion of 'basic needs,' demonstrated that by the second half of the 1960s:

[19] Rist, *History of Development*, 165.

[20] Cullather, *The Hungry World*, 238.

[21] Matthias Schmelzer, *The Hegemony of Growth: The OECD and the Making of the Economic Growth Paradigm* (Cambridge: Cambridge University Press, 2016), 271; Ekbladh, *The Great American Mission*, 224.

[22] Vijay Prashad, *The Darker Nations: A People's History of the Third World* (New York: The New Press, 2007), 191–199; Rist, *History of Development*, 123–139.

[23] Julius K. Nyerere, *Socialism and Rural Development* (Dar es Salaam: Printed by the Govt. Printer, 1967), 4.

> Whereas the dominant strategy proposes a single path of 'development', what is now happening is a *diversification of 'developments'*. The theoretical sequence of modernization is replaced with a multiplicity of new practices that spring forth at the crossroads of history and cultures.[24]

Out of the fragmentation of developmental ideas of the mid-1960s, new attitudes towards development emerged in different parts of the world. This global phenomenon guided Australian aid through the significant political changes in PNG.[25]

Papua New Guinea: Development and Independence

The late 1960s saw increased momentum for Papua New Guinean independence, both in PNG and amongst Australian policymakers. The earlier rhetoric claiming that it would be 'generations' until the Indigenous population could govern themselves largely disappeared. This was due to a combination of factors, ranging from international pressures for decolonisation, manifested in the UN Trusteeship Council, to changing attitudes towards colonial administration amongst federal policymakers. The combination of new attitudes in Canberra and increased Indigenous agitation for independence produced self-government in 1973 and full independence in 1975.[26] The granting of self-government was closely linked to an evolution in developmental thought. At the time of independence, the Papua New Guinean budget was still heavily reliant upon Australian economic assistance. However, a more diverse range of ideas informed Australian policy than in the first two decades following the Second World War. From the mid-1960s onwards, visitors from international organisations such as the World Bank took a greater interest in the development of PNG. In addition, Indigenous leaders in PNG became more vocal in regard to their vision of developmental policy after independence. These viewpoints had an increasing impact on Australian developmental policy.

[24] Rist, *History of Development*, 137 [Emphasis in original].

[25] Patrick Kilby explains the role of ACFOA's *Development News Digest* in driving Australian engagement with new developmental ideas. Patrick Kilby, *NGOs and Political Change: A History of the Australian Council for International Development* (Acton, ACT: ANU Press, 2015), 52.

[26] Downs, *The Australian Trusteeship Papua New Guinea, 1945–75*, 496–498.

As we saw in Chapter 4, throughout the 1950s and early 1960s Paul Hasluck and Territories officials maintained the view that development was a prerequisite to self-government. By the end of the decade, this situation had changed, as the opposition Labor Party had committed to a policy of immediate moves towards self-government if elected.[27] This pressure led the Coalition government, under Prime Minister John Gorton and new Minister for External Territories Andrew Peacock, to repudiate the previous approach, and to promise continued aid even if PNG lacked economic self-sufficiency at the time of independence. In 1970, Gorton visited PNG. While there, the Department of External Territories provided the Prime Minister with a policy brief that explained: "Constitutional progress towards self-government will not alter Australia's intention to assist the political, social and economic advancement of the Territory."[28] This reversal in policy reflected political pressures, both in Canberra and PNG, but the developmental considerations behind Australian aid remained consistent. The Australian grant to PNG continued to form the bulk of Australian aid, comprising around two-thirds of the foreign aid budget in the first half of the 1970s.[29] Orthodox ideas continued to exert influence, as shown by Gorton's claims that continued improvement in tea, coffee and cocoa production would "help to boost economic development and give better lives to everyone."[30] This was an approach reminiscent of the Hasluck era. Nevertheless, as the pace towards independence began to quicken, Australian policymakers were exposed to the new ideas emerging in the field of development. This produced some innovative policy suggestions throughout the final years of the Australian administration of PNG.

The 'basic needs' approach found a receptive audience in Australian planning for PNG. Department of External Territories staff, working on a five-year development program for 1970–1975, began to place greater emphasis on the impact of economic policy on the lives of ordinary

[27] K.E. Beazley to J.A. Burnett, July 2, 1970, NAA: A452, 1970/3068.

[28] Department of External Territories, "Early Self-government," July 3, 1970, NAA: A452, 1970/3068.

[29] *Official Year Book of the Commonwealth of Australia* (Canberra: Commonwealth Bureau of Census and Statistics, 1973), 118. This statistic also demonstrates the degree to which Australian colonial development funding had become accepted as foreign aid.

[30] Department of External Territories, "Prime Minister's Speech—Kieta Local Government Council," July 1970, NAA: A1838, 1970/3068.

people. Responding to criticisms of early drafts that failed to acknowledge these factors, a departmental officer added a passage to the draft program: "Economic development is largely meaningless if it does not improve the lot of ordinary men and women and it may actually be self-defeating if it creates more problems than it solves."[31] Language such as this fits with Samuel Moyn and Julia Dehm's analysis of basic needs discourse, which targeted poverty alleviation, while not necessarily tackling the structural causes of global inequality.[32]

The increasing importance of direct expenditure aimed at improving the lives of "ordinary men and women" can be seen in the increase of the social and community development budget from $170,000 in 1970–1971 to over $2.5 million in 1973–1974.[33] Projects supported by this funding ranged from improvements to housing to provisions for child welfare. Community centres were to be built throughout PNG, from Port Moresby to Lae. Youth activities attracted funding, including the expansion of existing school leaver programs, which had the objectives of maintaining student morale, inculcating "habits of responsibility and reliability," and assisting them to find employment. It was expected that the community centres would require around $35,000 to run by 1975/76, while the school leaver program would only require a budget of around $10,000.[34] These programs shared the broad developmental objectives of earlier policy, as seen through the behavioural goals of the school leaver program. However, they also marked a shift away from the programs associated with the earlier Hasluck period, thanks to the emphasis on directly improving the lives of Indigenous Papua New Guineans. Community development policy in PNG, which required closer involvement with the Indigenous population, was a product of the evolution of development thinking at the beginning of the 1970s. This was a shift away

[31] A. McIntosh, "Social Development in Papua and New Guinea," February 25, 1971, NAA: A452, 1970/4775.

[32] Moyn, *Not Enough*; Julia Dehm, "Highlighting Inequalities in the Histories of Human Rights: Contestations Over Justice, Needs and Rights in the 1970s," *Leiden Journal of International Law* 31, no. 4 (2018): 878–879.

[33] A. McIntosh Memorandum, "Revised Department Program—Section 15.7.1—Department of Social Development and Home Affairs," February 2, 1971, NAA: A452, 1970/4775.

[34] D.M. Fenbury, "Second Five Year Plan, 1973–1978—Department of Social Development and Home Affairs," February 4, 1972, NAA: A452, 1970/4775.

from the earlier emphasis on modernisation, which aimed at national economic growth and often gave little consideration to the consequences for individuals.

Self-Reliance and the Faber Report

The shift in development policy in PNG was partly a product of the growing interest of international organisations in the soon-to-be independent territory. While the UN Trusteeship Council had always exerted its oversight of Australian actions in PNG, it was really the visit of the World Bank mission in 1963 that marked the beginning of a shift away from the Australian monopoly over developmental planning in the territory.[35] The Australian administration of PNG came under more intense scrutiny as the global process of decolonisation accelerated throughout the 1960s. After a visit to a number of African countries in 1964, Arthur Tange reflected on what he perceived as the "hopeless dilemma" that faced Australia. He held that Australia either kept control of PNG and faced the charge of 'colonialism,' or it prematurely granted independence and would be accused of 'neo-colonialism.'[36] One consequence of this was the intensification of efforts to achieve independence at a sooner date than was perhaps expected in the early 1960s.[37]

In the face of this international scrutiny, Australian officials invited a UN Development Program/World Bank mission, headed by the British economist and administrator, Michael Faber. Faber, a prominent development expert and former administrator in the newly independent Zambia, was chosen for his "international standing in the field of development economics and... wide knowledge of underdeveloped countries and of

[35] World Bank, *The Economic Development of the Territory of Papua and New Guinea* (Canberra: Department of Territories, 1964).

[36] A.H. Tange to P.M.C. Hasluck, August 28, 1964, NLA, Tange Papers, MS 9847, Box 6.

[37] On a visit to PNG in 1967 Mildred Watt, the wife of former Secretary of the Department of External Affairs Alan Watt, contrasted the "the liberal and paternal Hasluck pattern" to the situation of the late 1960s, marked by a "view to self-sufficiency and self-government." Mildred Watt, PNG Diary, June 23, 1967, NLA, Watt Papers, MS 3788, Box 1.

world economic trends affecting them."[38] The Faber Report, as it became known, was influential in guiding Papua New Guinean leaders in their planning for independence. It called for a plan that drew on both orthodox and new developmental ideas, and its principal recommendation is worth quoting in full:

> In short, we propose the development of a mixed capitalist economy in which there are *two* important sources of dynamic transformation – one is the modern enclave (our bureaucratic sector) drawing on imported capital, technology and skills, the other is the endogenous evolution of small-scale rural and urban activities (both petty capitalist and collective in different sectors); the role of the government will be to attract, control and draw resources from the modern enclave and to devote a major part of its own material and administrative resources towards creating the environment in which informal activities may flourish.[39]

Faber and his colleagues contrasted their ideas "with any modernisation theory which thinks of the transformation process solely as the need to graft a western-type modern sector (including what we have called the 'small firm' sector) on to an assumed indigenous subsistence economy."[40] They also suggested that greater attention be paid to promoting "crafts and service industries," in contrast to the existing emphasis on "wage employment, entrepreneurship and agriculture."[41] This process had been followed in other newly independent countries and reflected the growing

[38] "United Nations Development Programme (Technical Assistance)—Commonwealth Government of Australia (on Behalf of Papua New Guinea): Request for Country Project No. 71," n.d. [Around February 1972], NAA: A452, 1972/2133; "Michael Faber Obituary," *The Guardian*, March 26, 2015, http://www.theguardian.com/politics/2015/mar/25/michael-faber.

[39] World Bank and United Nations Development Programme, *A Report on Development Strategies for Papua New Guinea: Prepared by a Mission from the Overseas Development Group (University of East Anglia) for the International Bank for Reconstruction and Development Acting as Agency for the United Nations Development Programme* (Port Moresby: IBRD, 1973), 27. Hereafter cited as *Faber Report* [Italics in original].

[40] *Faber Report*, 27.

[41] DRAFT, The Overseas Development Group (University of East Anglia) for the IBRD acting as executive agency for The UNDP, "Report to Advise Upon Strategies for the Next Development Programme (1973–1978) for Papua New Guinea," June 1972, NAA: A452, 1972/2133.

emphasis on developmental strategies that took Indigenous traditions and practices into account.

The incorporation of traditional practices into developmental policy was at the heart of the self-reliance movement, which was most closely associated at this time with Nyerere's Tanzania.[42] This idea had become increasingly attractive to leaders throughout the Global South. As a consequence of his emphasis on traditional practices, the Faber Report argued for an increased focus on "localisation/indigenisation, rather than on growth," marking a departure from the orthodox Rostovian model of modernisation.[43] It was also critical of the size of the central administrative bureaucracy, which was another product of Australian developmental policy. While the Australian administration relied on a public service modelled on the metropolitan example, the Report noted that this would not be appropriate given the budgetary and technical constraints that would exist in a newly independent PNG. Overall, the Faber Report recommended increased Indigenous participation in economic development and a shift away from emulating Australian-style development in PNG.

The Australian response to the Faber Report was mixed, reflecting the varied state of developmental thinking during this period. In a Department of External Territories meeting, held on August 15, 1972, some officials expressed their opposition to the ideas conveyed in the Report. One critic felt that the Report was "disappointing" and "superficial" and argued that "growth is not necessarily inconsistent with indigenous participation."[44] The same critic observed the influence of self-reliance ideas in the Faber Report, noting that it aimed to "impose an African model" on PNG.[45] Such commentary demonstrates how particular ways of thinking, once accepted, were difficult to overcome. The Secretary of the Department, David Hay, was more diplomatic in his comments. He recognised that the "proposed strategies will probably be very acceptable to Papua

[42] Rist, *History of Development*, 125; Nyerere, *Socialism and Rural Development*, 4.

[43] "Report to Advise Upon Strategies for the Next Development Programme (1973–1978) for Papua New Guinea."

[44] Department of External Territories, "UNDP Report: Some Notes of a Discussion on 15th August," NAA: A452, 1972/2133.

[45] Department of External Territories, "UNDP Report."

New Guineans."[46] The Faber Report's criticism of Australian developmental policy challenged the long-held claim that Australia's policy in PNG was disinterested and selfless.[47] At the heart of the report's challenge was the suggestion that the growth model of development was not in the best interests of PNG. The Faber Report, with its shift away from the development orthodoxy, was indicative of the swirling field of ideas that confronted Australian policymakers by the early 1970s.

The Department of Foreign Affairs also took an interest in the Faber Report. Examining the Report in the context of aid policy, Foreign Affairs was more accepting of its recommendations. In summarising the key recommendations, Neil Hope of the Department's Aid Branch emphasised that Papua New Guinean development shared numerous features with that of other developing countries. Hope identified that "Papua New Guinea is unique, but many of its problems are not... What is needed as much as anything is a change of attitude and a new and clearer formulation of objectives."[48] This view reflected Foreign Affairs' recognition of the changing field of international development. It also illustrated their qualified acknowledgement of the External Territories' long-held view of PNG as 'unique.'

Their different attitudes towards the Faber Report notwithstanding, both Foreign Affairs and External Territories acknowledged its appeal to PNG's leaders. Hope noted that "there have been many indications that PNG leaders have adopted its recommendations as a guide to future policy."[49] This was indeed the case, as the Faber Report formed the basis for the Somare Government's early foray into developmental policy, the Eight Point Plan. As the founding leader of the pro-independence Pangu Pati, itself inspired by Kenyan examples, Somare visited Africa in 1969 as part of the PNG Select Committee on Constitutional Development. He travelled through Kenya, Tanzania, Uganda and Ghana. Despite the fact that the trip was organised through Australian diplomatic missions and was therefore quite strictly controlled, Somare was

[46] Department of External Territories, "UNDP Report."

[47] "Colonialism in Reverse," *Canberra Times*, October 19, 1966.

[48] Summary of Faber Report, attached to Neil Hope to Loveday, Spratt, and Nicholson, "Aid to PNG—The Faber Report," June 13, 1973, NAA: A452, 1973/291.

[49] Neil Hope to Loveday, Spratt, Nicholson, "Aid to PNG—The Faber Report," June 13, 1973, NAA: A452, 1973/291.

deeply influenced by his experiences. In his 1975 memoir he wrote, "it was inspiring for me to visit black countries where people managed their own affairs," and that one day "we would be worthy to stand next to countries that had produced Nyerere, Kaunda, Mboya, and Nkrumah."[50] Given his exposure to these international experiences, Somare was introduced to the possibilities offered new ideas such as Nyerere's conception of self-reliance, with its emphasis on finding a balance between traditional practices and development.

James Griffin has summarised Somare's plan in the following terms: "Succinctly, the eight aims were localisation, equal distribution of incomes and services, decentralisation, small-scale industry, self-reliance in production, self-reliance in the raising of revenue, equality for women and government control of the economy where necessary."[51] These policies adhered to Julius Nyerere's approach to development, which stressed that:

> Just as each village would be able to do certain things on its own, and for others would benefit from co-operating with similar villages nearby, so there are some things in which the nation as a whole has to co-operate... The job of Government would therefore be to help these self-reliant communities and to organize their co-operation with others.[52]

A number of Papua New Guinean leaders had visited Tanzania in the 1970s, and Nyerere came to Australia in 1974 at the same time as PNG was preparing for independence.[53] Somare's Eight Point Plan, which was guided by the self-reliance approach, was a product of Australian and Papua New Guinean leaders' engagement with new ideas in international development.

[50] Michael Somare, *Sana: An Autobiography of Michael Somare* (Port Moresby: Niugini Press, 1975), 75–76.

[51] Griffin, Nelson, and Firth, *Papua New Guinea*, 188–189.

[52] Nyerere, *Socialism and Rural Development*, 20.

[53] Downs, *The Australian Trusteeship Papua New Guinea, 1945–75*, 415.

The Establishment of the Australian Council for Overseas Aid

For the first two decades following the Second World War, Australian overseas developmental assistance was almost exclusively in the hands of the federal government. There were small groups of volunteers who travelled overseas to places like Indonesia to provide technical assistance, with the oldest and most famous being the Volunteer Graduate Scheme (VGS), founded by Herb Feith in 1950.[54] NGOs, including Community Aid Abroad, had also begun fundraising for overseas welfare projects. Nevertheless, these groups attracted only small numbers of supporters, and their resources were dwarfed by those available to the Australian government. The primacy of governmental aid was in keeping with the dominant conceptions of development during the period, which placed economic growth as the primary goal of international development.[55] This resulted in large-scale infrastructure programs such as hydroelectric schemes and industrial projects, which in many ways resembled the developmental aims of countries in the Global North.[56]

Large-scale projects came under increasing scrutiny by the second half of the 1960s. Around the same time that the effectiveness of large-scale development programs was coming under criticism, NGOs began to assume increased public prominence. In Australia, these groups interacted through ACFOA. Emerging out of a conference organised by John Crawford in April 1964, ACFOA sought to co-ordinate the work of voluntary aid organisations in Australia.[57] Nancy Anderson, Crawford's long-term assistant, played a vital role in the establishment of ACFOA. Inaugural member organisations included Community Aid Abroad, Freedom From Hunger Campaign, Overseas Service Bureau, along with numerous church relief organisations. Just as was happening overseas, these NGOs

[54] Purdey, *From Vienna to Yogyakarta*, 75–79; Agnieszka Sobocinska, "A New Kind of Mission: The Volunteer Graduate Scheme and the Cultural History of International Development," *Australian Journal of Politics and History* 62, no. 3 (2016); Agnieszka Sobocinska, "How to Win Friends and Influence Nations: The International History of Development Volunteering," *Journal of Global History* 12, no. 1 (2017): 49–50; Sutherland, "The Dynamics of Aid and Development," 50–81.

[55] Rist, *History of Development*, 25–46.

[56] Cullather, *The Hungry World*, 108–113.

[57] John Crawford, Press release, April 23, 1964, NLA, ACFOA Papers, MS 9347, Box 1. Kilby, *NGOs and Political Change*, 35–39.

were taking a greater interest in developmental assistance.[58] ACFOA believed NGOs could break down "institutional barriers" by:

> Providing direct financial and technical assistance to small, local projects at the 'grass roots' level which may have a valuable educational effect, helping village farmers to acquire techniques adapted to local conditions and enabling them to take advantage of large-scale water conservation or fertilizer projects etc.[59]

Many organisations took a closer interest in the 'basic needs' of people in developing countries, although there was a clear awareness of the connection between this approach and the objective of promoting growth in terms of GNP.

In its early years, ACFOA also sought to co-ordinate their activities with the government. Jim Webb, president of the Overseas Service Bureau, one of the founding member organisations of ACFOA, noted that NGOs could provide forms of aid that governments could not. Because of this:

> ACFOA is also of the view that, as voluntary agencies and Government departments develop understanding of each other, the role of the voluntary organization as an agency of aid can be recognized as a part of the overseas aid programme of the nation.[60]

For Australia, poverty alleviation and basic needs were to be the responsibility of NGOs. This work would be complementary to the developmental assistance provided by the government. As a result, ACFOA believed NGOs contributed to the overall effectiveness of Australian aid, despite the small resources at their disposal.[61]

[58] Barnett, *Empire of Humanity*, 123–124.

[59] Nancy Anderson, "Voluntary Foreign Aid Seminar, April 20–21, 1964: Review Paper Notes," NLA, ACFOA Papers, MS 9347, Box 1.

[60] ACFOA Paper, "The Objectives and Relationships with Government," March 1966, attached to Minutes of ACFOA Executive Meeting, May 3, 1966, NAA: A1838, 2101/5/1 PART 2.

[61] This was somewhat borne out by the spending figures provided at the 1964 conference, where it was stated that the combined resources of all the participating NGOs was "somewhat over £3 million," with the vast bulk of these funds belonging to church groups, compared to the governmental spending of over £45 million in the year 1963/4.

The Department of External Affairs saw potential in establishing ties with ACFOA. Paul Hasluck attended early conferences and some contacts were established with Departmental officials, such as H.D. White. ACFOA's willingness to work with the government was part of an international pattern. By the mid-1960s, many NGOs worked with governments throughout the West, mainly due to the fact that states exerted a profound degree of control over the provision of aid.[62] By working closely with governments, NGOs could expect better developmental results than if they attempted to go it alone in developing countries. ACFOA also sought recognition as an official body to secure tax-exempt status on donations.[63] As with many features of Australian aid during the age of international development, developmental and political imperatives existed simultaneously.

The growing critique of large-scale government aid projects affected the relationship between ACFOA and the government. Whereas the mid-1960s were filled with sentiments of co-operation between government and NGOs, by 1972 ACFOA was deeply critical, claiming:

> Many believe that voluntary aid is far more effective than Government aid in bringing about real and practical development to people, for despite genuine efforts to the contrary the Government is regarded as impersonal and mostly appears to be soulless.[64]

As Faye Sutherland's analysis has shown, NGOs became increasingly frustrated with the official approach towards aid during this time.[65] As another sign of this frustration, ACFOA developed close ties with prominent Australian dependency theorists, Rex Mortimer and Herb

Nancy Anderson, "Voluntary Foreign Aid Seminar, April 20–21, 1964—Review Paper Notes," NLA, ACFOA Papers, MS 9347, Box 1.

62 Barnett, *Empire of Humanity*, 118–131.

63 The campaign for tax exemption forms a substantial part of the correspondence found in Box 1 of the ACFOA papers at the NLA.

64 ACFOA Submission, For the Consideration of the Sub-Committee of the Joint Committee on Foreign Affairs of the Subject: What is the most effective form of foreign aid, bi-lateral or multi-lateral, 1972, NLA, ACFOA Papers, MS 9347, Box 1.

65 Sutherland, "The Dynamics of Aid and Development."

Feith.[66] As the government persisted with large programs that supposedly promoted economic growth, ACFOA became more firmly convinced of the need to tackle the causes of poverty at a grass-roots level.[67] While there were pragmatic reasons behind the growing distance between ACFOA and the Department of Foreign Affairs, such as over the absence of official financial support, differences over developmental ideas were pivotal in separating the two institutions.[68] The contrast between ACFOA with its 'basic needs' approach and the Foreign Affairs adherence to the orthodox growth model was more powerful than the political forces that drew them together.

ACFOA and 'Basic Needs'

The growing awareness of the "urgent and expanding needs of peoples in many parts of the world" was central to the establishment of ACFOA.[69] In 1966, ACFOA drafted a 'standing policy' paper on development and relief aid, and part of it was devoted to a critique of official aid programs. The central point of the critique was:

> International aid, whether for relief or development is not just a question of impersonal economic relationships. It involves and requires an acute and sympathetic awareness of human needs and aspirations. This personal dimension must not be lost sight of no matter how vast and impersonal the problems may seem.[70]

Comments such as these reflected the growing view that aid provided by governments was underpinned by economic theories that did not take the

[66] Appendix to Minutes of ACFOA Council Meeting, 25–26 August 1973, NLA, ACFOA Papers, MS 9347, Box 54. Jemma Purdey discusses the power of Mortimer's ideas with ACFOA member organisations such as Community Aid Abroad. Purdey, *From Vienna to Yogyakarta*, 362–364.

[67] Sutherland, "The Dynamics of Aid and Development," 68, 180.

[68] Kilby, *NGOs and Political Change*, 132. An undated "History of ACFOA" document held in the ACFOA Papers at the NLA explains that the annual grant provided from the government remained below $20,000 between 1968 and 1973, "History of ACFOA," n.d., NLA, ACFOA Papers, MS 9347, Box 2.

[69] ACFOA, Draft Constitution, February 1965, NLA, ACFOA Papers, MS 9347, Box 1.

[70] "ACFOA Standing Policy on Development and Relief Aid," March 1966, NAA: A1838, 2101/5/1 PART 2.

human aspects of development into consideration. This advocacy for the 'basic needs' conception of development assistance was ACFOA's primary contribution to the intellectual discourse on development in Australia in the second half of the 1960s.

The developmental basis for co-operation between ACFOA and the Department of External Affairs was the mutual recognition that both groups specialised in different forms of overseas aid. In his address to the ACFOA conference on the "Respective Roles of Government, United Nations and Non-Government Agencies," Hasluck admitted that voluntary organisations were often best equipped to help foreign countries with "their worst social blots."[71] On the other hand, Hasluck argued that large-scale infrastructure projects, such as road-building or other construction projects, were "a field which the voluntary agencies are not equipped to enter."[72] The departmental view placed NGOs as a supplement to the official aid program, with voluntary agencies filling the gaps left by 'official' aid. Importantly, this was a clear recognition of the different developmental approaches, with the Commonwealth restating its belief in the orthodoxy of growth and voluntary organisations taking charge at a more grass-roots level.

This division of responsibilities led to the enlistment of ACFOA in providing civil assistance in South Vietnam. Following extensive negotiations between ACFOA and External Affairs, aid workers were sent to South Vietnam to continue technical assistance programs that had lost momentum as the conflict escalated.[73] By 1967, the Commonwealth Government had paid ACFOA $18,000 to assist in the establishment of an office in South Vietnam.[74] The purpose of the office was to co-ordinate the work of ACFOA's member organisations, thereby supplementing the civil aid being provided by the government, which mainly revolved around the provision of a surgical team and a water supply

[71] Hasluck speech, "Respective Roles of Government, United Nations and Non-Government Agencies, and Opportunities for Co-operation in Overseas Aid Activities," ACFOA Conference, November 11, 1965, NAA: A1209, 1965/6531 PART 1.

[72] Hasluck, "Respective Roles of Government, United Nations and Non-Government Agencies."

[73] "Committee on Aid Will Go to Vietnam," *Canberra Times*, October 31, 1966.

[74] "History of ACFOA," n.d. [written in the late 1970s], NLA, ACFOA Papers, MS 9347, Box 2.

project in Bien Hoa, projects valued at around $1.2 million.[75] ACFOA provided assistance to the government in co-ordinating these projects, although by the end of the 1960s the collaboration between the government and ACFOA became unworkable due to intensified opposition to the war and dangerous conditions in South Vietnam.[76] As can be seen in the relative financial figures, the government's support for voluntary aid was insignificant compared to its own expenditure, despite Hasluck suggesting that Commonwealth assistance to ACFOA "could be expected to produce big increases in voluntary aid efforts."[77] For the Department of External Affairs in the second half of the 1960s, the 'basic needs' approach provided by ACFOA and its member NGOs merely filled the gap left by official aid.

While ACFOA's engagement with the Department of External Affairs indicated a degree of compromise towards the orthodox approach to development, alternative concepts steadily assumed greater prominence. This was perhaps most pronounced in their 1972 submission to the Parliamentary Joint Committee on Foreign Affairs. Titled "What is the most effective form of aid, bi-lateral or multi-lateral?", the submission criticised 'traditional' aid policies in terms set by dependency theory:

> There must be a change of attitude in the developed countries and in the decision-making centres of the developing countries. Work for development must not be allowed to continue what has become the pattern of established traditional attitudes without its being submitted to the scrutiny of the criteria of justice and equality. Aid programmes must seek to promote social justice.[78]

According to Patrick Kilby, the acceptance of these ideas was facilitated by a "heady period of social change in Australia," which by the 1970s produced a more "radical edge" amongst ACFOA's members.[79] In

[75] Department of External Affairs, "Australian Economic Aid to Viet Nam," n.d., NAA: A1209, 1965/6531 PART 1.

[76] Kilby, *NGOs and Political Change*, 41–42.

[77] "Major Boost in Vietnam Aid," *Canberra Times*, February 2, 1967.

[78] ACFOA Submission, For the Consideration of the Sub-Committee of the Joint Committee on Foreign Affairs of the Subject: What is the most effective form of foreign aid, bi-lateral or multi-lateral, 1972, NLA, ACFOA Papers, MS 9347, Box 1.

[79] Kilby, *NGOs and Political Change*, 66–67.

keeping with the influence of international forces during this period, the shift to a more radical politics in Australia followed from similar changes amongst NGOs in the UK and the United States.[80] In many ways, the critical approach provided by the anti-modernisation model (which manifested itself most clearly in Australia as anti-growth), with its emphasis on the social consequences of development assistance, suited the 'basic needs' approach of ACFOA.

Ultimately, the first decade of ACFOA's existence exemplified the changes that took place in Australian engagement with international development in the late 1960s and early 1970s. Established in 1965, ACFOA arrived at a time when the modernisation paradigm was still influential both within and outside official circles. The grass-roots approach of voluntary NGOs was thus conceived of as a supplement to official developmental assistance. By the beginning of the 1970s, however, the 'basic needs' concept became closely associated with more critical developmental approaches. ACFOA, in tune with the evolution of developmental ideas, became much more sceptical of the effectiveness of the official aid program.[81] The break between ACFOA and the Commonwealth Government was therefore a product of the shifting nature of international development.

Creating a Stand-Alone Australian Aid Agency: The Establishment of the ADAA

The previous sections have demonstrated that the late 1960s and early 1970s were marked by the arrival of new forces in the field of Australian aid policy. While the emerging voices of NGOs and Indigenous leaders in PNG called for aid that met basic needs or that promoted self-reliance, government officials in Canberra also continued to search for ways to improve Australian developmental assistance. The 1964–1965

[80] Matthew Hilton, "Ken Loach and the Save the Children Film: Humanitarianism, Imperialism, and the Changing Role of Charity in Postwar Britain," *The Journal of Modern History* 87, no. 2 (2015): 360–361; Akira Iriye, *Global Community: The Role of International Organizations in the Making of the Contemporary World* (Berkeley: University of California Press, 2002), 113–116.

[81] Box 2 of the ACFOA Papers held at NLA contains numerous documents that provide information on British and American institutional arrangements for the provision of developmental assistance.

inter-departmental aid review considered a number of reforms to aid policy. In the short-term, development policy continued to be driven by an emphasis on growth as it had since the end of the Second World War. The 1972 election of the Whitlam Labor Government provided an opportunity for significant reform in the field of foreign aid. Throughout the late 1960s and early 1970s, Labor politicians consistently targeted the aid policy of the Coalition governments, particularly in taking up the call for a minimum of one per cent of GNP to be spent on foreign assistance.[82] These calls, alongside the increased prominence of ACFOA, presented the rare situation where Australian foreign aid policy was the subject of considerable public interest. In this context, the Labor Party made it clear in their 1972 election platform that significant reforms would take place in the field of overseas aid.[83]

The clearest symbol of these reforms was the establishment of a stand-alone Australian aid agency, the ADAA. Its establishment corresponded with two important international trends. First, the ADAA was a late entrant into the international process of countries establishing stand-alone aid bureaucracies. The United States' Agency for International Development was established in 1961, the British Ministry of Overseas Development in 1964 and the Canadian International Development Agency in 1968.[84] By establishing a separate agency dedicated to the provision of foreign aid, the Whitlam Government placed development at the centre of their vision of Australian overseas economic assistance. Looking back at the brief existence of the ADAA, former Aid Branch official and Whitlam's Private Secretary, Peter Wilenski, argued that a separate aid agency would ensure "that developmental aspects (including the social and income distribution effects of aid) received a high priority in formulating aid programmes."[85]

[82] "Major ALP Policy Switch," *Canberra Times*, July 18, 1967.

[83] E.G. Whitlam, Cabinet Submission No. 634, "Administration of Australia's Foreign Aid," August 29, 1973, NAA: A571, 1973/2215 PART 16.

[84] Ekbladh, *The Great American Mission*, 192; Cumming, *Aid to Africa*, 71–72; Spicer, "Clubmanship Upstaged," 32.

[85] Peter Wilenski, "Infanticide in the Bureaucracy: The Australian Development Assistance Agency," in *Decisions: Case Studies in Australian Public Policy*, ed. Solomon Encel, Peter Wilenski, and B.B. Schaffer (Melbourne: Longman Cheshire, 1981), 104.

Secondly, the incorporation of colonial development expertise into the ADAA, most clearly expressed in the appointment of the Administrator of PNG Les Johnson to be the first head of the Agency, was in keeping with the international practice of bringing colonial officials into aid institutions.[86] The developmental goals of late colonial rule were very close to those of post-war aid programs. It therefore made sense for bureaucracies throughout the world to make use of the developmental 'expertise' of colonial officials. In the Australian context, this argument was buttressed by the expectation that after 1975 PNG would continue to receive around seventy-five per cent of Australian foreign aid.

Domestically, the forces driving the establishment of the ADAA ranged from the political to the intellectual to the pragmatic. On a political level, ALP criticism of the previous government's handling of foreign aid policy created momentum for significant change in the administration of Australian overseas assistance. On an intellectual level, the ADAA emerged out of a recognition of the limitations of the existing aid policy, with the problems of 'underdevelopment' seemingly as pressing as they were in 1950, when the Colombo Plan was formed. This could be seen in the Foreign Affairs observation that, outside of aid to Indonesia and PNG, "most of our aid has been a conglomeration of small, and often unrelated projects."[87] This was a long-held concern amongst Australian policymakers and had been at the heart of the 1965 aid review. Finally, on a pragmatic level, the independence of PNG necessitated a bureaucratic reshuffle away from the dual forces of the Departments of External Territories and Foreign Affairs.

Prior to the 1972 election, the ALP had pledged to "reorganise" the provision of Australian aid. W.L. Morrison, a former External Affairs official and Labor Minister for External Territories, played an important role in driving ALP aid policy. According to Wilenski, Morrison's work in External Affairs convinced him of "the extent to which the developmental aspects of aid were ignored in the Department and of the lack of professionalism in its aid branch."[88] Morrison's arguments found a receptive

[86] Gorman, "Britain, India, and the United Nations," 488; Dimier, *The Invention of a European Development Aid Bureaucracy*.

[87] A.R. Parsons, memorandum for Minister of Foreign Affairs, "Future Foreign Aid Programmes," January 16, 1973, NAA: M3383, 73.

[88] Wilenski, "Infanticide in the Bureaucracy," 102.

audience in Whitlam, and the ALP Federal Platform pledged reorganisation of Australian aid within the context of "accepting the United Nations programme to work towards a national contribution of one per cent of gross national product."[89] When combined with the ALP's acknowledgement that "the quantity of aid is not the full measure of its effectiveness," the incoming government conceived of aid in a different way to the Coalition governments of the previous two decades. In order to implement these changes, the new government sought to reform the aid bureaucracy. This was in keeping with the recommendations of the 1964–1965 aid review, commentary coming from ACFOA, as well as by additional comments made by John Crawford in other forums.[90] For instance, Crawford was invited by the Department of Foreign Affairs to present his views during the planning process, and he firmly indicated a preference for a "separate Department or Bureau responsible to the Foreign Minister but *not* to the Permanent Head of Foreign Affairs."[91] Comments such as these demonstrated both a concern over bureaucratic autonomy for the new agency and a desire to separate Australian aid from the diplomatic imperatives of Foreign Affairs. The structure suggested by Crawford as well as several others, such as Wilenski, prevailed, and the ADAA was formed as an autonomous agency that reported to the Foreign Minister.[92]

By separating Australian aid from the diplomatic imperatives of Foreign Affairs, the ADAA was able to emphasise the developmental aspects of economic assistance. In their 1975–1976 Annual Report, the ADAA explained that:

> Although Australia gives assistance in emergency situations for the alleviation of human suffering in the short term, the success of the aid program

[89] Extracts from Federal Platform of Australian Labor Party relative to overseas aid, attached to W.L. Morrison to E.G. Whitlam, March 8, 1973, NAA: A571, 1973/2215 PART 16.

[90] "Australian External Aid, Report to the Minister for External Affairs by the Inter-Departmental Committee to Review Australian External Aid," March 1965, 109, NAA: A4311, 147/1.

[91] J.G. Crawford, Report on Aid Administration, June 6, 1973, NAA: M3383, 73 [Emphasis in original].

[92] "Report of the Task Force on a Unified Aid Administration," May 1973, NAA: M3383, 73.

> depends ultimately on the contribution it can make to building up the capacity of developing countries to achieve self-sustaining growth.[93]

This reference to Rostow's modernisation theory suggests a degree of intellectual continuity in the aims of Australian aid, but the ADAA also implemented some policy reforms. Perhaps the most significant change was the shift away from the Colombo Plan scholarship scheme towards providing resources for the training of students in developing countries themselves.[94] The ADAA also took over the control of Australian assistance to PNG, following the closing of the Department of External Territories after the granting of self-government to PNG in 1973. With regard to specific aid projects, Nancy Viviani and Peter Wilenski identify only minor changes in the types of programs supported under the ADAA, but emphasise the increased environment of "innovation and experimentation which would lead to a great involvement of Australian aid in social welfare programs and to an impact on 'people's' problems rather than a government's problems."[95] The ADAA offered a promising sign to those who sought to bring developmental imperatives to the forefront of Australian aid policy.

Debates over the autonomy of the ADAA demonstrated that Foreign Affairs retained a concern for the political objectives of Australian aid. As Departmental Secretary Keith Waller argued:

> While in the selection and implementation of individual projects our objectives are essentially 'economic', decisions on the geographical distribution of foreign aid, the concentration on South East Asia, day-to-day decisions

[93] Australian Development Assistance Agency, *Annual Report, 1975–76* (Canberra: Australian Govt. Pub. Service, 1977), 1. Jon Piccini connects this shift to growing scepticism amongst Australian diplomats over the effectiveness of the scholarship scheme. Jon Piccini, *Transnational Protest, Australia and the 1960s: Global Protest* (London: Palgrave Macmillan, 2016), 197–199.

[94] Australian Development Assistance Agency, *Annual Report, 1975–76*, 18–19.

[95] N. Viviani and P. Wilenski, "Politicians, Bureaucrats and Foreign Aid: A Case Study," in *International Aid: Some Political, Administrative and Technical Realities*, ed. R.T. Shand and H.V. Richter (Canberra: Development Studies Centre, A.N.U., 1979), 120–121.

> on food aid, projects and training, can only be assessed in foreign policy terms.[96]

Waller's comments demonstrated the ongoing tension between developmental and political considerations in Australian aid. The fact that the Department of Foreign Affairs was unsuccessful in maintaining direct control over foreign aid indicated that the new Labor Government was less willing to allow political imperatives to drive Australian developmental assistance.

The change of government produced a shift in the long-held conflict between Treasury and External/Foreign Affairs over aid spending. Unlike his predecessors, who had believed that Australian aid contributions had to be limited by Australia's domestic needs, the new Federal Treasurer, Frank Crean, was an adherent of the 'basic needs' approach to development. The Treasurer wrote, "I would like to see Australia's aid used more effectively and would like to ensure that it is provided in such a way as to reach the under-privileged people within the developing countries."[97] While the Treasury Department continued to hold on to attitudes established in the decades of Coalition government, Crean's receptiveness to overseas developmental assistance was a new feature.[98] It also demonstrated an official engagement with some of the newer approaches towards developmental assistance.

The looming independence of PNG was a further driver in the establishment of the ADAA. As the largest recipient of Australian aid spending, and with the firm view that this situation would persist well into the future, PNG held a 'special' place in aid policy. The closing of the Department of External Territories raised questions over how the developmental expertise of its employees would be retained. The Chairman of the Public Service Board, Alan Cooley, recommended that:

[96] J.K. Waller, memorandum for Minister of Foreign Affairs, "Administration of Aid Programmes," n.d. [written in the first half of 1973], NAA: M3383, 73.

[97] Frank Crean to E.G. Whitlam, September 5, 1973, NAA: M3383, 73.

[98] Jenny Hocking provides a thorough account of the tensions experienced in the Federal Bureaucracy following the election of the new Labor Government in *Gough Whitlam*, 37.

> It is considered that with the change in the relations between Australia and Papua New Guinea, Australia's economic aid activities should be concentrated in an International Development Agency styled after the Overseas Development Administration in the United Kingdom and the Canadian International Development Agency. The objectives would be to achieve overall co-ordination of aid activities and at the same time, to raise the status of the function and to increase the quality of resources allocated to it.[99]

Further evidence of PNG's significance to the reforms of Australian aid can be seen in the decision to appoint Les Johnson, the final Administrator of the Territory, as Director-General of the ADAA.[100] Through such an appointment, a degree of continuity was established between earlier colonial development policies and the new bilateral aid relationship. As was the case throughout the decades following the Second World War, events in PNG were central to the Australian attitude and policy regarding overseas development.

The ADAA and the Clash Between Developmental and Political Imperatives

In 1976, the ADAA was renamed the Australian Development Assistance Bureau (ADAB) and incorporated back into Foreign Affairs under new Coalition Prime Minister Malcolm Fraser. The ADAA's brief existence reflects a short period where the tension between political and developmental objectives within Australian aid favoured the latter. As Faye Sutherland has argued: "Whatever ADAA might have been[,] Labor policy did at least align government thinking on aid more closely with current global development analysis."[101] We have already seen this through the 'innovative' environment that the ADAA sought to foster. New ideas could also be found in the work of the ADAA Advisory Board, which was chaired by John Crawford and included staff members from government departments, as well as from ACFOA. According to the Board's 1974 report, the ADAA was working towards the target that:

[99] "Overseas Aid Function," attached to Alan Cooley to E.G. Whitlam, May 16, 1973, NAA: M3383, 73.

[100] "Agency to Oversee Aid," *Canberra Times*, September 19, 1973.

[101] Sutherland, "The Dynamics of Aid and Development," 219.

> In the longer-term aid should contribute to self-reliance in the recipient country through the development of human and other potential... The encouragement of self-reliance in the sense of decreasing dependence on the regular input of foreign aid is in the political and economic interests of donor and recipient countries alike.[102]

Of course, the transition from 'help' to 'self-help' had been central to developmental assistance since President Truman's Point Four speech.[103] Yet, the combination of new ideas with significant bureaucratic reform gave Australian aid a different look just as the age of international development was coming to an end.

That is not to say that all debate about the nature and size of Australian aid had ended. Long-held concerns over the effectiveness of aid programs continued. In a conversation between Jim Ingram, First Assistant Secretary of the ADAA's Bilateral Programs and Operations Division, and a Treasury Department official, Ingram commented that:

> The people in the Policy Secretariat had no practical experience with projects but they continually took up whatever were the latest fashions, e.g. aid must help the poorest sections of the community, it must go to the rural areas etc. While these objectives were highly desirable, they were often completely irrelevant when it came to the design of an Australian aid project, which was usually so small that it could have no impact on income distribution or other high-minded objectives except in a very remote fashion.[104]

This revealing comment speaks to the engagement of ADAA officials with the new developmentalism of the early 1970s, while also highlighting the difficulties in implementing the various approaches through policy. The ADAA in 1975, much like the Department of External Affairs with the Colombo Plan in 1950, was the location for Australian bureaucrats with an interest in development to attempt to implement developmental theories on a limited budget. As was the case throughout the period from 1945 to 1975, Australian aid was guided by international trends

[102] "Getting Aid to Those Who Really Need It," *Canberra Times*, March 22, 1974.

[103] Rist comments on how self-reliance shares a contradiction with more orthodox approaches to aid, in that it created "a paradoxical situation where what was done contradicted the declared goal." Rist, *History of Development*, 133.

[104] R.H. Dean, Minutes of conversation with Jim Ingram, October 14, 1975, NAA: A571, 1973/2215 PART 16.

in development, but had to contend with political and bureaucratic obstacles.

Australian Aid at the End of the Age of International Development

The final decade of the age of international development was marked by the rise of new ideas that put further pressure on the orthodox foundations of Australian aid. These new ideas found their way into Australian aid policy, as seen in the newfound recognition of basic needs and the acceptance that PNG's development might not adhere strictly to the Australian model. However, there was also a degree of continuity. In 1974–1975, PNG and the Colombo Plan accounted for almost $210 million out of Australia's overall bilateral aid budget of $278 million.[105] Small project aid continued to comprise the majority of Australia's economic assistance, while significant numbers of students continued to be sent to Australia under the Colombo Plan scholarship scheme. By mid-1975, there were 1775 Colombo Plan scholars in Australian educational institutions, with a grand total of 15,041 coming to Australia between 1950 and 1975.[106] PNG continued to be dependent on Australian aid, but there was now a much greater emphasis on the desires of the Indigenous population. These changes, alongside the arrival of the first Labor Government in over two decades, drove the establishment of the ADAA.

The creation of the ADAA reflected a desire for developmental objectives to take precedence over political goals. By taking the responsibility for Australian aid away from the Department of Foreign Affairs, the Whitlam Labor Government signalled their intentions to give aid policy a clearer developmental basis. Similarly, the increased significance of NGOs organised under ACFOA by the 1970s indicated that the diplomatic objectives of Australian aid were less significant than the developmental. Finally, PNG's independence caused a significant bureaucratic reshuffle that brought significant amounts of developmental experience into the new ADAA. The intersection of all of these events ensured the ascendancy of development in Australian aid policy. While this ascendancy was short lived, it can be seen as the culmination of three decades of intellectual and political adaptation.

[105] *Official Year Book of the Commonwealth of Australia* (Canberra: Commonwealth Bureau of Census and Statistics, 1976), 127.

[106] *Official Year Book of the Commonwealth of Australia*, 128.

CHAPTER 8

Conclusion

Between 1945 and 1975, developmental imperatives were at the forefront of Australian foreign and colonial policies. While political considerations were a part of aid policy throughout this period, they existed alongside concerns over development. Australia's involvement in the age of international development was motivated by more than just self-interest and a desire for Asian engagement. Humanitarian concern for the plight of people living in poverty combined with increased academic interest in the process of development to guide Australian policymakers in the provision of economic assistance. This combination of forces was found in Australia's policy towards both PNG and Southeast Asia.

Looking at the Colombo Plan or Australian policy in PNG only tells part of the story. Development provided the link between these two areas of government spending. While the two areas of Australian aid were not closely associated by policymakers throughout the 1950s, by the mid-1960s they had begun to acknowledge that assistance to PNG closely resembled Colombo Plan aid. Paul Hasluck's experience as both Minister for Territories and External Affairs provided a personal link between PNG and the Colombo Plan. By bringing PNG into the history of Australian aid between 1945 and 1975, this book has highlighted the close links between colonial development and post-war foreign aid policies. While there were important differences between the two areas of assistance, they formed two complementary strands in post-war Australian aid.

N. Ferns, *Australia in the Age of International Development, 1945–1975*, Security, Conflict and Cooperation in the Contemporary World, https://doi.org/10.1007/978-3-030-50228-7_8

Both the New Deal in PNG and the Colombo Plan emerged out of the complex interaction between the post-Atlantic Charter concern with global poverty and the recognition amongst policymakers that promoting development throughout the poorer parts of the world was in the national interest. By 1950, the twin strands of Australian aid policy had been put into place. The 1950s were marked by a process of consolidation both in PNG and in the Colombo Plan. After existing alongside one another with minimal interaction, by the mid-1960s PNG was quickly incorporated into Australian policy towards the developing world. Considerations over the development of PNG had an effect on the Middle Zone policy at UNCTAD, as it undermined McEwen's claim that Australia was not a "developed" country. The 1964–1965 aid review brought out the developmental and political arguments for counting spending on PNG as a form of aid. By the 1970s, PNG was on course to become independent and the colonial expertise established in Australia over the previous two decades was incorporated into the ADAA.

In going beyond the orthodox assumption that the Colombo Plan was the dominant component of Australian aid in the decades following the Second World War, I challenge the dominance of political imperatives in Australian aid policy. Instead, I have focused on the developmental considerations behind Australia's spending on development in PNG and Asia. There was often tension between these imperatives, as Australian policymakers were regularly driven by a combination of political and developmental factors. At times the political factors were dominant, such as in Spender's arguments for the establishment of the Colombo Plan. At other times developmental considerations took priority, as in the establishment and brief existence of the ADAA. At all times, however, both imperatives were present. While the political aspects of Australian aid have received substantial historical attention, the developmental side of the debate has been under-examined. This book has restored this balance, establishing a more comprehensive understanding of Australian aid policy between 1945 and 1975.

This tension continues to be felt in Australian aid policy, as developmental imperatives compete with an emphasis on the political benefits that come from aid spending. This is the case today, as the Coalition government's aid policy under recent Foreign Affairs Minister Julie Bishop placed a clear emphasis on the political objectives of foreign aid. Under Bishop, the Australian Agency for International Development (AusAID) was incorporated into the Department of Foreign Affairs and Trade

(DFAT) in order to align Australian "diplomatic, trade, and development efforts" as part of an attempt to strengthen "economic diplomacy."[1] Similar imperatives can be found in Australian concern over increased Chinese interest in providing aid to countries like PNG.[2] Examining the history of Australian aid helps to understand contemporary policy. As Joseph Hodge writes:

> Historians are not in the business of predicting what will happen, but what we *can* do is examine the historical context and complexities of current policy prescriptions more deeply, which, if nothing else, will alert those interested enough to listen to the potential pitfalls and ramifications of certain actions.[3]

The history of Australian foreign aid and colonial policy during the age of international development therefore not only informs our understanding of that period, but also provides valuable information that can guide contemporary development practice.

Australian aid was informed by international political and intellectual trends throughout the age of international development. While domestic political interests and diplomatic benefits undoubtedly motivated the establishment of the Colombo Plan and Australian policy in PNG, international forces were often just as influential. Australian experts and policymakers were deeply interested in overseas trends, and they had a clear sense of how Australian policy fitted into a broader international context.

Whether it was in the sphere of colonial development or through the Colombo Plan, advances in Australian aid policy were closely related to shifts in development theory and practice overseas, particularly in the United States and the UK. It was no coincidence that Eddie Ward and his Department of External Territories decided to implement a New Deal for

[1] Department of Foreign Affairs and Trade, *Australian Aid: Promoting Prosperity, Reducing Poverty, Enhancing Stability* (Canberra: Department of Foreign Affairs and Trade, 2014), iii.

[2] "China's Aid to Papua New Guinea Threatens Australia's Influence," *The Guardian*, July 3, 2018, https://www.theguardian.com/world/2018/jul/02/chinas-aid-to-papua-new-guinea-threatens-australias-influence.

[3] Joseph Morgan Hodge, "Writing the History of Development (Part 2: Longer, Deeper, Wider)," *Humanity: An International Journal of Human Rights, Humanitarianism, and Development* 7, no. 1 (2016): 160.

PNG after the war. As international concerns over the plight of colonised peoples coalesced with the newfound developmental imperatives, colonial development under the auspices of trusteeship became a central component of colonial practice throughout the world. The Hasluck era in PNG coincided with the rise of the modernisation paradigm of development. This phenomenon in international development informed Hasluck's emphasis on agriculture and education, while also challenging his conception of uniform development. Similarly, the Colombo Plan emerged out of international forces that drew developmental theory into foreign policy. By the mid-1960s, the rising challenge of dependency theory was felt keenly in Australia. McEwen's Middle Zone policy was both a response to these ideas and an attempt to present an Australian counter to the dichotomy of international development. The 1964–1965 aid review followed similar investigations in the United States and the UK. It also provided a forum for the different developmental approaches within the Canberra bureaucracy to emerge, many of which were informed by ideas that originated overseas. This culminated in the emergence of new ideas and institutions in the final decade of the age of international development. In a similar way to the international influence of ideas of trusteeship and modernisation, the basic needs and self-reliance approaches illustrated the power of international trends on Australian policy.

In Australia between 1945 and 1975, an increasing number of scholars became interested in developmental economics in the post-war decades, observing and engaging in a global conversation that encouraged theoretical and policy advances Importantly, these scholars were also very closely involved with Australian policymaking institutions, ensuring that public policy was informed by academic expertise. This established an important trend that persisted through to the early 1970s. Australian economists including Douglas Copland, John Crawford, Heinz Arndt and Rex Mortimer engaged with international theoretical trends, and the broad meaning of "development" underwent a constant process of evolution and re-evaluation. This impacted upon Australian policymakers.

Throughout the age of international development, a number of different positions on development emerged within the Commonwealth bureaucracy. Officials within External Affairs engaged with international trends, advocating what has broadly been referred to as a "growth" model of development. According to this view, increased financial and technical assistance to poorer countries was expected to enable states to undergo the development process. In contrast to the External Affairs emphasis on the developmental needs of other nations, Treasury and Trade and Industry acknowledged the need for international development so long as it also benefitted Australia. Presenting Australia as a "developing" country, these departments were far more likely to engage with the self-interested arguments behind overseas assistance, as they aimed to get the most "bang" for their aid "buck." Finally, Territories maintained what they perceived as the extremely difficult task of bringing PNG out of its "primitive" state into a modern society that would eventually be prepared for independence. Guided by the principles of trusteeship, Territories highlighted the special "responsibility" Australia had in PNG, favouring a gradual approach until the progress towards independence suddenly accelerated in the 1960s. These ideological differences within the Commonwealth bureaucracy had a profound influence over developmental policies.

Ultimately, this book adds to the story of Australian aid by looking beyond the political dimensions of the Colombo Plan. It has shown that Australian assistance to PNG was the dominant form of Australian aid, and that policymakers in Canberra paid close attention to the constantly evolving field of international development. Thus, this book tells us as much about the age of international development as it does Australian aid between 1945 and 1975. The Australian case study reveals the close interaction between colonial governance and post-war development practice. It also demonstrates how ideas flowed around the world and impacted upon debates over aid policy. International notions of trusteeship, modernisation and dependency all found their way into the Commonwealth bureaucracy and were adopted or challenged by different government departments. The Australian story was one of adaptation and evolution, of debate and compromise. No idea was hegemonic, and no policy was static. The evolution of Australian aid policy throughout the age of international development illustrated the close engagement of Australian experts and policymakers with the rest of the world. While national and regional interests were always present, the developmental considerations of Australian aid were a product of international forces.

Bibliography

Archival Sources

National Archives of Australia, Canberra

A452 – Department of Territories: Correspondence Files, 1951–1975

1957/950 – Canberra Comments - Article - Development in Papua and New Guinea.

1957/3985 – Education - General - Papua and New Guinea.

1958/3188 – Lutheran Mission - New Guinea - Economic development of Papua and New Guinea indigenous people.

1958/4106 – Trusteeship Council Resolutions - Economic advancement - New Guinea.

1960/374 – Forward planning for development in Papua and New Guinea.

1960/2803 – Tactics in United Nations, regarding Trusteeship and Non-Self-Governing Territories.

1960/4427 – Plan for accelerated development in education in Papua and New Guinea.

1960/5670 – Proposed 'Colombo Plan' for the Pacific under the South Pacific Commission.

1961/928 – Survey of Papua and New Guinea by the International Bank.

1961/6694 – Address by the Minister to the NSW Branch of the Economic Society of Australia - Economic development of Papua and New Guinea.

1962/5561 – Policy re political development in Papua and New Guinea.

1963/7763 – United Nations conference on trade and development.

N. Ferns, *Australia in the Age of International Development, 1945–1975*, Security, Conflict and Cooperation in the Contemporary World, https://doi.org/10.1007/978-3-030-50228-7

1964/2692 – Brief for the Australian delegation to the United Nations conference on trade and development.
1970/3068 – Visit to Papua New Guinea by the Prime Minister - July 1970 - briefs and speeches.
1970/4775 – Papua New Guinea Development Programme - 1970/1971 to 1971/1975 - Social Development and Home Affairs section.
1972/2133 – U.N.D.P./I.B.R.D. [United Nations Development Program/International Bank for Reconstruction and Development] - East Anglia University - visit to Papua New Guinea by four experts 1972.
1973/291 – CP - Policy and finance - Policy towards countries - Papua/New Guinea - Report on development strategies for Papua New Guinea 1973 (The 'Faber Report').

A518 – Department of External Territories: Correspondence Files, 1928–1956

A58/3/3 – Commodities - Cocoa - Papua and New Guinea - Proposals for development - G.L. McClure.
A114/1/1 PART 1 – Establishment and organisation of the Australian School of Pacific Administration.
A114/1/1 PART 2 – Establishment and organisation of the Australian School of Pacific Administration.
A927/1 – Economic Development of the Territories - Organisation - Formation of 1949 Committees.
B927/1 PART 1 – Economic Development of the Territories - Organisation - General organisation of work.
C2/1/1 – Advancement of Native Agriculture - Papua & New Guinea.
R815/1/1 PART 1 – Post War Reconstruction - Australian Pacific Territories Research Council.
T800/1/7 – Papua and New Guinea - Administration - Proposed visit of Minister of External Territories to Papua and New Guinea (Honourable Ward, E.J.).

A571 – Department of the Treasury: Correspondence Files, 1901–1976

1947/1529 PART 2 – Post UNRRA Relief Part 2.
1973/2215 PART 16 – Establishment of the Australian Development Assistance Agency.

A989 – Department of External Affairs: Correspondence Files, 1942–1945

1943/735/651 – PWR [Post War Reconstruction] - Australian Institute of International Affairs - Reports.

A1068 – Department of External Affairs: Correspondence Files, 1947

DL47/5/6 – South East Asia.
R47/3/1 – UNRRA - UNRRA Policy. General Policy.

A1209 – Prime Minister's Department: Correspondence Files, 1957–

1957/5406 – Colombo Plan - Australian Policy.
1965/6531 PART 1 – Aid for Vietnam - Other (than military).

A1313 – Department of Trade and Industry: Correspondence Files, 1959–1989

1964/2380 PART 1 – UNCTAD [United Nations Conference on Trade and Development] - Australian position.
1964/2388 – UNCTAD [United Nations Conference on Trade and Development] - notes for the Secretary.

A1838 – Department of External Affairs: Correspondence Files, 1948–1989

301/9 – Territory of Papua and New Guinea - Administration and Government - Inter-Departmental Committee for the co-ordination of plans for the development of Papua and New Guinea.
532/5/2/2 – Conference of British Commonwealth Foreign Ministers - Colombo, January 1950 - Brief for the Australian delegation - The Honourable P C Spender K.C. - Australian Minister for External Affairs.
740/4/5 PART 1 – Colombo Plan.
909/8/1/5 – Dependent territories - visit of Sir Hugh Foot [head of UN Visiting Mission to New Guinea and Nauru; consultations with Departments of External Affairs and Territories, e.g. on anti-colonialism in UN].
2020/1/2 PART 1 – Colombo Plan Policy (1957–1961).
2020/1/2 PART 3 – Colombo Plan - Policy and procedure - General policy.
2020/1/2 PART 4 – Colombo Plan policy and procedure - Policy - General.
2020/1/12 PART 1 – Technical Co-operation Scheme - Australian effort - Progress Report [on the Colombo Plan].
2020/1/12 PART 3 – Colombo Plan - Australian Progress Reports.

2020/1/24 PART 2 – Policy Review of Australian External Aid Programs.
2020/1/24 PART 3 – Policy Review of Australian External Aid Programs.
2020/1/24/1 PART 1 – Policy - Review of Australian External Aid Programme - Information from overseas posts.
2020/1/24/1 PART 2 – Policy review of Australian external aid programme - Information from overseas posts.
2020/1/24/2 – Policy review of Australian External Aid Programme - Submission by Department not represented on the Committee.
2020/1/24/20 – CP Review of Australian External Aid - Set (3) Preliminary Documentation, Description Origin and purposes of Australian External Aid.
2020/1/24/23 – Colombo Plan - Review of Australian External Aid - Set Number 3 - Documents 46–73.
2020/1/33 – Colombo Plan - Aid Policy - Advisory Committee.
2036/5 PART 9 – Colombo Plan - Indonesia - Economic aid - General.
2101/5/1 PART 2 – Australian Voluntary Aid Co-ordinating Bodies - Australian Council for Overseas Aid.
3004/11 PART 1 – South East Asia - Australian Policy towards South East Asia - General.

A3092 – Australian Embassy, Washington: Correspondence Files, 1958–

221/1/4/7/6 – Development assistance group.

A3318 – Department of External Affairs, London: Correspondence Files, 1948–1950

L1950/3/2/28 – [Political and Economic - British Commonwealth Relations] Commonwealth Foreign Ministers Meetings - Colombo, 1950.

A4311 – Cumpston Collection of documents relating to the history of Australian foreign policy, 1960–1969

147/1 – Australian External Aid, Report to the Minister for External Affairs by the Inter-Departmental Committee to Review Australian External Aid.

A4639 – Fourth Menzies Ministry - folders of Cabinet submissions and associated decisions, 1949–1951

37 – Meeting of British Commonwealth Foreign Ministers, Colombo, January 1950.

A9879 – Department of Trade: Papers relating to Post War economic matters, particularly General Agreement on Tariffs and Trade (GATT), 1927–1956

2202/E PART 1 – Colombo Plan. Economic assistance to South and South East Asia. British Commonwealth Consultative Committee documents.

A10617 – Colombo Plan: Records of Meetings of the Consultative Committee, 1950–1971

1950/1 – [Colombo Plan] Meeting of Commonwealth Foreign Ministers, January 1950 - Conference Papers.
1950/5 – [Colombo Plan] British Commonwealth Consultative Committee [2nd Meeting, Sydney] - main meeting - proceedings part 1.

M3383 – Folders of papers maintained by Dr Wilenski while Principal Private Secretary to Prime Minister, Mr Whitlam, 1972–1974

73 – Dr Peter Steven WILENSKI, AC - Australian Development Assistance Agency.

STATE LIBRARY OF NEW SOUTH WALES, MITCHELL LIBRARY

MLMSS 4268—H.C. Coombs Papers.
MS 1309—H.V. Evatt Papers.

NATIONAL ARCHIVES OF THE UNITED STATES, COLLEGE PARK, MARYLAND

Decimal File, 1950–54, Record Group 59, Central File for State Department Records.

NATIONAL LIBRARY OF AUSTRALIA, CANBERRA

MS 802—H.C. Coombs Papers.
MS 2396—E.J. Ward Papers.
MS 3788—Alan Watt Papers.
MS 4514—John Crawford Papers.
MS 7662—L.R. McIntyre Papers.
MS 7851—William McMahon Ball Papers.
MS 9347—Australian Council for Overseas Aid Papers.
MS 9847—Arthur Tange Papers.

United Nations Archives, New York

United Nations Archives. S-0288-0021-05. Office of the Chef de Cabinet fonds. Economic and Social Affairs—subject files. United Nations Conference on Trade and Development—institutional arrangements.

———. S-0552-0007-0005. United Nations Conference on Trade and Development (UNCTAD) and United Nations Industrial Development Organisation (UNIDO).

———. S-0858-0003-01. Secretary-General U Thant fonds. Commissions, Committees, and Conferences. Conference on Trade and Development.

———. S-0858-0003-02. Secretary-General U Thant fonds. Commissions, Committees, and Conferences.

Statistical Collections

Official Year Book of the Commonwealth of Australia. Canberra: Commonwealth Bureau of Census and Statistics, 1966.

Official Year Book of the Commonwealth of Australia. Canberra: Commonwealth Bureau of Census and Statistics, 1970.

Official Year Book of the Commonwealth of Australia. Canberra: Commonwealth Bureau of Census and Statistics, 1973.

Official Year Book of the Commonwealth of Australia. Canberra: Commonwealth Bureau of Census and Statistics, 1976.

Media and Periodicals

Australian Financial Review, February 2, 1965.

Brisbane Courier-Mail, "Spender Plan Emerges," January 14, 1950.

Canberra Times, "Post-War New Deal for New Guinea Natives," September 23, 1943.

Canberra Times, October 30, 1957.

Canberra Times, "Colonialism in Reverse," October 19, 1966.

Canberra Times, "Committee on Aid Will Go to Vietnam," October 31, 1966.

Canberra Times, "Major Boost in Vietnam Aid," February 2, 1967.

Canberra Times, "Major ALP Policy Switch," July 18, 1967.

Canberra Times, "Agency to Oversee Aid," September 19, 1973.

Canberra Times, "Getting Aid to Those Who Really Need It," March 22, 1974.

Melbourne Age, October 31, 1953.

Pacific Islands Monthly, "Progress of Rehabilitation in Papua-New Guinea," January 18, 1946.

Pacific Islands Monthly, "New Guinea Progress is Shackled by Canberra," September 1, 1954.

Pacific Islands Monthly, "Minister Hasluck's Papua-New Guinea," September 1, 1956.
Sydney Morning Herald, "After UNRRA," May 14, 1947.
Sydney Morning Herald, February 10, 1965.
The Guardian, "Michael Faber Obituary," March 26, 2015.
The Guardian, "China's Aid to Papua New Guinea Threatens Australia's Influence," July 3, 2018.

Government Publications

Australian Development Assistance Agency. *Annual Report, 1975–76*. Canberra: Australian Govt. Pub. Service., 1977.
Commonwealth of Australia. *Commonwealth Parliamentary Debates*. House of Representatives, no. 27 (1945).
———. *Commonwealth Parliamentary Debates*. House of Representatives, no. 23 (1950).
———. *Commonwealth Parliamentary Debates*. House of Representatives, no. 36 (1952).
———. *Commonwealth Parliamentary Debates*. House of Representatives, no. 35 (1954).
———. *Commonwealth Parliamentary Debates*. House of Representatives, no. 38 (1954).
———. *Commonwealth Parliamentary Debates*. House of Representatives, no. 40 (1955).
———. *Commonwealth Parliamentary Debates*. House of Representatives, no. 40 (1959).
———. *Commonwealth Parliamentary Debates*. House of Representatives, no. 13 (1960).
———. *Commonwealth Parliamentary Debates*. House of Representatives, no. 41 (1960).
———. *Commonwealth Parliamentary Debates*. House of Representatives, no. 8 (1962).
———. *Commonwealth Parliamentary Debates*. House of Representatives, no. 18 (1962).
———. *Commonwealth Parliamentary Debates*. House of Representatives, no. 19 (1963).
———. *Commonwealth Parliamentary Debates*. House of Representatives, no. 20 (1963).
———. *Commonwealth Parliamentary Debates*. House of Representatives, no. 20 (1965).
———. *Our North, Our Future: White Paper on Developing Northern Australia*. Canberra: Commonwealth of Australia, 2015.

Department of External Affairs. *New Hope for Asia: The Colombo Plan for Co-Operative Economic Development in South and South-East Asia*. Sydney: F.H. Johnston, 1951.

Department of Foreign Affairs and Trade. *Australian Aid: Promoting Prosperity, Reducing Poverty, Enhancing Stability*. Canberra: Department of Foreign Affairs and Trade, 2014.

Organisation for Economic Co-operation and Development. *Development Co-operation Report 1999: Efforts and Policies of the Members of the Development Assistance Committee*. Paris: Organisation for Economic Co-operation and Development, 2000.

United Nations. *Proceedings of the United Nations Conference on Trade and Development, Geneva, 23 March–16 June 1964*. 8 vols. New York: United Nations, 1964.

United Nations Department of Economic Affairs, ed. *Economic Development in Selected Countries: Plans, Programmes and Agencies*. Vol. 2. Lake Success: United Nations, 1947.

———. *Measures for the Economic Development of Under-developed Countries: Report by a Group of Experts Appointed by the Secretary-General of the United Nations*. New York: United Nations Publications, 1951.

United Nations Economic Commission for Latin America. *The Economic Development of Latin America and Its Principal Problems*. Lake Success: United Nations Dept. of Economic Affairs, 1950.

United Nations Trusteeship Council. *Report of the Drafting Committee on the Report on the Administration of the Trust Territory of New Guinea for the Year 1 July 1946 to 30 June 1947*. Lake Success: United Nations, 1948.

United States Department of State. *Foreign Relations of the United States, 1950. East Asia and the Pacific*. Vol. 4. Washington, DC: Government Printing Office, 1976.

World Bank. *The Economic Development of the Territory of Papua and New Guinea*. Canberra: Department of Territories, 1964.

World Bank, and United Nations Development Programme. *A Report on Development Strategies for Papua New Guinea: Prepared by a Mission from the Overseas Development Group (University of East Anglia) for the International Bank for Reconstruction and Development acting as agency for the United Nations Development Programme*. Port Moresby: IBRD, 1973.

Theses

Sutherland, Faye. "The Dynamics of Aid and Development: Australian and Asian Responses to Poverty in the Region 1950s–1990s." PhD Thesis, University of NSW, 1997.

Wilkinson, Alan E. "The Politics of Australian Aid Policy, 1950–1972." PhD Thesis, ANU, 1976.

Published Primary Sources

Almond, Gabriel, and James S. Coleman, eds. *The Politics of Developing Areas*. Princeton: Princeton University Press, 1960.

Amarshi, Azeem, Kenneth Good, and Rex Mortimer. *Development and Dependency: The Political Economy of Papua New Guinea*. Melbourne; New York: Oxford University Press, 1979.

Arndt, H.W. "Australia—Developed, Developing or Midway?" *Economic Record* 41, no. 95 (1965): 318–340.

———. *A Small Rich Industrial Country: Studies in Australian Development, Aid and Trade*. Melbourne; Canberra: Cheshire, 1968.

———. *A Course Through Life*. Canberra: National Centre for Development Studies, Australian National University, 1985.

Belshaw, Cyril S. "Native Administration in South-Eastern Papua." *Australian Outlook* 5, no. 2 (1951): 106–115.

———. "Community Development in Papua." *Australian Outlook* 6, no. 1 (1952): 50–59.

Belshaw, James P. Review of *Possibilities of Economic Progress*, by A.J. Youngson. *Economic Record* 35, no. 3 (1959): 448.

Bettison, David George. "The People of Papua-New Guinea." In *The Independence of Papua-New Guinea: What are the Pre-requisites?—Four Lectures Presented Under the Auspices of the Public Lectures Committee of the Australian National University*, edited by David George Bettison, E.K. Fisk, F.J. West, and J.G. Crawford. Sydney: Angus and Robertson, 1962.

Blyth, C.A. Review of *The Economics of Take-off into Sustained Growth*, edited by W.W. Rostow. *Australian Outlook* 40, no. 4 (1964): 611–613.

Burton, John W. *The Alternative: A Dynamic Approach to our Relations with Asia*. Sydney: Morgans Publications, 1954.

Carr-Gregg, John. "The Colombo Plan: A Commonwealth Program for Southeast Asia." *International Conciliation*, no. 467 (1951): 3–55.

Clark, Colin, and John Crawford. *The National Income of Australia*. Sydney: Angus & Robertson, 1938.

Cleland, Rachel. *Pathways to Independence: Story of Official and Family Life in Papua New Guinea from 1951 to 1975*. Cottesloe: R. Cleland, 1985.

Clunies Ross, Anthony. *One Per Cent: The Case for Greater Australian Foreign Aid*. Melbourne: Melbourne University Press, 1963.

Coombs, H.C. *Trial Balance*. South Melbourne: Macmillan, 1981.

Copland, D.B. "Balance of Production in the Australian Post-War Economy." *Economic Record* 25, no. 2 (1949): 1–6.

———. *The Changing Structure of the Western Economy*. Montreal: McGill University Press, 1963.

Crawford, J.G. "Emerging Issues in New Guinea." In *The Independence of Papua-New Guinea: What Are the Pre-requisites?—Four Lectures Presented Under the Auspices of the Public Lectures Committee of the Australian National University*, edited by David George Bettison, E.K. Fisk, F.J. West, and J.G. Crawford. Sydney: Angus and Robertson, 1962.

———. *Australian Trade Policy 1942–1966: A Documentary History*. Canberra: Australian National University Press, 1968.

Crawford, J.G., and A.A. Ross. *Wartime Agriculture in Australia and New Zealand 1939–50*. Stanford, CA: Stanford University Press, 1954.

Fisk, E.K. "The Economy of Papua-New Guinea." In *The Independence of Papua-New Guinea: What are the Pre-requisites?—Four Lectures Presented Under the Auspices of the Public Lectures Committee of the Australian National University*, edited by David George Bettison, E.K. Fisk, F.J. West, and J.G. Crawford. Sydney: Angus and Robertson, 1962.

Fitzpatrick, Brian. *The British Empire in Australia: An Economic History 1834–1939*. Melbourne: Melbourne University Press in association with Oxford University Press, 1941.

Frank, Andre Gunder. *Capitalism and Underdevelopment in Latin America: Historical Studies of Chile and Brazil*. Rev. ed. Harmondsworth: Penguin, 1971.

Fry, T.P. "Papua and Mandated New Guinea Today." *Pacific Affairs* 19, no. 2 (1946): 146–164.

Hasluck, Paul. *Australian Policy in Papua and New Guinea*. University of Sydney, 1956.

———. "The Economic Development of Papua and New Guinea." *Australian Outlook* 16, no. 1 (1962): 5–25.

———. *A Time for Building: Australian Administration in Papua and New Guinea, 1951–1963*. Carlton, VIC: Melbourne University Press, 1976.

Hefford, R.K. "Foreign Aid—Australia's Contribution." *Economic Record* 38, no. 2 (1962): 246–257.

Kerr, J.R. "The Political Future of New Guinea." *Australian Outlook* 13, no. 3 (1959): 181–192.

Lederer, Katrin, Johan Galtung, and David Antal. *Human Needs: A Contribution to the Current Debate*. Koenigstein/Ts.: 1980.

Legge, J.D. *Australian Colonial Policy: A Survey of Native Administration and European Development in Papua*. Sydney: Angus & Robertson, 1956.

Lerner, Daniel. *The Passing of Traditional Society: Modernizing the Middle East*. Glencoe, IL: Free Press, 1958.

Lewis, W. Arthur. *Principles of Economic Planning*. Washington, DC: Public Affairs Press, 1951.

———. *The Theory of Economic Growth*. London: Allen & Unwin, 1955.

Leyser, J. "Australia and the Post-War Settlement in South-East Asia." *Australian Outlook* 3, no. 3 (1949): 183–189.

Lowe, David, and Daniel Oakman, eds. *Australia and the Colombo Plan, 1949-1957*. Barton, ACT: Department of Foreign Affairs and Trade, 2004.

Lugard, F.D. *The Principle of Trusteeship for Backward Races*. Marlborough, UK: Adam Matthew Digital, 2007.

Mair, Lucy. *Australia in New Guinea*. London; Melbourne: Christophers, 1948.

Mandelbaum, Kurt. *The Industrialisation of Backward Areas*. Oxford: B. Blackwell, 1945.

McDonald, A.H., ed. *Trusteeship in the Pacific*. Sydney: Angus & Robertson, 1949.

Merrill, Dennis, ed. *Documentary History of the Truman Presidency*. Vol. 27. Bethesda, MD: University Publications of America, 1995.

Millikan, Max Franklin, and W.W. Rostow. *A Proposal: Key to an Effective Foreign Policy*. New York, NY: Harper, 1957.

Mortimer, Rex. "From Ball to Arndt: The Liberal Impasse in Australian Scholarship on Southeast Asia." In *Showcase State: The Illusion of Indonesia's "Accelerated Modernisation"*, edited by Rex Mortimer. Sydney: Angus & Robertson, 1973.

———, ed. *Showcase State: The Illusion of Indonesia's "Accelerated Modernisation"*. Sydney: Angus & Robertson, 1973.

Murray, Hubert. *Papua of To-day: Or an Australian Colony in the Making*. London: P.S. King & Son, 1925.

Murray, J.K. "In Retrospect 1945–1952: Papua-New Guinea and Territory of Papua and New Guinea." In *The History of Melanesia*, edited by Ken Inglis. Port Moresby: University of Papua New Guinea, 1969.

Myrdal, Gunnar. "Economic Nationalism and Internationalism." *Australian Outlook* 11, no. 4 (1957): 3-50.

———. *Asian Drama: An Inquiry into the Poverty of Nations*. 3 vols. New York: Pantheon, 1968.

Neale, R.G. "Australian Interests In and Attitudes Towards Economic Assistance to Asia." In *Australian Policies Toward Asia: Australian Papers, Institute of Pacific Relations Conference, 1954*, edited by Gordon Greenwood. Melbourne: Australian Institute of International Affairs, 1954.

Nyerere, Julius K. *Socialism and Rural Development*. Dar es Salaam: Printed by the Govt. Printer, 1967.

Prebisch, Raul. *Towards a New Trade Policy for Development*. New York: United Nations, 1964.

Pye, Lucian W. *Personality, and Nation Building: Burma's Search for Identity*. New Haven: Yale University Press, 1962.

Rosenstein-Rodan, P.N. "The International Development of Economically Backward Areas." *International Affairs* 20, no. 2 (1944): 157–165.

Rostow, W.W. *The Stages of Economic Growth: A Non-Communist Manifesto.* London: Cambridge University Press, 1960.

Shann, E.O.G. *An Economic History of Australia.* Cambridge: Cambridge University Press, 1930.

Shannon, Ian. "Economic Aid." *Australian Outlook* 17, no. 3 (1963): 328–338.

Shaw, A.G.L. *The Economic Development of Australia.* Rev. ed. London: Longmans, Green, 1946.

Singh, L.P. *The Colombo Plan: Some Political Aspects.* Canberra: Department of International Relations, Research School of Pacific Studies, Australian National University, 1963.

Somare, Michael. *Sana: An Autobiography of Michael Somare.* Port Moresby: Niugini Press, 1975.

Spate, O.H.K., C.S. Belshaw, and T.W. Swan. *Some Problems of Development in New Guinea: Report of a Working Committee of the Australian National University.* Canberra: Australian National University, 1953.

Spender, Percy. *Exercises in Diplomacy: The ANZUS Treaty and the Colombo Plan.* Sydney: Sydney University Press, 1969.

Staley, Eugene. *World Economy in Transition.* New York: Council on Foreign Relations, 1939.

———. *World Economic Development: Effects on Advanced Industrial Countries.* Montreal: International Labour Office, 1944.

———. *The Future of Underdeveloped Countries: Political Implications of Economic Development.* Rev. ed. New York: Praeger, 1961.

Stanner, W.E.H. Review of *Costa Rica: A Study in Economic Development*, by Stacy May, et al. *Australian Outlook* 9, no. 4 (1955): 252.

Tan, Augustine H.H. "Special Development Problems of a Plural Society: The Malayan Example—A Comment." *Economic Record* 40, no. 1 (1964): 114–121.

Tange, Arthur. *Defence Policy-Making: A Close-up View, 1950–1980.* Canberra: ANU E Press, 2008.

"Trusteeship Agreement for the Territory of New Guinea." In *Australia and Papua New Guinea*, edited by W.J. Hudson. Sydney: Sydney University Press, 1971.

Ward, E.E. "The Economic Commission for Asia and the Far East." *Australian Outlook* 2, no. 3 (1948): 139–146.

———. "The Colombo Plan." *Australian Outlook* 5, no. 4 (1951): 191–202.

Wood, G.L., ed. *Australia: Its Resources and Development.* New York: Macmillan, 1947.

Internet Sources

Academy of the Social Sciences in Australia. "Dr Fred Fisk." http://www.assa.edu.au/fellowship/fellow/deceased/94.

Association for Social Anthropology in Australia. "Cyril S. Belshaw." http://www.soc.hawaii.edu/asao/pacific/honoraryf/belshaw.htm.

Atlantic Charter. August 14, 1941. http://avalon.law.yale.edu/wwii/atlantic.asp.

Boadle, Donald. "Bury, Leslie Harry Ernest (1913–1986)." Australian Dictionary of Biography, National Centre of Biography, Australian National University. http://adb.anu.edu.au/biography/bury-leslie-harry-ernest-12270/text22027, published first in hardcopy 2007.

Farquharson, John. "Hay, Sir David Osborne (1916–2009)." Obituaries Australia, National Centre of Biography, Australian National University. http://oa.anu.edu.au/obituary/hay-sir-david-osborne-474/text475.

Grundy, Peter C. "Lambert, Cecil Ralph (Eski) (1899–1971)." Australian Dictionary of Biography, National Centre of Biography, Australian National University. http://adb.anu.edu.au/biography/lambert-cecil-ralph-eski-10774/text19105, published first in hardcopy 2000.

Hutchison, D.E. "Currie, Sir George Alexander (1896–1984)." Australian Dictionary of Biography, National Centre of Biography, Australian National University. http://adb.anu.edu.au/biography/currie-sir-george-alexander-12384/text22257, published first in hardcopy 2007.

Irving, T.H. "Mortimer, Rex Alfred (1926–1979)." Australian Dictionary of Biography, National Centre of Biography, Australian National University. http://adb.anu.edu.au/biography/mortimer-rex-alfred-11181/text19925, published first in hardcopy 2000.

Lloyd, C.J. "McEwen, Sir John (1900–1980)." Australian Dictionary of Biography, National Centre of Biography, Australian National University. http://adb.anu.edu.au/biography/mcewen-sir-john-10948/text9455, published first in hardcopy 2000.

McMullin, Ross. "Ward, Edward John (Eddie) (1899–1963)." Australian Dictionary of Biography, National Centre of Biography, Australian National University. http://adb.anu.edu.au/biography/ward-edward-john-eddie-11959/text21435, published first in hardcopy 2002.

Miller, J.D.B. "Crawford, Sir John Grenfell (Jack) (1910–1984)." Australian Dictionary of Biography, National Centre of Biography, Australian National University. http://adb.anu.edu.au/biography/crawford-sir-john-grenfell-jack-1391/text22223, published first in hardcopy 2007.

Nelson, H.N. "Cleland, Sir Donald Mackinnon (Don) (1901–1975)." Australian Dictionary of Biography, National Centre of Biography, Australian National University. http://adb.anu.edu.au/biography/cleland-sir-donald-mackinnon-don-9762/text17247, published first in hardcopy 1993.

Ryan, Peter. "Conlon, Alfred Austin Joseph (Alf) (1908–1961)." Australian Dictionary of Biography, National Centre of Biography, Australian National University. http://adb.anu.edu.au/biography/conlon-alfred-austin-joseph-alf-9804/text17331, published in hardcopy 1993.

United Nations Charter, art. 73. http://www.un.org/en/sections/un-charter/chapter-xi/.

United States Department of State. "Address by John F. Kennedy to the UN General Assembly, September 25, 1961." http://www.state.gov/p/io/potusunga/207241.htm.

University of Queensland Faculty of Business and Law. "Dr James Cumes." http://bel.uq.edu.au/james-cumes.

Published Secondary Sources

Akita, Shigeru, Gerold Krozewski, and Shoichi Watanabe, ed. *The Transformation of the International Order of Asia: Decolonization, the Cold War, and the Colombo Plan*. Milton Park, Abingdon, Oxon: Routledge, 2014.

Arndt, H.W. "Economic Development: A Semantic History." *Economic Development and Cultural Change* 29, no. 3 (1981): 457–466.

———. *Economic Development: The History of an Idea*. Chicago: University of Chicago Press, 1987.

Bain, William. "The Idea of Trusteeship in International Society." *The Round Table* 92, no. 368 (2003): 67–76.

Baldwin, David A. *Economic Development and American Foreign Policy, 1943–62*. Chicago: University of Chicago Press, 1966.

Barnett, Michael N. *Empire of Humanity: A History of Humanitarianism*. Ithaca, New York: Cornell University Press, 2011.

Beaumont, Joan. "Making Australian Foreign Policy, 1941–69." In *Ministers, Mandarins and Diplomats: Australian Foreign Policy Making, 1941–1969*, edited by Joan Beaumont, Christopher Waters, David Lowe, and Garry Woodard. Melbourne: Melbourne University Press, 2003.

Beaumont, Joan, Christopher Waters, David Lowe, and Garry Woodard, eds. *Ministers, Mandarins and Diplomats: Australian Foreign Policy Making, 1941–1969*. Melbourne: Melbourne University Press, 2003.

Boisen, Camilla. "The Changing Moral Justification of Empire: From the Right to Colonise to the Obligation to Civilise." *History of European Ideas* 39, no. 3 (2013): 335–353.

Bolton, G.C. *Paul Hasluck: A Life*. Crawley: UWA Publishing, 2014.

Borgwardt, Elizabeth. *A New Deal for the World: America's Vision for Human Rights*. Cambridge, MA: Belknap Press of Harvard University Press, 2005.

Brown, Nicholas. *Governing Prosperity: Social Change and Social Analysis in Australia in the 1950s*. Cambridge: Cambridge University Press, 1995.

———. "Student, Expert, Peacekeeper: Three Versions of International Engagement." *Australian Journal of Politics and History* 57, no. 1 (2011): 34–52.

Campbell, I.C. "The ASOPA Controversy: A Pivot of Australian Policy for Papua and New Guinea, 1945–49." *The Journal of Pacific History* 35, no. 1 (2000): 83–99.

Capling, Ann. *Australia and the Global Trade System: From Havana to Seattle.* Cambridge: Cambridge University Press, 2001.

Close-Barry, Kirstie. *A Mission Divided: Race, Culture and Colonialism in Fiji's Methodist Mission.* Acton: ANU Press, 2015.

Cooper, Frederick. *Decolonization and African Society: The Labor Question in French and British Africa.* Cambridge: Cambridge University Press, 1996.

———. "Writing the History of Development." *Journal of Modern European History* 8, no. 1 (2010): 5–23.

Corbett, Jack. *Australia's Foreign Aid Dilemma: Humanitarian Aspirations Confront Democratic Legitimacy.* Abingdon: Routledge, 2017.

Crawford, Neta C. "Decolonization Through Trusteeship: The Legacy of Ralph Bunche." In *Trustee for the Human Community: Ralph J. Bunche, the United Nations, and the Decolonization of Africa*, edited by Robert A. Hill and Edmond J. Keller. Athens: Ohio University Press, 2010.

Cullather, Nick. *The Hungry World: America's Cold War Battle Against Poverty in Asia.* Cambridge, MA: Harvard University Press, 2010.

———. "Research Note: Development? It's History." *Diplomatic History* 24, no. 4 (2000): 641–653.

Cumming, Gordon. *Aid to Africa: French and British Policies from the Cold War to the New Millennium.* Aldershot: Ashgate, 2001.

Darian-Smith, Kate. "World War 2 and Post-War Reconstruction." In *The Cambridge History of Australia*, edited by Alison Bashford and Stuart Macintyre. Port Melbourne: Cambridge University Press, 2013.

Dehm, Julia. "Highlighting Inequalities in the Histories of Human Rights: Contestations Over Justice, Needs and Rights in the 1970s." *Leiden Journal of International Law* 31, no. 4 (2018): 871–895.

Dell, Sidney. "The Origins of UNCTAD." In *UNCTAD and the South-North Dialogue: The First Twenty Years, Essays in Memory of W.R. Malinowski*, edited by Michael Zammit Cutajar. New York: Pergamon Press, 1985.

Denoon, Donald. *A Trial Separation: Australia and the Decolonisation of Papua New Guinea.* Canberra: ANU E Press, 2012.

Denoon, Donald, Philippa Mein Smith, and Marivic Wyndham. *A History of Australia, New Zealand, and the Pacific.* Malden, MA: Blackwell Publishers, 2000.

Dimier, Veronique. *The Invention of a European Development Aid Bureaucracy: Recycling Empire.* Basingstoke: Palgrave Macmillan, 2014.

Dosman, Edgar J. *The Life and Times of Raul Prebisch, 1901–1986*. Montreal: McGill-Queen's University Press, 2008.

Downs, Ian. *The Australian Trusteeship Papua New Guinea, 1945–75*. Canberra: Australian Government Publishing Service, 1980.

Edwards, P.G. *Arthur Tange: Last of the Mandarins*. Crows Nest, NSW: Allen & Unwin, 2006.

Edwards, P.G., and Gregory Pemberton. *Crises and Commitments: The Politics and Diplomacy of Australia's Involvement in Southeast Asian Conflicts, 1948–1965*. North Sydney: Allen & Unwin, 1992.

Ekbladh, David. *The Great American Mission: Modernization and the Construction of an American World Order, 1914 to the Present*. Princeton: Princeton University Press, 2010.

Engerman, David C. "West Meets East: The Center for International Studies and Indian Economic Development." In *Staging Growth: Modernization, Development, and the Global Cold War*, edited by David C. Engerman, Nils Gilman, Mark H. Haefele, and Michael E. Latham. Amherst: University of Massachusetts Press, 2003.

Fassin, Didier. *Humanitarian Reason: A Moral History of the Present*. Berkeley: University of California Press, 2012.

Fernandes, Clinton. *Island off the Coast of Asia: Instruments of Statecraft in Australian Foreign Policy*. Clayton: Monash University Publishing, 2018.

Frey, Marc. "Control, Legitimacy, and the Securing of Interests: European Development Policy in South-East Asia from the Late Colonial Period to the Early 1960s." *Contemporary European History* 12, no. 4 (2003): 395–412.

Frost, Lionel. "The Economy." In *The Cambridge History of Australia*, edited by Alison Bashford and Stuart Macintyre. Port Melbourne: Cambridge University Press, 2013.

Gifford, P. "The Cold War Across Asia." In *Facing North: A Century of Australian Engagement with Asia*, edited by David Goldsworthy and P.G. Edwards. Carlton South, VIC: Melbourne University Press, 2001.

Gilman, Nils. *Mandarins of the Future: Modernization Theory in Cold War America*. Baltimore: Johns Hopkins University Press, 2003.

———. "The New International Economic Order: A Reintroduction." *Humanity: An International Journal of Human Rights, Humanitarianism, and Development* 6, no. 1 (2015): 1–16.

Golding, Peter. *Black Jack McEwen: Political Gladiator*. Carlton South, VIC: Melbourne University Press, 1996.

Gorman, Daniel. "Britain, India, and the United Nations: Colonialism and the Development of International Governance, 1945–1960." *Journal of Global History* 9, no. 3 (2014): 471–490.

Griffin, James, Hank Nelson, and Stewart Firth. *Papua New Guinea: A Political History*. Richmond: Heinemann Educational Australia, 1979.

Groenewegen, Peter D., and Bruce J. McFarlane. *A History of Australian Economic Thought*. London: Routledge, 2011.

Gyngell, Allan. *Fear of Abandonment: Australia in the World Since 1942*. Carlton: La Trobe University Press, 2017.

Hall, Stuart. "The Neoliberal Revolution." *Soundings*, no. 48 (2011): 9–27.

Hameiri, Shahar. "Risk Management, Neo-liberalism and the Securitisation of the Australian Aid Program." *Australian Journal of International Affairs* 62, no. 3 (2008): 357–371.

Harper, Marjorie. *Douglas Copland: Scholar, Economist, Diplomat*. Carlton: Miegunyah Press, 2013.

Harris, Stuart. "Australia and the New International Economic Order." *Australian Outlook* 32, no. 1 (1978): 24–40.

Havinden, Michael Ashley, and David Meredith. *Colonialism and Development: Britain and Its Tropical Colonies, 1850–1960*. London: Routledge, 1993.

Henry, Adam. *The Gatekeepers of Australian Foreign Policy 1950–1966*. North Melbourne, VIC: Australian Scholarly Publishing, 2015.

———. "John Burton: Forgotten Mandarin?". In *The Seven Dwarfs and the Age of the Mandarins: Australian Government Administration in the Post-war Reconstruction Era*, edited by Samuel Furphy. Acton, ACT: ANU Press, 2015.

Hilton, Matthew. "Ken Loach and the Save the Children Film: Humanitarianism, Imperialism, and the Changing Role of Charity in Postwar Britain." *The Journal of Modern History* 87, no. 2 (2015): 357–394.

———, ed. *The Politics of Expertise: How NGOs Shaped Modern Britain*. Oxford: Oxford University Press, 2013.

Hocking, Jenny. *Gough Whitlam: His Time—The Biography Volume II*. Carlton: Miegunyah Press, 2012.

Hodge, Joseph Morgan. *Triumph of the Expert: Agrarian Doctrines of Development and the Legacies of British Colonialism*. Athens: Ohio University Press, 2007.

———. "Writing the History of Development (Part 1: The First Wave)." *Humanity: An International Journal of Human Rights, Humanitarianism, and Development* 6, no. 3 (2015): 429–463.

———. "Writing the History of Development (Part 2: Longer, Deeper, Wider)." *Humanity: An International Journal of Human Rights, Humanitarianism, and Development* 7, no. 1 (2016): 125–174.

Hodge, Joseph Morgan, and Gerard Hodl. "Introduction." In *Developing Africa: Concepts and Practices in Twentieth-Century Colonialism*, edited by Joseph M. Hodge, Gerard Hodl, and Martina Kopf. Manchester, MA: Manchester University Press, 2014.

Hodge, Joseph Morgan, Gerard Hodl, and Martina Kopf, eds. *Developing Africa: Concepts and Practices in Twentieth-Century Colonialism*. Manchester, MA: Manchester University Press, 2014.

Hoyle, Arthur. *Eddie Ward: The Truest Labor Man*. Canberra: A. Hoyle, 1994.
Hudson, W.J. *Casey*. Melbourne: Oxford University Press, 1986.
Hudson, W.J., and Jill Daven. "Papua and New Guinea Since 1945." In *Australia and Papua New Guinea*, edited by W.J. Hudson. Sydney: Sydney University Press, 1971.
Immerwahr, Daniel. *Thinking Small: The United States and the Lure of Community Development*. Cambridge, MA: Harvard University Press, 2015.
Ingham, Barbara, and Paul Mosley. *Sir Arthur Lewis: A Biography*. London: Palgrave Macmillan, 2013.
Iriye, Akira. *Global Community: The Role of International Organizations in the Making of the Contemporary World*. Berkeley: University of California Press, 2002.
Jarrett, F.G. *The Evolution of Australia's Aid Program*. Canberra: Australian Development Studies Network, 1994.
Jinks, Brian. "Alfred Conlon, the Directorate of Research and New Guinea." *Journal of Australian Studies* 7, no. 12 (1983): 21–33.
Kilby, Patrick. *NGOs and Political Change: A History of the Australian Council for International Development*. Acton, ACT: ANU Press, 2015.
Latham, Michael E. *Modernization as Ideology: American Social Science and "Nation Building" in the Kennedy Era*. Chapel Hill, NC: University of North Carolina Press, 2000.
Legge, J.D. "The Murray Period: Papua 1906-40." In *Australia and Papua New Guinea*, edited by W.J. Hudson. Sydney: Sydney University Press, 1971.
Low, D.A., and J.M. Lonsdale. "Introduction: Towards the New Order 1945–1963." In *History of East Africa*, edited by D.A. Low and Alison Smith. Oxford: Clarendon Press, 1976.
Lowe, David. "Percy Spender and the Colombo Plan 1950." *Australian Journal of Politics and History* 40, no. 2 (1994).
———, ed. *Australia and the End of Empires: The Impact of Decolonisation in Australia's Near North, 1945–65*. Geelong, VIC: Deakin University Press, 1996.
———. "The Colombo Plan." In *Australia and the End of Empires: The Impact of Decolonisation in Australia's Near North, 1945–65*, edited by David Lowe. Geelong, VIC: Deakin University Press, 1996.
———. "Canberra's Colombo Plan: Public Images of Australia's Relations with Post-colonial South and Southeast Asia in the 1950s." *South Asia: Journal of South Asian Studies* 25, no. 2 (2002): 183–204.
———. *Australian Between Empires: The Life of Percy Spender*. London: Pickering & Chatto, 2010.
———. "Journalists and the Stirring of Australian Public Diplomacy: The Colombo Plan Towards the 1960s." *Journal of Contemporary History* 48, no. 1 (2013): 175–190.

———. "Australia's Colombo Plans, Old and New: International Students as Foreign Relations." *International Journal of Cultural Policy* 21, no. 4 (2015): 448–462.

Macintyre, Stuart. *Australia's Boldest Experiment: War and Reconstruction in the 1940s*. Sydney, NSW: NewSouth Publishing, 2015.

MacWilliam, Scott. *Securing Village Life: Development in Late Colonial Papua New Guinea*. Canberra, ANU E Press, 2013.

Mazower, Mark. *No Enchanted Palace: The End of Empire and the Ideological Origins of the United Nations*. Princeton: Princeton University Press, 2009.

McGregor, Russell. *Environment, Race, and Nationhood in Australia: Revisiting the Empty North*. New York: Palgrave Macmillan, 2016.

Meaney, Neville. "Australia, the Great Powers and the Coming of the Cold War." *Australian Journal of Politics and History* 38, no. 3 (1992): 316–333.

Meier, Gerald M., and Dudley Seers, eds. *Pioneers in Development*. New York: Oxford University Press, 1984.

Millmow, Alex. "Douglas Copland's Battle with the Younger Brethren of Economists." *Australian Economic History Review* 53, no. 2 (2013): 187–209.

Milne, David. *America's Rasputin: Walt Rostow and the Vietnam War*. New York: Hill and Wang, 2008.

Moon, Suzanne. *Technology and Ethical Idealism: A History of Development in the Netherlands East Indies*. Leiden: CNWS Publications, 2007.

Morgan, D.J. *Changes in British Aid Policy, 1951–1970*. London: Macmillan, 1980.

Moyn, Samuel. *Not Enough: Human Rights in an Unequal World*. Cambridge: Belknap Press, 2018.

Nelson, Hank. *Taim Bilong Masta: The Australian Involvement with Papua New Guinea*. Crows Nest: ABC Enterprises, 1990.

O'Brien, Robert, and Marc Williams. *Global Political Economy: Evolution and Dynamics*. 3rd ed. New York: Palgrave Macmillan, 2010.

Oakman, Daniel. *Facing Asia: A History of the Colombo Plan*. Canberra: Pandanus Books, 2004.

Pemberton, Gregory. *All the Way: Australia's Road to Vietnam*. Sydney: Allen & Unwin, 1987.

Piccini, Jon. *Transnational Protest, Australia and the 1960s: Global Protest*. London: Palgrave Macmillan, 2016.

Porter, Robert. *Paul Hasluck: A Political Biography*. Nedlands: University of Western Australia Press, 1993.

Prashad, Vijay. *The Darker Nations: A People's History of the Third World*. New York: The New Press, 2007.

———. *The Poorer Nations: A Possible History of the Global South*. London; New York: Verso, 2012.

Purdey, Jemma. *From Vienna to Yogyakarta: The Life of Herb Feith*. Sydney: University of New South Wales Press, 2011.

Pybus, Cassandra. "Conlon's Remarkable Circus." In *Scholars at War: Australasian Social Scientists, 1939–1945*, edited by Geoffrey Gray, Doug Munro, and Christine Winter. Canberra: ANU E Press, 2012.

Renwick, Chris. *Bread for All: The Origins of the Welfare State*. London: Penguin, 2017.

Rist, Gilbert. *The History of Development: From Western Origins to Global Faith*. 3rd ed. London; New York: Zed, 2008.

Roe, Margriet. "Papua-New Guinea and War 1941–5." In *Australia and Papua New Guinea*, edited by W.J. Hudson. Sydney: Sydney University Press, 1971.

Rosser, Andrew. "Neo-liberalism and the Politics of Australian Aid Policy-Making." *Australian Journal of International Affairs* 62, no. 3 (2008): 372–385.

Rowse, Tim. *Nugget Coombs: A Reforming Life*. Cambridge: Cambridge University Press, 2002.

Said, Edward W. *Orientalism*. London: Penguin, 1995.

Schmelzer, Matthias. *The Hegemony of Growth: The OECD and the Making of the Economic Growth Paradigm*. Cambridge: Cambridge University Press, 2016.

Sexton, Michael. *The Great Crash: The Short Life and Sudden Death of the Whitlam Government*. Rev. ed. Melbourne: Scribe, 2005.

Shlomowitz, Ralph. "Mortality and Indentured Labour in Papua (1885–1941) and New Guinea (1920–1941)." *The Journal of Pacific History* 23, no. 1 (1988): 70–79.

Simpson, Bradley R. *Economists with Guns: Authoritarian Development and U.S.-Indonesian Relations, 1960–1968*. Stanford, CA: Stanford University Press, 2008.

Sligo, Graeme. *The Backroom Boys: Alfred Conlon and Army's Directorate of Research and Civil Affairs, 1942–46*. Newport, NSW: Big Sky Publishing, 2013.

Sobocinska, Agnieszka. "A New Kind of Mission: The Volunteer Graduate Scheme and the Cultural History of International Development." *Australian Journal of Politics and History* 62, no. 3 (2016): 369–387.

———. "How to Win Friends and Influence Nations: The International History of Development Volunteering." *Journal of Global History* 12, no. 1 (2017): 49–73.

Spicer, Keith. "Clubmanship Upstaged: Canada's Twenty Years in the Colombo Plan." *International Journal* 25, no. 1 (1969): 23–33.

Spratt, Elwyn. *Eddie Ward: Firebrand of East Sydney*. Adelaide: Rigby, 1965.

Tarling, Nicholas. "The United Kingdom and the Origins of the Colombo Plan." *The Journal of Commonwealth and Comparative Politics* 24, no. 1 (1986): 3–34.

Taylor, Ian, and Karen Smith. *United Nations Conference on Trade and Development (UNCTAD)*. New York: Routledge, 2007.

Thompson, John, ed. *Alfred Conlon: A Memorial by Some of His Friends*. Sydney: Benevolent Society of New South Wales, 1963.

Tomlinson, Jim. "The Commonwealth, the Balance of Payments and the Politics of International Poverty: British Aid Policy, 1958–1971." *Contemporary European History* 12, no. 4 (2003): 413–429.

Toye, John, and Richard Toye. "The Origins and Interpretation of the Prebisch-Singer Thesis." *History of Political Economy* 35, no. 3 (2003): 437–467.

Tyrrell, Ian R. *Reforming the World: The Creation of America's Moral Empire*. Princeton: Princeton University Press, 2010.

Viner, Jacob, George Meany, Fowler Hamilton, Otto Passman, and Paul Hoffman. "The Report of the Clay Committee on Foreign Aid: A Symposium." *Political Science Quarterly* 78, no. 3 (1963): 321–361.

Viviani, N., and P. Wilenski. "Politicians, Bureaucrats and Foreign Aid: A Case Study." In *International Aid: Some Political, Administrative and Technical Realities*, edited by R.T. Shand and H.V. Richter. Canberra: Development Studies Centre, ANU, 1979.

Ward, Stuart. *Australia and the British Embrace: The Demise of the Imperial Ideal*. Carlton South, VIC: Melbourne University Press, 2001.

Waters, Christopher. "The MacMahon Ball Mission to East Asia 1948." *Australian Journal of Politics and History* 40, no. 3 (1994): 351–363.

———. "A Failure of Imagination: R.G. Casey and Australian Plans for Counter-Subversion in Asia, 1954–1956." *Australian Journal of Politics and History* 45, no. 3 (1999): 347–363.

Webster, David. "Development Advisors in a Time of Cold War and Decolonization: The United Nations Technical Assistance Administration, 1950–59." *Journal of Global History* 6, no. 2 (2011): 249–272.

Whitwell, Greg. *The Treasury Line*. Sydney: Allen & Unwin, 1986.

Wilenski, Peter. "Infanticide in the Bureaucracy: The Australian Development Assistance Agency." In *Decisions: Case Studies in Australian Public Policy*, edited by Solomon Encel, Peter Wilenski, and B.B. Schaffer. Melbourne: Longman Cheshire, 1981.

Williams, Marc. *Third World Cooperation: The Group of 77 in UNCTAD*. London: Pinter Publishers, 1991.

Wright, Huntley. "Protecting the National Interest: The Labor Government and the Reform of Australia's Colonial Policy, 1942–45." *Labour History* 82 (May 2002): 65–79.

Index

N. Ferns, *Australia in the Age of International Development, 1945–1975*, Security, Conflict and Cooperation in the Contemporary World, https://doi.org/10.1007/978-3-030-50228-7

The manufacturer's authorised representative in the EU is Springer Nature Customer Service Centre GmbH, Europaplatz 3, 69115 Heidelberg, Germany. If you have any concerns regarding our products, please contact ProductSafety@springernature.com

Printed and bound by CPI Group (UK) Ltd, Croydon, CR0 4YY
30/09/2026
02225502-0005